The Losing War

SUNY series, James N. Rosenau series in Global Politics

David C. Earnest, editor

The Losing War

Plan Colombia and Beyond

Jonathan D. Rosen

Published by State University of New York Press, Albany

Printed in the United States of America

For information, contact State University of New York Press, Albany, NY
www.sunypress.edu

Production by Ryan Morris
Marketing by Michael Campochiaro

Library of Congress Cataloging-in-Publication Data

Rosen, Jonathan D.
    The losing war : Plan Colombia and beyond / Jonathan D. Rosen.
        pages cm. — (SUNY series, James N. Rosenau series in global politics)
    Includes bibliographical references and index.
    ISBN 978-1-4384-5299-9 (hardcover : alk. paper)
    ISBN 978-1-4384-5298-2 (pbk : alk. paper)
    ISBN 978-1-4384-5300-2 (e-book)
    1. Drug control—Colombia.   2. Insurgency—Colombia.   3. Counterinsurgency—
Colombia.   4. Fuerzas Armadas Revolucionarias de Colombia.   5. National
security—Colombia.   6. Colombia—Politics and government—21st century.
7. Economic assistance, American—Colombia.   8. Military assistance,
American—Colombia.   I. Title.

    HV5840.C7R67 2014
    363.4509861—dc23   2013042570

10 9 8 7 6 5 4 3 2 1

Contents

Timeline

1994 – Election of President Ernesto Samper of Colombia

1995 – U.S. decertifies Colombia

1996 – U.S. decertifies Colombia

1997 – U.S. decertifies Colombia

1998 – Election of President Andrés Pastrana of Colombia

2000 – Plan Colombia signed into law

2001 – George W. Bush launches global war on terrorism

2002 – Election of Álvaro Uribe

2003 – *Plan Patriota*

2007 – U.S. signs into law the Mérida Initiative ("Plan Mexico")

2008 – Election of Barack Obama

2010 – Election of Juan Manuel Santos

2011 – No mention of Plan Colombia in U.S. budget proposal

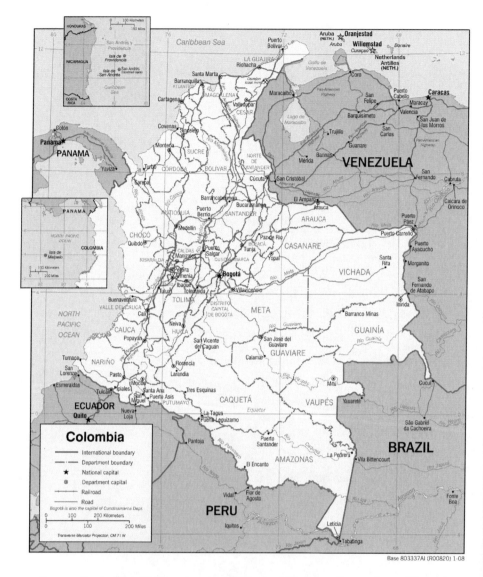

Source: Central Intelligence Agency. Public domain. (https://www.cia.gov/library/
publications/cia-maps-publications/Colombia.html).

Acknowledgments

This book is a revised and altered version of my dissertation. I would like to thank my dissertation committee members, Elvira María Restrepo, Bradford McGuinn, Ambler Moss, and Roger Kanet for all their help. I would like to give special thanks to the chair of the committee and my mentor, Bruce M. Bagley. It has been a true honor and privilege to work with Dr. Bagley, and I would not have been able to publish this book without his leadership, guidance, and encouragement. Thank you, Dr. Bagley, for always making time for me despite your busy schedule.

I also would like to thank Vanessa Rayan for her editorial assistance and Nicolás Velásquez for his research assistance in chapter 7.

A special thanks to Hanna Kassab for his support, encouragement, and helpful comments in the dissertation seminar.

I also would like to thank Michael Rinella of SUNY Press for his confidence in my book project and providing me with this excellent opportunity. In addition, I would like to thank the staff at SUNY Press for their hard work, dedication, and assistance in preparing the manuscript. They were extremely professional and helped improve the quality of the book. Finally, I want to thank the Universidad del Mar, Huatulco, Mexico, especially the Institute of International Studies. A special thanks to the Rector of the University, Dr. Modesto Seara Vázquez, for his guidance and leadership. It has been an honor and privilege to work at UMAR.

1

Introduction

For several decades, Colombia has been at the epicenter of the U.S.-led "war on drugs." At various points in its history, Colombia appeared to be on the verge of becoming a narco-state as drug lords, such as Pablo Escobar, roamed free and could virtually do whatever they wanted. Drug traffickers killed many Colombians and used other tactics, such as bribery and extortion. The U.S. wanted to stop drug trafficking in Colombia, which continued despite the death of Pablo Escobar and the collapse of the Medellín and Cali cartels.[1] In 2000, President Clinton signed into law Plan Colombia, providing the Colombians with billions of dollars in aid to combat drug trafficking. Plan Colombia has been one of the most exhaustive drug packages ever passed. This work provides a critical analysis of Plan Colombia, which sought to reduce the cultivation, trafficking, and production of drugs by 50 percent.[2] Despite spending more than $8 billion, Plan Colombia failed to achieve its drug objectives: drugs remain cheaper and more readily available than ever before.[3]

This work examines the origins and outcomes of Plan Colombia from 2000 to 2012, using the theoretical concepts and methodological tools drawn from international relations theory and comparative politics to examine the critical junctures and evolution of Plan Colombia from its initial approval in July 13, 2000, by the U.S. Congress through its implementation from Andrés Pastrana (1998–2002), Álvaro Uribe (2002–2010), until the Juan Manuel Santos administration (2010–April 2012).

While much has been written on the formation of Plan Colombia, not a single work exists that examines Plan Colombia from beginning to end. Critics might question why policymakers, analysts, and academics care about Plan Colombia. In other words, what relevance does Plan Colombia have today? Anybody who reads the news recognizes that Mexico, not Colombia, has become the epicenter and focus of the war on drugs. This work argues that Plan Colombia is crucial for understanding why the violence has shifted to Mexico. In some sense, Mexico appears to be the Colombia of the 1990s. In addition, the lessons from Plan Colombia can be applied to other areas today that are experiencing large levels of organized crime and violence as a result of drug trafficking (for example, West Africa).

We must first briefly examine why studying Colombia is necessary for policymakers and academics. Colombia is a critical case in the U.S.-led war on drugs for six reasons.

1. Colombia has been a longtime security threat dating back to the cold war before the emergence of drug trafficking in the country.

2. During the 1970s and beyond, the country became and remains today deeply entrenched in drug cultivation, processing, and trafficking, thus presenting new post–cold war security concerns for the United States.

3. Colombia constitutes a microcosm of the failures and successes of the U.S.-led war on drugs.

4. Colombia is located in an important strategic area because it borders the Panama Canal and Brazil, which is a major economic power in the region. Security challenges that transpire in Colombia, therefore, can threaten trade and prosperity for the region.

5. Colombia remains the principal ally of the United States.

6. Colombia is a democracy and Washington does not want its allies to become anti-democratic.

Organization of the Book

This work provides an exhaustive examination of Plan Colombia from beginning to end, which no other work today does. It is organized around several key puzzles or questions that subsequently each become chapters. The concluding chapter analyzes the notion of whether Plan Colombia should be used as a model for other countries. Should policymakers and politicians take the core concepts of Plan Colombia and apply them to other countries such as Mexico and Afghanistan? In other words, it seeks to answer the "so what?" question, exploring the lessons of Plan Colombia, and determine what analysts should learn from this case. This is something that the United States has failed to do as it continues to implement the same failed strategies again and again.

Puzzle One: Origins of Plan Colombia

Beginning in 1995, the U.S. government decertified Colombia and the Ernesto Samper administration three consecutive years for failing to comply with the requirements set forth by the United States. In July 2000, during the Andrés Pastrana administration, the U.S. Congress approved and President Clinton signed into law a bill designed specifically to assist Colombia combat drug trafficking.[4] This initiative is known as "Plan Colombia." The first puzzle seeks to analyze and examine what transpired between 1995 and 2000 that led to the creation and signing of Plan Colombia into law by the United States. Why did President Clinton sign Plan Colombia into law and provide the Colombians with billions of dollars in aid after decertifying the country three consecutive years?[5]

Puzzle Two: From Drug Trafficking to Narco-Terrorism

The September 11, 2001, terrorist attacks by Muslim extremists fundamentally changed U.S. foreign policy, as the Bush administration focused on the "war on terrorism," thereby subordinating the war on drugs to the war on terrorism. President Álvaro Uribe was inaugurated as the new president of Colombia on August 7, 2002. From the beginning of his presidency, Uribe had very different goals and objectives than his predecessor. Specifically, Uribe sought not only to combat drug trafficking within Colombia but also what he referred to as "narco-terrorism." Why did the discrepancies evaporate between the United States and Colombia? Why did the United States accept the new strategy Uribe designed? How is it that the less powerful country, Colombia, was able to set the agenda?[6]

Puzzle Three: Beyond Plan Colombia

By the end of the decade, President Bush (2009) and President Uribe (2010) ended their respective presidential terms. Toward the end of the Bush administration and the beginning of the Obama administration, the United States has reduced its aid to Colombia. How did the Colombians perceive and evaluate Plan Colombia in terms of its successes and failures? Were the initial goals of the United States and the Colombians achieved? If so, how were these goals achieved? Why did the policies change from Uribe to Santos?[7]

Puzzle Four: Theory and Method

In the aftermath of the transition, Obama pledged to support Colombia. In reality, he has sought to desecuritize[8] Colombia as a major security issue and priority for the U.S. government. Why did the United States cut funding to Plan Colombia and attempt to desecuritize Colombia? How have efforts been made to desecuritize Colombia? Have Obama's efforts been successful?

Methodological Approach and Techniques

Colombia is an important case because it lies at the epicenter of the U.S.-led war on drugs and has been a major security concern for the United States. This work uses diachronic analysis to examine the critical moments of Plan Colombia.[9] This book is not a complete history of Plan Colombia, but it does focus on the critical junctures. Plan Colombia provides scholars and policymakers with various important lessons for other countries. Obviously, a single-case study has some limitations, such as the ability to draw generalizable theories that can be tested in other countries. Comparing Colombia to other cases could be a fruitful research topic. On the other hand, multiple case studies complicate the research design because one has to answer several important questions with regard to the justification of cases chosen. For instance, which countries are chosen and why? Does the researcher compare countries based on most similar or most different cases? How does one avoid issues such as selection bias and selecting on the dependent variable? In sum, this book does not use multiple case studies, but rather focuses on key moments or critical junctures in Colombia, which has been and continues to be a crucial country for drug production as well as trafficking.[10]

In terms of methodological techniques, this endeavor adopts process tracing to examine the critical junctures of Plan Colombia. Process tracing enables researchers to evaluate and determine the causal mechanisms. This work also draws on both primary and secondary sources to examine the critical junctures of Plan Colombia. This project, for instance, analyzes research from both U.S. and Colombian government documents. The Government Accountability Office and United Nations (UN) reports, in particular, have been consulted and provide a plethora of information with regard to coca cultivation and overall trends in drug trafficking.

In addition, this work uses techniques from constructivism, primarily the analysis of speech acts by authoritative figures to trace the desecuritization process. This project consulted interviews from newspapers, speeches, and other documents and examined the statements made by key leaders, such as President Obama. This work, however, does not use content analysis, which is another methodological technique constructivists use, which requires extensive numerical analysis of content, such as the frequency in which an issue appears in a newspaper.[11]

This work also uses other qualitative methods, such as open-ended interviews with various experts, such as academics and government officials involved in policy formation and research and who are experts in each stage of the process and formation of Plan Colombia.[12] Open-ended interviews, using the snowball technique, provide the interviewee with the opportunity to answer questions and provide useful insights into Plan Colombia.[13] The individuals selected for interviews are from Colombia and the United States, which provides a methodologically sound sample of individuals who can present the entire picture of Plan Colombia. Each person interviewed was an expert in U.S. foreign policy toward Colombia or the war on drugs as well as the internal armed conflict in Colombia. The goal was not to survey and interview the people in Colombia, but rather to interview policy experts and scholars who would provide keen insights into Plan Colombia.[14]

Levels of Analysis

This book analyzes the origins of Plan Colombia and its evolution over time and uses process tracing to analyze Plan Colombia and the various key moments. In essence, this work analyzes U.S. foreign policy toward Colombia. Foreign policy lies at the dividing line between international relations (IR) and comparative politics. Laura Neack emphasizes the importance of "levels of analysis" and the need to distinguish between the levels of foreign policy.[15] The first level of analysis is theories of grand strategy because a theoretical approach is essential for understanding the long-term goals of a state, as well as the formation of Plan Colombia. IR theory, in particular, has been prone to these debates among contending theories and paradigms. In addition to realism and liberalism, soft constructivism also has explanatory power in terms of its ability to explain the perceptions and social constructions of the United States and Colombia.[16]

Theories of grand strategy alone are insufficient, and, therefore, this book employs various techniques and approaches from comparative politics to examine the internal dynamics and politics that impacted the formation and evolution of Plan Colombia. In other words, comprehending and analyzing the formation and evolution of Plan Colombia is impossible without examining the role of key institutions, such as the executive branch and Congress. This book not only examines the role of three U.S. presidents (Clinton, Bush, and Obama) and three Colombian presidents (Pastrana, Uribe, and Santos), but also examines the role of the U.S. Congress and how it helped impact the formation and evolution of Plan Colombia during these critical junctures.[17]

Midrange theories demonstrate that scholars cannot understand U.S. foreign policy and drug trafficking in Colombia without examining the internal dynamics within a country. Comparative politics requires one to have in-depth knowledge of the culture, history, and institutions within the state apparatus. Some of the following questions need to be examined: how do the institutions function? How is a policy made? Who are the actors involved in policymaking? What are the "rules of the game"? What institutions are involved in the policymaking process?[18]

Theoretical Approach

This book consciously adopts an eclectic theoretical approach. Today, the world in which we live is more complicated than ever, and in order to understand such a complex world, scholars need to employ different tools in order to explain events that occur. For IR scholars, IR theory is an important tool for understanding these phenomena and events that have transpired. Some individuals, particularly those outside of academia, believe that IR theory does not have much explanatory power and is merely an intellectual exercise among those in academia. In *The Tragedy of Great Power Politics*, John Mearsheimer quotes Paul Nitze who played a major role in foreign policy during the cold war era. Nitze wrote that "most of what has been written and taught under the heading of 'political science' by Americans since World War II has been . . . of limited value, if not counterproductive, as a guide to the actual conduct of policy."[19] Nitze's statement suggests that theory has little use in the "real world" and does not have any explanatory power. Instead, politicians and individuals who participate in the policymaking process should use their experiences, information analysis, and common sense when designing a policy or making an important decision. Mearsheimer responds to such critics of IR theory stating: "This view is wrongheaded. In fact, none of us could understand the world in which we live in or make intelligent decisions without theories. Indeed, all students and practitioners of international politics rely on theories to comprehend their surroundings. Some are aware of it and some are not, some admit and some do not; but there is no escaping the fact that we could not make sense of the complex world around us without simplifying theories."[20] Therefore, to understand the formation of Plan Colombia and how it evolved over time, this book applies IR theory as a lens or framework to explain this complicated case. IR scholars often use one theory or paradigm and fail to use other theoretical perspectives to explain their question. This work argues that scholars selectively choose those points that support their position while ignoring things that contradict it, which is a form of selection bias.[21] This is not the correct method to conduct social science research. In an interview at the University of California, Berkeley, Harry Kreisler asked Robert Pape whether he would classify himself as a realist. Pape responded that he does not like to label himself and believes that scholars should use the appropriate theories necessary to analyze and answer a question.[22] This is the practice that scholars should be engaged in, as opposed to finding cases that explain why their particular theory of choice has more explanatory power or relevance. The use of examples to justify the value or explanatory power of a particular theory is improper social science research. Critics of an eclectic approach argue that the paradigm or theory one uses determines the type of questions asked.

Neorealism

Neorealism has explanatory power in terms of its ability to explain state-to-state relations between Colombia and the United States. Realism clearly indicates that the United States has geostrategic goals, and that Colombia played a role in the grand strategy of the United States. Washington, for instance, viewed Colombia as a pillar of democracy and a crucial ally for its foreign policy in the region. Colombia also is a vital country for security in the region because it borders Venezuela, Brazil, and the Panama Canal. Security in Colombia, therefore, is a major priority in order to ensure stable trading zones. In addition, neorealism explains how a powerful country, such as the United States, can use its power to alter the goals of a policy. Realism also has several hypotheses regarding agenda-setting and how power impacts bilateral relations between a strong state and weaker power. According to realism, the hegemonic state, the United States in this case, will use its power to dictate the terms and conditions and dominate the agenda-setting process over the less powerful country. Therefore, the less powerful country will not be able to set the agenda and will be required to follow the orders of the hegemonic actor.[23] However, does the weaker country have the ability to set the agenda and maintain relative autonomy, contradicting realist logic? Realism has important contributions with regard to alliance politics. Realists argue that countries either balance against a power or bandwagon. According to realist logic, Colombia, a staunch ally of the United States, should join forces with the United States. This hypothesis will be tested in the subsequent pages.

Realism, however, has various other shortcomings in its ability to explain Plan Colombia. One serious shortcoming of neorealism is that it focuses on states as the unit of analysis and ignores other actors, such as drug traffickers. Bagley and Tokatlian argue that "in fact, multiple subnational and transnational actors are involved in this international industry, most of whom operate outside, if not in direct defiance, of national authorities through the hemisphere."[24] Bagley and Tokatlian also stress the importance of the market, whereas realists underestimate the importance of globalization and market forces. Even though they are illegal, drugs should be viewed as any other commodity in a legal market. Drug traffickers, therefore, will continue to supply drugs if the demand for such commodities continues to exist and the potential to earn money remains.[25]

Liberalism

Liberalism has various strands that are useful and help explain the formation, implementation, and evolution of Plan Colombia. The first strand of liberalism focuses on interdependence and helps explain the economic linkages that exist between Colombia and the United States, which is something that realist scholars have neglected. The relationship between the two can be characterized as one of asymmetric interdependence, as opposed to one of complex interdependence. Colombia is heavily reliant on the United States as a trade partner. In economic terms, Colombia only accounts for less than 1 percent of overall U.S. trade. That being said, Colombia is an important energy producer of coal and oil. Trade, however, is not the only indicator of economic interest because the United States has significant investments within Colombia.[26]

Liberalism is useful because it focuses on the economic linkages and highlights the asymmetric relationship between the United States and Colombia. The weaker countries, in this case Colombia, do have a degree of relative autonomy.[27] The greater the degree of independence that the weaker power has increases the ability of the weaker power to negotiate on certain issues. Interdependence is not only a tool of the hegemonic power, but the weaker actor, Colombia, can use interdependence to obtain various goals and concessions from the hegemonic actor. In other words, interdependence, when used correctly, can be an effective mechanism to extract or obtain certain resources.

The second strand of liberalism is referred to as neoliberal institutionalism and, as the name suggests, emphasizes the importance of institutions to promote cooperation, coordination, promote efficiency, and decrease transaction costs.[28] This type of liberalism is useful for understanding the attempts to institutionalize Plan Colombia. Said differently, the United States sought to construct a model of security between Colombia and the United States under the auspices of Plan Colombia that was institutionalized in this liberal sense. The institutionalization process enabled the United States and Colombia to increase connections between the two countries and promote cooperation and collaboration. For instance, the U.S. ambassador played a major role in Colombian relations and such cooperation could not have occurred without the institutionalization of Plan Colombia.[29]

Constructivism

Soft constructivism focuses on perceptions and the social construction of issues, such as national security priorities. Constructivism helps explain how the elites in Colombia and the United States perceived each other. Such perceptions help determine the nature and intensity of interactions. From a U.S. perspective, some individuals perceived Colombia as a failed state. From the Colombian perspective, Colombian elites believed that they needed the United States as an ally in order to receive the necessary support to combat drug trafficking and the various internal actors. Constructivism also clearly demonstrates that the United States was not only concerned with its national security interests but also the electoral dynamics within the United States. The Republicans challenged Clinton during his presidency, and Gore during his presidential campaign, arguing that they were not tough enough on drugs. The Democrats felt obligated to respond and prove that they were not "soft on crime." In addition, Washington perceived Colombia as a thriving democracy in the region, which also helped support U.S. values. In terms of hypothesis testing, constructivists would hypothesize that countries can collaborate despite different perceptions and social constructions as long as countries can find common linkages and grounds for cooperation.[30]

Lessons and Analytical Contributions

After analyzing the various critical junctures or key moments of Plan Colombia, this work will end with several policy recommendations that will make a significant contribution to the field. The empirical analysis of Plan Colombia is the first subject addressed in the policy recommendations suggestions. Determining whether Plan Colombia has achieved its objectives and can be defined as a success can be measured empirically. Statistical analysis, for instance, provides estimates about the number of hectares of coca produced in Colombia. This work calculates the money spent on drug trafficking and examines empirically whether drug production has increased or decreased. The initiatives to combat the *Fuerzas Armadas Revolucionarias de Colombia* (FARC) also can be empirically studied as the number of FARC members operating within Colombia can be estimated, as well as the revenue that illegal armed groups earn from illegal activities such as drug trafficking.

The second major policy recommendation is titled analytical recommendations and addresses the notion of autonomy. How does Colombia help scholars understand various IR concepts such as alliance politics? What does the Colombia case suggest for scholars of international relations and policy experts regarding the relations between hegemonic powers and weaker actors?

Finally, the third policy recommendation addresses the notion of lessons. What are the conclusions or lessons that can be drawn from Colombia? What does Plan Colombia teach scholars and policymakers about drug trafficking?

2

The Colombian Puzzle
in Historical Context

Before delving into the first puzzle of this book, a brief history of drug trafficking and organized crime within Colombia is needed.[1] We cannot understand the formation or the different critical junctures that impacted the evolution and transformation of Plan Colombia without having a basic understanding of the history and events that resulted in the formation of Plan Colombia. Colombia has a long history of violence and organized crime.[2] Over the 1990s, the U.S. government spent an estimated $1 billion attempting to combat drug cultivation and trafficking within Colombia. Despite these efforts, the area of coca under cultivation proliferated drastically.[3] Over the ten-year period from 1989 to 1998, the production of coca leaves within Colombia increased from 33,900 to 81,400 metric tons, which is an astounding 140 percent increase. Bruce Bagley states that "These dramatic increases in overall production reflected the fact that between 1996 and 1999, the total number of hectares of coca leaf under cultivation in Colombia rose by almost 100 percent, from 68,280 to 120,000 hectares."[4] These statistics are quite astounding, especially considering the billions of dollars of U.S. aid provided to Colombia over the decade to combat drug cultivation and trafficking.[5]

During the 1990s, Colombia had many other issues besides coca cultivation. In fact, Colombia continued to be the major cocaine refiner in the world during this period. Research indicates that Colombia supplied approximately "80 percent (220 metric tons) of the total cocaine imports (approximately 300 metric tons) smuggled into the United

States in 1999."[6] In addition to producing and trafficking cocaine, the Colombians also produced opium poppy, which is later refined into heroin. The 1998 statistics, however, reveal that the Colombians produced 61 metric tons of this good in one year alone, which is an astounding increase from no production only several years earlier. In terms of heroin production, Colombia was and continues to be only a minor producer and cultivator of heroin in the world. During this time period, scholars estimate that Colombia supplied only 2 percent of the heroin consumed around the world. Yet, the heroin produced in Colombia entered into the United States, particularly the eastern region.[7]

In 1989, the situation in Colombia began to spiral out of control when Liberal Party presidential candidate Luis Carlos Galán was assassinated. This tragic event represented the third presidential candidate the Medellín cartel assassinated before the 1990 elections. With U.S. support, the Colombian government attempted to dismantle the two major drug cartels operating within Colombia: the Medellín and Cali cartels. In the 1990s, the United States implemented the kingpin strategy, where the government focused on dismantling the leaders of the cartels operating within Colombia. The Colombians continued to track the notorious leader of the Medellín cartel, Pablo Escobar, and killed him in 1993.[8]

By the beginning of the 2000s, drug trafficking and violence continued in Colombia. Bagley argues that Colombia was one of the most dangerous and violent states in the world at the beginning of the 2000 and became a major concern for the United States from a security perspective.[9]

Drug Cultivation and Trafficking in Colombia

Despite the $1 billion in aid granted to Colombia during the 1990s, coca cultivation in the Andes continued to flourish, signaling the continued failures of the war on drugs. In 1998, for example, the number of metric tons of coca being cultivated in Colombia was 81,400, which represents a drastic increase over the 1990s. Just ten years earlier, reports estimate the number of metric tons being cultivated in Colombia at 33,900. These changes represent an astonishing 140 percent increase in coca cultivation. Politicians questioned how such massive increases in the area of coca under cultivation could occur every year despite U.S. funding and efforts to help the Colombians combat drug production and trafficking.[10]

Coca cultivation had shifted from Peru and Bolivia and moved to Colombia. In fact, Peru produced the majority of coca in the world during the mid-1980s whereas Colombia only cultivated approximately 10 percent of the global coca supply. In 1985, for example, Peru accounted for 65 percent of coca grown in the entire world.[11] Several important interdiction efforts targeted coca cultivation in Bolivia and Peru. In particular, two successful operations—Operation Blast Furnace and *Plan Dignidad*—resulted in the decrease of cultivation in Peru, but inevitably shifted coca cultivation to Colombia. With the support of the U.S. government, the Colombian government effectively dismantled what is referred to as the "air-bridge," which refers to the airspace that enabled coca paste to travel from Bolivia and Peru into Colombia where the paste could be refined and processed into cocaine. In 1995, Peru's President Alberto Fujimori authorized the Air Force to intervene and gave them permission to shoot aircraft flying between the two countries. The Air Force implemented the strategy with remarkable success, shooting down 25 airplanes and deterring aircraft from flying between the two countries.[12]

Bolivia also experienced major declines of coca production during this period. The interdiction efforts, however, had unintended consequences, forcing the drug traffickers to adapt. As a result of these partial victories, Colombia became the world's primary cultivator of coca.[13] In fact, Colombia accounted for approximately 90 percent of the coca produced in the world in the early 2000s.[14]

In addition to cultivating coca, Colombia also was—and remains— the leading refiner of cocaine in the world. Therefore, Colombia has dominated all aspects of the cocaine industry including cultivation, refinement, and trafficking for decades. At the end of the 1990s, researchers estimate that Colombia continued to dominate the cocaine industry, supplying 80 percent of the cocaine imported to the United States.[15]

Cocaine, however, is not the only product that the Colombians produce and traffic; Colombians also produce and participate in the trafficking of marijuana, the majority of which reaches the United States. Research indicates that the Colombians trafficked approximately 4,000 metric tons of marijuana into the United States in 1999 alone.[16] Yet, marijuana and heroin result in lower profits for drug traffickers than cocaine because Colombia produces smaller quantities of heroin and marijuana.

Along with marijuana, the production of opium, which is refined to produce heroin, also proliferated rapidly in Colombia over the decades. In 1998, for instance, the production of opium was estimated to be approximately 61 metric tons in Colombia, which is a 100 percent increase from previous years when the cultivation of opium was virtually nonexistent. In terms of the global heroin market, Colombia was—and remains—only a minor producer and distributor of heroin in the world market. Interestingly, the small percentage of heroin produced and trafficked—less than 2 percent—reached the eastern portion of the United States but did not enter the European market.[17]

The Defeat of the Colombian Kingpins

What is extremely baffling about Colombia is that drug cultivation and trafficking did not decrease even after the collapse of the two major cartels: Medellín and Cali. Why after such large amounts of money spent combatting drug trafficking and the collapse of the cartels would drug trafficking not decrease in the country? Certain key events led to serious efforts to dismantle the large cartels operating within Colombia. In 1989, the Medellín cartel assassinated Liberal Party presidential candidate Luis Carlos Galán. This was one of three assassinations of candidates campaigning for the Colombian presidency in 1990. The Barco administration attempted to combat the cartels, and the new policy became referred to as the kingpin strategy because the Colombians sought to dismantle these large cartels by going after the leaders. Killing the leaders would hasten the dismantling of the cartels, the logic being that the cartels could not function without their major leaders or *capos*. After endless monitoring and tracking of Pablo Escobar, the Colombians intercepted a call that he made, were able to determine his location, and killed him in 1993. Both Bogotá and Washington viewed the collapse of the Medellín cartel as a major success for security within Colombia. Under Escobar's leadership, the cartel's corrupt practices presented major security dilemmas for the democratic stability of Colombia. Not only did the cartel traffic drugs, but it also bribed government officials, judges, and other law enforcement authorities.[18] The Medellín cartel demonstrated that it was not afraid to use violence against government officials as well as political candidates. The collapse of both cartels represented a significant victory because it prevented Colombia from becoming a narco-state, or a state dominated by drug trafficking organizations.[19]

The dismantling of the Medellín cartel, however, created a vacuum and enabled the Cali cartel to fill the void created by the collapse of the more powerful Medellín cartel. The death of Pablo Escobar and the defeat of his powerful criminal organization enabled the Cali cartel to increase in strength and seize control of what was left of the organized criminal industry that remained from its rival—and more powerful—cartel. Differences existed between the Cali and Medellín cartels, with the major distinction being levels of violence. First, the

Cali cartel had fewer members than the much larger Medellín cartel, which had approximately 70,000 at the height of its power. Research indicates that the Cali cartel had approximately 5,000 members or 65,000 fewer than the Medellín cartel.[20] The Cali cartel was much less violent than Medellín, spending more effort influencing politicians through bribes and other elements of coercion. In fact, a major leader of the cartel, Miguel Rodríguez Orejuela, spent approximately $1 billion to bribe myriad individuals including but not limited to government officials, law enforcement officials, politicians, and judges.[21]

The Colombians also used the kingpin strategy against the Cali cartel, which eventually led to the collapse of this large organization. Even after the eventual dismantling of both cartels, drug trafficking continued within Colombia. While the kingpin strategy was successful in toppling the cartels, it created a vacuum and enabled smaller organizations to continue trafficking drugs.[22] The fragmentation of the cartels into smaller organizations has been referred to as the cockroach effect (just as cockroaches quickly scatter when a light is turned on in a darkened room, so did the drug cartels fragment).[23] Smaller cartels, or *cartelitos*, emerged and took control of the drug production and trafficking within Colombia. Experts estimate that 300 smaller organizations, or *cartelitos*, moved into fill the void created by the collapse of the two major Colombian cartels. Another consequence of the vacuum was that other organizations, such as the guerrillas, filled the void and took control of the cultivation of coca leaves within Colombia as well as the refining of the product.[24]

Importantly, the smaller organizations, or *cartelitos*, began to operate in areas of Colombia where the Colombian government had little or no control. The vast majority of Colombia is comprised of the Andes and jungle; the Colombian state was rather weak at this time and did not have the ability to administer law and order in remote regions of the country.[25] The smaller organizations took advantage of the weak Colombian state and continued to flourish.[26] Traditionally, weak states such as Colombia act as fruitful places for organized criminal networks to operate because the states do not have the capacity to stop such illegal activities.

Despite the victories against the major cartels, the smaller cartels created major problems for law enforcement and government officials. The *cartelitos* did not have a large structure and operations like the Cali and Medellín cartels. In essence, a smaller organizational structure makes giving orders to drug traffickers much easier. More importantly, law enforcement had significant challenges because of the dispersion phenomenon that existed as a result of the fragmentation of drug traffickers into smaller organizations.[27]

Domestic Dynamics: Internal Actors within Colombia

Colombia is a very complicated, yet fascinating, case study because many actors impact security and participate in drug trafficking within Colombia.[28] Colombia has a long history of violence,[29] and one cannot understand the political dynamics within Colombia without briefly understanding the actors involved in the internal conflict that has occurred for decades. One could spend an entire career studying and learning about the armed conflict within Colombia and the different actors. Many works have been written on the subject and this brief analysis does not begin to address the complexities of the internal conflict in Colombia.[30] It is, however, important to briefly mention the actors because they also participate in drug trafficking, and the money earned from the drug trade helps finance the internal conflict within Colombia.

The *Fuerzas Armadas Revolucionarias de Colombia* (FARC) is one of the major internal armed actors that has contributed to the internal strife. This leftist guerrilla organization claimed Marquetalia to be an independent "republic," where "guerrilla leaders held cabinet positions determined by their military experience and Marxist education."[31] The FARC had linkages with the Communist parties, but scholars have questioned the relationship between the two groups.[32] The FARC participates in various aspects of organized crime, such as kidnaping and extortion, in order to accumulate revenue. The FARC also receives income by taxing the peasants who cultivate coca. Importantly, however, the FARC does not participate in the drug trade outside of Colombia.[33]

Determining the profits earned by the FARC from drug trafficking and other illegal activities is a daunting task. Again, one should note that statistics are estimations. Different calculations exist for the profits earned and should be viewed as a range. Bagley estimates that the FARC earned approximately $400 million from its operations relating to drug trafficking at the end of the 1990s. He states: "By the end of the decade, Colombian government estimates placed the FARC's total earnings from the drug trade as high as $400 million per year—added to the estimated US $500 million per year that the FARC were believed to earn from their more 'traditional' guerrilla activities (e.g., collection of revolutionary 'taxes' on landowners, kidnapping, extortion, robbery, 'commissions' collected from local governments and businesses, and their own business investments), [the] FARC's total annual income in 1999 may have amounted to as much as U.S. $900 million."[34] Scholars, however, disagree whether the money earned from drug trafficking operations helps sustain the FARC. Analysts who think that drugs are crucial for FARC operations argue that the organization would be significantly weakened—if not depleted—without the vast resources earned from the drug trade. Critics of this argument counterargue that the FARC has many potential sources of income. If the FARC earns very minimal amounts of money from the drug trade, it would adapt and would increase other forms of organized crime, such as kidnapping, which are also quite lucrative.[35]

The profits earned from the drug trade have helped finance the FARC and have enabled it to expand and strengthen its operations throughout Colombia. In 1986, the FARC had an estimated 3,600 members in the organization, and its numbers continued to increase rapidly over time. By 1995, the FARC operated in 60 fronts within Colombia and had an estimated 7,000 members. By 1999, the FARC had approximately 10,000 combatants operating in Colombia. During its strongest period, the FARC had 17,000 combatants between 1999 and 2001.[36]

The FARC recognized that it was not strong enough to overthrow the Colombian government and implement a Marxist revolution. In order to continue the war against the government, FARC forces began to disperse throughout the regions and established different zones or front lines. As a result, the locations and operations of the FARC have shifted over time. The dispersion of the groups operating throughout Colombia leads one to question how the leadership exercises control over the different factions. With regard to this topic, Russell Crandall notes: "These dispersed groups—called *frentes*—have operated in a semi-autonomous manner since their inception, and doubtless, at times have little or no idea what type of operations—or even specific ideologies—other *frentes* are implementing. Moreover, there remains a great debate today in Colombia as to whether the central hierarchy of the FARC is always able to effectively control all of its *frentes*, which now number roughly 100."[37] Despite these concerns about organizational and control issues, the FARC today still remains a powerful actor and major player in Colombia.

The FARC, however, is not the only actor involved in the drug trade; various other organizations exist. The *Ejército de Liberación Nacional* (ELN) is the other major guerrilla organization operating within Colombia. The ELN has been described as a more "traditional" revolutionary group and can be compared to Castro's revolution in Cuba. The ELN also participates in organized criminal operations, such as extortion, and has turned to blowing up oil pipelines and extorting money from large corporations that conduct business in Colombia. However, the ELN differs from the FARC because it does not participate in drug trafficking activities.[38]

The paramilitaries are another major actor in Colombia. A 1968 decree enabled "the creation of civil defense forces to defend property against guerrilla incursions."[39] The paramilitaries have evolved over time, originally consisting of peasants who acted as a "self-defense" unit. The creation of the paramilitaries resulted from the weaknesses of the Colombian state and its inability to govern.[40] Crandall notes that the "new forms of paramilitary groups were born out of drug traffickers' resistance to guerrilla harassment; today they are no longer directly related to the drug cartels, but instead, consist of quasi-autonomous, drug revenue-supported groups committed to clearing the Colombian country-side of guerrilla influence."[41] Throughout its history, the FARC has threatened owners of land. The hostile relations between landowners and the guerrillas forced the landowners to fight back and combat the guerrilla organizations with their own paramilitaries.[42] In 1997, Carlos Castaño, a former member of the Medellín cartel, created *Las Autodefensas Unidas de Colombia* (AUC) in an attempt to improve the organization and structure of the paramilitaries in order to increase its presence in Colombia.

Colombia and Its History of Weak Institutions

Colombia has always suffered from a weak state with weak institutions that have been prone to corruption and have helped foster organized crime and other criminal activities. One potential reason why Colombia has weak institutions is the geographic complexity of the state. The rugged territory makes asserting control over rural areas more difficult for the Colombian state. Pizarro and Gaitán argue that "in a comparative, historic perspective, the Colombian state has always been small, poor, and weak."[43] They argue that geography has been a major factor in the weakness of the state, declaring that "first, it is a vast territory cross-cut by a very complex geography, one of the world's most hellish. This has given rise to a multitude of markets and scattered pockets of population."[44] The Colombian state apparatus remained poor for many years, which contributed to the government's inability to establish and enforce the law throughout the country. A poor state does not have the necessary resources to implement programs, strengthen institutions, and fund law enforcement initiatives, as these activities require resources. This lack of resources resulted in the Colombian state not having the ability to project itself throughout the vastly diverse geographic terrains. Pizarro and Gaitán credit the poverty of the state to the fact that Colombia did not have a major commodity to export to the global market until the beginning of the twentieth century, arguing: "It was not until the first decades of the twentieth century that Colombia was able to stabilize a product (coffee) for which there was demand on the world market. In addition, industrialization was slow in coming, and the state's resource base was very shaky."[45]

The Clinton Administration

This section moves from the overall history and focuses on answering the questions proposed in the development of Plan Colombia and how it came to fruition. It is appropriate to examine the various reasons why Plan Colombia was created and signed by President Clinton in 2000 after years of quarrelsome relations between the United States and Colombia. In order to understand the formation of the plan, one must begin with the relationship between the Samper and Clinton administrations.[46]

From the beginning, the Clinton administration had a negative view of Ernesto Samper because of his previous statements and positions on drug legalization.[47] Washington has had a long history of antidrug policies and rhetoric, and therefore viewed Samper as "soft" on the issue of drugs. As a result, the United States and Colombia did not always have great diplomatic relations, particularly during the middle of the 1990s. From the outset, the United States had a negative view of Ernesto Samper, who was the president of Colombia from 1994 through 1998, and questioned whether he could be an effective ally in combating drug trafficking in Colombia.[48] Samper allegedly was on the payroll of the drug cartels and used drug money to finance his presidential campaign. Additionally, Samper advocated for a rethinking of drug policies and supported the legalization of drugs.[49] In 1993, Deputy Assistant Secretary of State for Inter-American Affairs, Phil McLean, spoke with Samper about the problems that he confronted. McLean describes his discussion with Samper: "I said, 'Ernesto, you have a major, major problem with the United States: you're perceived as being soft on narcotics. This is the problem and there's only one way to fix it—you've gotta show that you're serious about this issue and to do this you're gonna have to do something about this particular issue. . . .' At that time there was no specific information that I knew of, and I was supposedly in the center of all the 'in' in intelligence on anything that implicated Samper."[50]

1994: Republicans Take over Congress

Realism demonstrates that the United States had geostrategic interests in Colombia and viewed it as a very important country for security within the region.[51] The Clinton administration and many politicians viewed drug trafficking from Colombia as a serious threat that needed to be addressed. The year 1994 represents a major turning point because the Republicans won the majority in the Congress, which is significant because the Republicans viewed the drug issue as a major priority and supported a tough U.S. foreign policy with regard to drug trafficking policy. One cannot understand the formation of Plan Colombia without taking into consideration the domestic pressures that President Clinton faced, particularly after the Republicans became the majority in Congress. Clinton did not want to be perceived as soft on the war on drugs and such pressures from Republicans forced him to strengthen his policy with regard to drugs. In addition, Al Gore ran for president in 2000, and he wanted to prove to the Republicans that he was deeply interested in the situation and to diffuse criticism among the electorate that he was soft on the issue of drugs. Plan Colombia, therefore, represented an opportunity to demonstrate that he was serious about U.S. geostrategic interests within Latin America and viewed U.S. national security as a priority. In sum, realism has no explanatory power with regard to the internal dynamics of the state. Only through using a comparative politics perspective can scholars understand the events that led to the formation of Plan Colombia.[52]

Ernesto Samper Toughens Stance on Drugs

Samper knew that the United States viewed him as soft on drugs, and this forced him to be tougher on drugs in order to appease the United States and help silence his critics. Crandall notes that Samper, in fact, was forced to implement harsher policies than ever envisioned, stating: "These actions also reveal Samper's profound lack of credibility on the drug issue in Washington. Knowing that critics both in Colombia and Washington were highly dubious about Samper's willingness to fight the war on drugs, Samper was forced to go further than either he or the United States had ever imagined. Thus we have the paradoxical situation whereby this supposedly narco-compromised president ended up, whether he liked it or not, being a reliable and predictable ally with Washington vis-à-vis the drug war."[53] This quote demonstrates that Samper actually became tougher on the war on drugs than many people would have ever expected. Also, one could argue that Samper was forced to do more than any of his predecessors with regard to drugs in order to maintain relations with the United States.[54]

Counterproductive Policies: The U.S. Decertifies Colombia

In 1995, 1996, and 1997, the U.S. government decertified Colombia for being uncooperative in the war on drugs. Many experts have criticized decertifying a country because it can remove access to money for countries that are vulnerable and require access to markets, trade, and foreign aid. As a result, a country can experience dire consequences if a U.S. president decertifies it. Decertification results in the suspension of foreign assistance from the United States, but, one must recognize that this neither includes money used for drug-related assistance, nor does it count for humanitarian aid. In addition, decertification results in the United States opposing loans from various institutions being granted to the country that fails to comply. However, one should note that the United States issued a national interest waiver in an attempt to avoid complete decertification.[55] Decertification also can impact the reputation of a country in the international arena, and, in turn, could hinder potential investors from investing within the country. In sum, "the impact of decertification on U.S. aid is immediate and direct: non-exempt aid is automatically suspended."[56]

Washington and the Samper administration had many differences in terms of their views regarding the results and progress of the war on drugs. On the one hand, the Clinton administration viewed Samper as a major threat to potential progress on the war on drugs. On the other hand, the Samper administration believed that it had made a tremendous amount of progress, particularly with the collapse of the Cali cartel. For Samper, the collapse of the cartel represented a significant victory and signified the ability of the Americans and the Colombians to work together and cooperate on certain issues and goals.[57] For instance, the U.S. Drug Enforcement Administration as well as the Central Intelligence Agency participated in the defeat of the cartel and the capture or defeat of major leaders working for the cartels.[58]

The certification process has been very controversial and has been viewed by many as the U.S. exercising its authority and forcing other "backward" countries to follow the rules. Adrián Bonilla argues that the United States believes that it has the responsibility to use its hegemonic power to intervene in backward countries and help them fix their problems. The realist assumptions of the United States have led other individuals to argue that the United States often behaves as a "bully," forcing weaker countries to comply in order to have access to various privileges.[59] As the most powerful country in the region, the United States had the ability to coerce Samper into enacting certain policies because the Colombians needed the aid from Washington. In order to receive the aid, the Colombian government had to meet U.S. standards. The United States viewed Samper as someone who could be controlled, and perhaps, even manipulated to comply with U.S. geostrategic interests. Decertification also can cause resentment among countries that the United States officially de-certifies because such countries often do not approve of being objectified and judged by the hegemonic actor, the United States.

Conclusion

Ultimately, this chapter has demonstrated that Colombia is a complex country,[60] and one cannot examine the war on drugs without analyzing the various actors within Colombia because some of these actors also participate in drug trafficking. The FARC, for instance, uses the revenues obtained from drugs to help finance its operations. Therefore, one cannot separate the internal actors from drug trafficking because they are uniquely intertwined.

This chapter also examined the contentious relations with Samper. The Republican takeover of Congress led Clinton to attempt to demonstrate his toughness against drugs in order to avoid the label of being soft on drugs. The next chapter examines why the United States signed Plan Colombia into law providing the Colombian government with billions of dollars after decertifying the country three consecutive years.

3

The Origins of Plan Colombia

Beginning in 1995, the U.S. government decertified Colombia and the Ernesto Samper administration three consecutive years for failing to comply with the requirements it set forth. In July 2000, during the Pastrana administration, the U.S. Congress approved and President Clinton signed into law a bill designed specifically to assist Colombia combat drug trafficking, which is known as Plan Colombia. This chapter explores the events that occurred between 1995 and 2000, which resulted in the creation and signing of Plan Colombia into law by the United States. Why did President Clinton sign Plan Colombia into law, thereby providing the Colombians with billions of dollars in aid after decertifying the country three successive years?

The Pastrana Administration

President Andrés Pastrana, the successor to Samper, took office in 1998 and represented an opportunity for a change in strategy. According to Marc Chernick, Pastrana had two main objectives: peace and the desire to improve relations with the United States. Pastrana came to power in Colombia and wanted to help Colombia solve its internal conflict that has resulted in a tremendous amount of violence and suffering in Colombia and has lasted for decades.[1] In addition, Pastrana wanted to improve relations with the United States. Washington understood that drug cultivation and trafficking still occurred in large numbers in Colombia despite the kingpin strategy and the successful operations that led to the dismantling of the major cartels operating within Colombia.[2] The United States learned from its mistakes with the Samper

23

administration, and Washington recognized that its "efforts to publicly undermine Ernesto Samper had resulted in an undermining of the Colombian state at the very time that the guerrilla and paramilitary groups were becoming stronger than ever."[3] Indeed, the new leader in Colombia provided the United States with a new opportunity to improve relations between the two countries and combat drug trafficking. The United States viewed Pastrana as a noteworthy ally in the fight against drug trafficking and organized crime. From the outset, the relations between Pastrana and the United States began on far better terms than the Samper administration, particularly because Pastrana was not connected to drug traffickers, which was not the case of his predecessor.[4] Pastrana also recognized the need to develop a solution to the internal conflict in Colombia, and he was able to leverage the United States and plead that Colombia was in dire need of assistance. In other words, Colombia was on the verge of collapse, and Pastrana convinced the United States that Colombia could not combat the problems without the necessary resources from Washington.

By 1999, the internal conflict in Colombia had devastating effects on the Colombian economy; the GDP decreased by 4.2 percent in Colombia, which represented the worst economic performance that Colombia had experienced since the Great Depression. The GDP decrease coincided with drastic increases in the levels of unemployment and individuals living in poverty. In 1999, for example, Colombia experienced a staggering 18 percent unemployment rate, and the poverty rate proliferated by 57.5 percent over a five-year period.[5] In addition to the economic instability as a result of the internal violence, neighboring countries became concerned about security levels, worrying that the internal conflict in Colombia would impact security in the region. DeShazo, Primiani, and McLean argue, "Neighboring countries began to feel the effects of violence in Colombia as the internal armed conflict took on an increasing regional dimension. FARC units frequently violated national borders, especially in remote areas such as the Darién in Panama, to rest and refit."[6]

Pastrana Travels North

President Clinton invited Pastrana to the White House shortly after he came to power. It appears as though Clinton wanted to increase his soft power and demonstrate that he sought an improved relationship with Pastrana, a relationship that would be much less quarrelsome than that between Washington and the Samper administration. At the White House in 1998, Pastrana stated: "On behalf of our people, I would like to express our thanks to the people of the United States,

and personally, I'd like to state that although I've only been President
for 3 months now, it would be very difficult I think for Nohra and I to
be welcomed so warmly anywhere else. I came here with the hope of
forging an alliance with President Clinton and the United States, and
I will leave having established a true friendship with the President,
and I hope with his Nation."[7] As the events transpired, it became
evident that Pastrana did not represent an equal partner, but rather
had to comply with Washington's demands and vision of how to fight
the drug war in order to receive money for counternarcotic initiatives.
Pastrana and the United States, however, differed on their goals and
objectives. Pastrana came to power desiring peace in Colombia and
viewed socioeconomic inequalities as a major problem within Colombia
that needed to be addressed.[8] For Pastrana, the need for land reform
and resources to address the economic and social issues occurring in
Colombia, particularly in the rural areas, became a primary concern,
and he proposed large amounts of aid to address the various inequalities in the rural regions of Colombia, wanting to replicate a Marshal
Plan for rural Colombia in order to increase the economic prosperity
of people living in the region.[9] In a 1998 press conference in Colombia,
Pastrana stated:

> We are committed to a peace process which is difficult, but
> we are committed to it, and we will forge ahead. We know
> the country we've received is in a financial situation worse
> than any in Colombia's history. We know we have to take
> harsh measures, and we will take them. We will protect the
> poorest sectors. Clearly, there are instructions to be given
> to ministers for all the social areas, those that have to do
> with social investment, with poverty, with health and edu-
> cation, with building houses; and matters of social interest
> are matters within the budget on which we are not going
> to try to reduce our expenses but try to keep them up and
> strengthen them. And we will have to make a major effort
> from the viewpoint of the administration, as we are doing,
> to cut our expenses, to cut a number of things.[10]

In 1998, Pastrana began peace negotiations with the FARC in
an effort to end the long conflict. Pastrana and FARC representative
Manuel Marulanda Velez entered into peace talks and agreed to establish a demilitarized zone, or *zona de despeje*, in Caquetá. Pastrana
described the situation, stating:

> I think that it's very important to be able to establish a
> dialog, a direct dialog with President Clinton, with the

Secretary of State, with General McCaffrey, with the
National Security Council Adviser, especially with this whole
demilitarized area which, according to Colombian law, can
be established so that the representatives of the guerrilla
movement can come to that area so we can guarantee their
life, so that the representatives of Government can go to
that area and their lives will also be guaranteed. We can
have international observers present in this demilitarized
area, as well as journalists who will also be attending.[11]

When asked if the United States was willing to lead the peace process
effort in Colombia, President Clinton responded:

Well, I would like to do anything that I can, but I think
the President has taken the lead in a way that is, I think,
innovative and very heartening to the rest of us. Again, I
hope that those who have been involved in the turmoil in
Colombia will take his offer in good faith. From the point
of view of the United States, I think we should be in a supporting role however we can be of help. One of the things
that we would very much like is the United States citizens
who have been kidnaped. If they are alive, we'd like them
released. If they're not, we'd like them accounted for. That
would help us a great deal.[12]

Pastrana's intentions backfired and, in effect, the demilitarized
zone prevented Pastrana and the military from operating within this
42,000 square kilometer zone (26,097 miles), roughly the size of Switzerland. According to Pastrana, the zone signified the peaceful intentions
of the Colombian government and the desire for peace negotiations. In
reality, the zone enabled the FARC to operate without any intervention or negative repercussions from the Colombian government, and
therefore, served as an area of central command for the FARC. The
FARC quickly placed 5,000 troops in the demilitarized zone and, in
essence, could do whatever they wanted in this large swatch of territory. In addition, the FARC took this opportunity to rearm and store
weapons in this zone.[13]

This zone provided the FARC with a massive territory where they
could organize and plan various attacks. Pastrana and his administration had no control over the region, and, in reality, this area became a
separate FARC-controlled state. As time passed, the FARC continued to
operate in this region, and Pastrana failed to make progress with the
FARC in terms of negotiations. In 1998, General McCaffrey described
the situation in Colombia as "out of control, a flipping nightmare."[14]

Pastrana's approval ratings also decreased drastically as a result of the failures of the peace negotiations and the disastrous demilitarized zone. By the end of 1999, Pastrana's approval rating decreased from 42 percent to 22 percent.[15]

By the summer of 1999, Pastrana spoke with Washington and emphasized that Colombia desperately needed assistance. The United States urged Pastrana to develop an initiative that Washington could discuss and review.[16] Pastrana developed the plan that became known as Plan Colombia in 1999. Pastrana had several major objectives and issues that he had to address upon assuming office. During this time, the Colombian economy was quite weak. He understood that issue of drugs had to be confronted, but he believed that the peace process was vital for this to happen. Pastrana also had to address the humanitarian crisis occurring in Colombia.[17] Therefore, his version of Plan Colombia focused on peace first, then developmental issues, and finally drug trafficking. Pastrana believed that peace had to be achieved first and then developmental assistance in order to improve Colombia's economic status. Some scholars believe that, in reality, separating the drug issue from the internal conflict is difficult because the FARC financed the conflict with revenue earned from the illicit drug business. Sandra Borda argues, "I don't think that it was ever possible to differentiate both things [drugs and the internal conflict] that clearly."[18]

Pastrana constructed a plan where drug trafficking and organized crime played a tertiary role, preparing several versions of Plan Colombia for the various potential donors.[19] Pastrana stated that Plan Colombia would be a $7.5 billion plan with the intention of helping the Colombian economy, as well as promoting peace and other programs, such as social development programs. Pastrana designed the plan believing that the U.S. government would provide $4 billion, and the international community would provide the rest of the money. When describing Plan Colombia and its formation, Arlene Ticker states, "I don't think Plan Colombia again was ever conceived as a counternarcotics policy by the Colombian government at least in its main components. For me the ultimate goal was state strengthening and particularly military strengthening."[20] Pastrana traveled to Washington, D.C., to promote his version of Plan Colombia, which barely mentioned the role of the military and focused much more attention on the different forms of economic and social aid that could help create peace in Colombia. While drug trafficking certainly impacted Colombia, combating drug cultivation and trafficking did not constitute a major initiative for President Pastrana.[21] When describing the plan Pastrana designed, Chernick states, "If you look at that, it was not much of a strategy, but it was a nice overall vision. It is hard to find fault with that Plan."[22]

Still, one cannot understand the formulation of Plan Colombia without examining the international issues at hand as well as the domestic politics within both countries. The nature of the issue enabled and provided the Colombians with greater relative autonomy in the early stages of Plan Colombia during its formulation because Colombia had become tired of the war and Pastrana wanted peace. Plan Colombia also appeared to be an excellent initiative and opportunity for the United States to combat drug trafficking in Colombia. Republicans in Congress criticized President Clinton for being "soft" on drugs. Republicans portrayed the president as a soft liberal who admitted to trying marijuana—but not inhaling—during his time in England.[23] Such statements made Clinton an easy target. The Religious Right, in particular, then and now, remains a prominent force for wholesome and traditional American values and morality. In sum, Plan Colombia provided Clinton with a forum to demonstrate that he was serious about combating drug trafficking, and, indeed, should not be labeled as soft on the issue of drugs.

Congress debated Plan Colombia and its strategy. Marc Chernick, one of the experts on Colombia who testified before Congress, explained that Pastrana's vision of Plan Colombia and his notion that peace would assist against drug production and trafficking would be an effective policy to combat narcotics. Chernick argued, "The reaction from the Congress was this is nuts. We are going to make peace with the narco-guerrillas and we are going to fund that, and they were totally hostile, completely hostile."[24] After the debate in Congress, which occurred in late spring of 2000, Plan Colombia underwent a fundamental transformation.

The transformation of Plan Colombia and reformulation of the policy Pastrana designed was in large part a result of "drug czar" Barry McCaffrey's efforts and influence. McCaffrey viewed Colombia as a problem country and knew that it would not be popular for the United States to become involved in Colombia's internal conflict. McCaffrey, director of the Office of National Drug Control Policy (ONDCP), was key to the process and helped influence President Clinton. Chernick explained, "Barry McCaffrey from inside the White House took control of this. . . . McCaffrey saw this as an opportunity. He understood that some sort of U.S. assistance program supporting peace in Colombia was not going to fly."[25] The United States needed to combat drugs first and not involve itself in the internal conflict in Colombia. McCaffrey recognized that Congress would support a strong antinarcotics strategy, and as a result of his efforts, Washington fundamentally altered Plan Colombia and transformed it into an antinarcotics policy.

McCaffrey's influence resulted in the Clinton administration disagreeing with the formula or strategy for Plan Colombia. First,

Plan Colombia appeared vague and did not emphasize the war on drugs enough. The Clinton administration reengineered the formula, making the number one priority and focus combating drug trafficking through supply-side programs and expanded "Plan Colombia to a wider strategy of strengthening the role of the state in the fight against drugs."[26] The Clinton administration had a different concept of the problem and solution and used its power to alter Plan Colombia and invert the initial formula Pastrana designed. Washington downplayed the interdependent nature of the drug problem, and, instead, viewed the major problem to be the supply of drugs coming from Latin America, particularly Colombia, and wanted to avoid becoming involved in the complicated internal dynamics within Colombia. The United States could not afford to become involved in another Vietnam-style conflict.[27] As a result, the Clinton administration clearly distinguished the counternarcotics initiatives in Colombia from deeper involvement in the complicated internal situation that had been ongoing for decades. Assistant Secretary of Defense, Brian Sheridan, summarized the sentiments during his testimony in early 2000, stating: "'The targets are the narco-traffickers, those individuals and organizations that are involved in the cultivation of coca or opium poppy and the subsequent production and transportation of cocaine and heroin to the U.S. Only those armed elements that forcibly inhibit or confront counterdrug operations will be engaged, be they narco-traffickers, insurgent organizations, or illegal self-defense forces. I know that some are concerned that we are being drawn into quagmire. Let me assure you, we are not.'"[28] This quote demonstrates that policy experts and politicians remembered the lessons from Vietnam and did not want to intervene in the internal dynamics in another country. Focusing on drug trafficking enabled Washington to combat drugs and attempt to stop the cultivation and eventual trafficking of drugs over the U.S. border without becoming involved in the more than four decades-long civil conflict.

U.S. Congressional Debate

House of Representatives members did not make drastic alterations to the bill President Clinton proposed. Some members, however, attempted to make changes and alter the flow of money. Nancy Pelosi (D-CA) argued that more money needed to be spent on domestic aspects such as programs to help addicts receive treatment and rehabilitation in order to return to their lives and become productive members of society.[29] The argument and logic behind supporting demand-reduction programs is that drug traffickers operate because they have a market.

As every student of economics knows, the law of supply and demand will dictate the levels of production of a product. Fewer "gringos" addicted to drugs in the United States, therefore, would help curb the number of users demanding drugs. Despite her valiant efforts, Pelosi's attempt to funnel money into programs designed to treat addicts and rehabilitate them into productive members of society ultimately failed.

The debate in the Senate resulted in various amendments to the bill Clinton proposed. Some senators wanted to address human rights issues. Patrick Leahy (D–VT), in particular, became a champion of human rights issues and expressed concern with Colombia's long history of human rights abuses. Leahy proposed that the Secretary of State would "have to certify the Colombian military officers accused of committing human rights violations were being tried in civilian courts, and that the Colombian Armed Forces was terminating links between the military and paramilitary groups."[30] The human rights initiatives resulted in small amounts of aid being devoted to this issue and led to minor decreases in the military budget. However, human rights issues did not constitute a major component of Plan Colombia. The military components of Plan Colombia always remained a crucial aspect of the bill, because Washington wanted to provide Colombia with the appropriate resources necessary to combat drug trafficking to decrease the flow of drugs entering the United States.[31]

Colombian Ambassador Luis Alberto Moreno is another key person who deserves credit for the passing of Plan Colombia. Moreno was very effective and made himself known to the members of the U.S. Congress. In addition to his excellent diplomatic skills, Moreno recognized that Colombia desperately needed money from the Clinton administration. He became a staunch advocate of Plan Colombia because he viewed the Clinton administration as an important ally for Colombia.[32]

After the numerous debates and concessions, Congress passed Plan Colombia and sent it to President Clinton for ratification. On July 13, 2000, Clinton signed Plan Colombia—or H.R. 4425—into law, which provided Colombia with significant amounts of aid to combat drug trafficking. Plan Colombia, in essence, became a U.S.-led initiative because all of the international donors refused to support such a plan. However, U.S. officials continued to emphasize that Plan Colombia would be a counternarcotics initiative, and the United States would not become involved in the internal dynamics within Colombia. Drug czar Barry McCaffrey declared, "The primary focus on this supplemental effort is to provide support for Colombia's intensifying counter drug [sic] efforts. As a matter of Administration policy, the United States will not support Colombian counterinsurgency efforts."[33]

Understanding the Formation of Plan Colombia

In reality, Washington created Plan Colombia and devised the strategy according to its goals and objectives. Importantly, a Spanish version did not exist until several months after the document had been created in English, which proves that the United States set the agenda and developed Plan Colombia according to the goals, priorities, and strategies of Washington.[34]

Realism helps explain the role of power and the ability of stronger states to set the agenda. For realists, strong states can do what they want, while weaker states must comply with policy and do what they must.[35] Altering Plan Colombia was easy for the United States. After the end of the cold war, the United States emerged as the most powerful country in the world. As the hegemon, the United States was able to use its power to invert the formula.

The United States also intervened in Plan Colombia based on certain inherent assumptions about the superpower's role in the international system. Adrián Bonilla argues that the United States thought that it had not only the right but also the responsibility to intervene in countries experiencing problems, or "backward countries," and should use its power to "fix" the problems within other countries. These realist assumptions are in line with the decades-old U.S. view of Latin America as a subservient region. Since the Monroe Doctrine in the early 1800s, Latin America has been the "backyard" of the United States, and therefore, the United States felt it had the right and responsibility to control its weaker neighbors to the south.[36] In sum, the hegemonic actor, the United States, was able to shift the formula and set the agenda by virtue of its position as an international superpower. On the other hand, the weaker actor, Colombia, could not set its own agenda and inevitably followed along and abided by the decisions of the stronger power.[37] Therefore, the Colombians had no choice but to appease the stronger power in order to receive money to combat drug trafficking in Colombia.

The stronger power, the United States, did not collaborate with the Colombians and work with the government in order to develop a joint plan that satisfied both countries. For the United States, marketing Plan Colombia as a key part of a Colombian-led initiative became paramount. Clearly, the United States neither wanted to have its "soft" power decline within Colombia, nor did it want to be accused of agenda-setting in the region.[38] Nothing, however, could have been further from the truth. The United States solicited advice from neither the Colombians nor the international community. Instead, it had a vision of what needed to be done in order to decrease the security risks and stop drugs from being cultivated and trafficked within its borders.

Realism further explains why the United States did not work through institutions, instead focusing on state-to-state relations with Colombia. For realists, states are the unit of analysis in the international system. While realists recognize that cooperation occurs between countries, they are skeptical of institutions. In the *False Promises of Institutions*, John Mearsheimer argues that institutions are a forum for power politics. Realists are critical of institutions because of the potential for free riders and defecting. Mearsheimer emphasizes that states care about relative gains vis-à-vis other states because the world is zero-sum. Therefore, states are not concerned about absolute gains, but instead they want to gain an advantage over their competitors.[39]

In addition to explaining the formation of the plan, realism also has explanatory power in terms of understanding the components of Plan Colombia. For realists, a state's primary goal is to survive in the anarchic international system. The United States viewed drug trafficking in Colombia as a serious threat to national security, regional security, as well as security in Colombia, and needed a solution to the problem. Washington did not want drug trafficking organizations to impact its security or its position as the sole world superpower.[40]

Although realism explains the power dynamics and the long-term goals or grand strategy of the United States, one needs to understand the role of economics and how economic considerations impacted Plan Colombia. Colombia is a vital country in terms of security because it borders on various important trading partners, including as Venezuela and Brazil.[41] In addition, Colombia neighbors the Panama Canal, which is a major transit point and crucial geographic location for trade. The United States has an interest in stability in the region and does not want the economic trade interrupted because it could hinder the prosperity and security within the United States. Colombia is more dependent on the United States for aid, trade, and access to markets, and, therefore, the relationship is not one of complex interdependence. In terms of the numeric percentages, Colombia accounts for less than 1 percent of U.S. trade. In addition to trade, the United States also has many economic investments in Colombia, and, therefore, stability is necessary in order to attract investors.[42]

Realism, however, fails to account for the perceptions among elite actors. Identifying the problem and developing a solution are constructivist issues. Since the Reagan administration, the United States has viewed drug trafficking and organized crime in Colombia as a major issue for U.S. national security and managed to securitize the war on drugs.[43] An analysis of the speech acts and an examination of the money allocated to combatting the war on drugs demonstrates that President Regan successfully securitized the war on drugs. Critics, such as Ethan Nadelmann, argue that the war on drugs should not be viewed or constructed as a security issue, but rather it should be seen as a health problem.[44] Less money should be spent on supply-side policies and more money should be allocated to treatment, prevention, and education. Supply-side policies have continued to dominate U.S. drug policies since the Reagan administration.[45] For Washington, the logic is that the United States would not have a major drug problem if the Colombians did not produce and traffic these noxious substances. According to this logic, then, the only way to win the war on drugs is not only to stop the cultivation of the drugs through eradication programs, but also to combat the cartels through interdiction programs as well as incarcerating drug traffickers.

Financing of Plan Colombia

The Europeans did not approve of Plan Colombia and provided no financial aid. The Europeans did, however, provide Colombia with some money for programs addressing developmental issues, but they did not view this aid as part of Plan Colombia.[46] The main program that finances Plan Colombia, known as the Andean Counterdrug Initiative (ACI), from 2000 to 2005 provided Colombia with $2.8 billion.[47] Colombia also received resources from the Foreign Military Financing (FMF), and in 2005 the combined total aid from ACI and FMF was $4.5 billion.[48]

Components of Plan Colombia

The final version of Plan Colombia passed by the U.S. Congress and signed into law by Clinton had ten major elements or components:

1. an economic strategy;

2. an international strategy;

3. a peace strategy;

4. a human development strategy;

5. a fiscal and financial strategy, including austerity and economic adjustment measures;

6. a military strategy;

7. a judicial and human rights strategy;

8. a social participation strategy;

9. a counternarcotics strategy; and

10. an alternative development strategy.

However, these ten components did not receive equal weight as Washington allocated 80 percent of the funds for Plan Colombia for "hard" components, as opposed to soft issues such as human rights and alternative development.[49]

Military Components of Plan Colombia

In order to fight the war on drugs, Washington has relied on its relationship with militaries in other countries. Adam Isacson argues that "the drug war, which is evolving into a larger battle against organized-crime groups that finance themselves with drug proceeds, has enabled the U.S. government to maintain the close military-to-military relationships forged during the cold war, a period when many generals served as heads of government."[50] Armed forces have continued to play a major role in combating drug trafficking, often blurring the lines between the traditional functions of the police and the military. In essence, the drug war represents a decline in the progress made during the transitions from authoritarian regimes to democracies in Latin America because the military reverted to assuming a role that it invoked in the past prior to the transitions.[51] Said differently, Isacson states:

> The turn to militaries to patrol the streets, to man check-points, to carry out searches and seizures, and to arrest and interrogate suspects is a step backward for the region. A key characteristic of the past 30 years' transitions to democracy has been the removal of soldiers from tasks that would have them in constant contact with the population in daily life. Many countries' police forces were moved from defense to public-security or interior ministries, with civilian chiefs and separate police academies."[52]

Importantly, the police and military, by definition, have different roles. The police force is designed to maintain and enforce the law; for instance, the police investigate crimes of different levels of severity ranging from murder to theft. The military, conversely, defends the state from external enemies. For example, it defends a country from foreign invaders to protect the sovereignty and survival of the country.[53] Analysts argue that the situation becomes dangerous when the two units blend together and a clear distinction is not made.[54]

The United States has a long history of maintaining separate roles for the military and the police; in fact, laws ensure that this distinction is maintained. The Posse Comitatus Act prohibits the government from using soldiers to conduct policing activities, unless the U.S. president orders the military to perform policing duties in times of extreme danger or uncertainty.[55] In sum, the military component of Plan Colombia accounted for a great deal of the funds.[56] In July 2000, the U.S. Congress passed emergency supplemental package P.L. 106–246, which provided the Colombian government with $1.3 billion to help combat drug production and trafficking in Colombia, as well as other countries in the Andean region, which historically have been major cultivators of coca. Colombia received $860 million of the $1.3 billion from the emergency-aid package. The vast majority of the money for the aid, $632 million, was allocated to assist the military combat drug trafficking. Meanwhile, the United States placed limitations on the number of troops that could be deployed to Colombia with the initial support package.[57] The military components of Plan Colombia would only continue to increase, particularly with the election of Álvaro Uribe, who wanted to combat the FARC and merged the war on drugs with the war on terrorism. The next chapter outlines the evolution of Plan Colombia and offers an in-depth analysis of the role of the military.

Aerial Eradication

A major component of Plan Colombia is the eradication of coca crops that are later processed into cocaine. Three main forms of eradication exist: voluntary manual, forced manual, and aerial spraying. Until 2007, aerial spraying was a crucial component of Plan Colombia and billions of dollars have been spent on flying airplanes over Colombia and spraying herbicides in order to destroy coca being cultivated.[58] However, aerial spraying efforts are not new in Colombia, having begun in the 1970s to eradicate the cultivation of cannabis crops. Aerial spraying enabled pilots to spray large number of hectares from the air with a version of Roundup®, a common herbicide designed to kill weeds that can be purchased in stores. The airplanes began spraying an effective concentration of Roundup Ultra®, a compound of Cosmo-Flux and glyphosate, which is a weak type of organic acid.[59] Research indicates that glyphosate has disastrous health impacts and has led to various cases of poisoning. Buffin and Jewell discuss the problem of toxicity, stating: "Some literature suggests that glyphosate can cause chronic health effects in laboratory animals. Lifetime glyphosate feeding studies have shown reduced weight gain, liver and kidney effects and degradation of the eye lens. These effects were significant only at the higher doses tested. . . . In spite of animal tests showing a low mammalian toxicity, significant poisoning effects caused by both intentional and accidental exposure to glyphosate have been recorded in humans and laboratory animals."[60] Further research demonstrates that glyphosate can have negative health impacts on reproduction. Research on animals found that glyphosate can indeed reduce the sperm count for men. Other research has suggested that glyphosate also can cause problems with pregnancy. Monsanto, the company that produces the product, denies the claims and argues that the product has been tested and is safe.[61]

Destroying coca crops by aerial spraying also has damaging effects on the environment. Research indicates that Roundup Ultra® is damaging to the environment. At times, the wind factor is uncontrollable, and it can blow the herbicides to different regions.[62] The State Department asserts that the aerial spraying programs are executed in a manner that minimizes harm and spray drift. Ramírez Lemus, Stanton, and Walsh argue that spray drift is a major problem that Washington underplays, stating: "However, the sheer number and consistency of the reports of damage lend them credibility, and many complaints have been verified by Colombian state agencies, intergovernmental commissions, or independent parties. Herbicide spray drift is a [sic] probably a major cause of the damage; models created by the U.S. Environmental Protection Agency (EPA) show that herbicide can drift up to 600 feet downwind from their targets. Although, on paper, a procedure exists to compensate small farmers whose legal crops are destroyed by spraying, in practice it has not functioned."[63] As a result of the spray drift, Roundup Ultra® can enter into the water, polluting the water and causing significant damages to the ecosystem. The chemicals in the herbicides have had negative impacts on various crops and resulted in damages to their production, which is an integral part of the food supply. Experts maintain that spraying such herbicides can have numerous health impacts, and research demonstrates that glyphosate can lead to respiratory problems, damage to the nervous system, digestive problems, and skin infections.[64]

Despite the research regarding the consequences of aerial spraying, the U.S. government continues to ignore the major ramifications that the aerial spraying program has had on Colombia's environment as well as on the health of its citizens. The EPA has conducted several studies regarding the health impacts, but critics have noted that the EPA studies have major problems in terms of objectivity and accuracy. For instance, the EPA conducts studies based on information provided by the State Department. The EPA, however, lacks the appropriate resources to measure the number of hectares sprayed and relies on the data collected by the U.S. government or other agencies. Since the EPA cannot collect data, conducting a rigorous and objective study is difficult. In addition, the EPA lacks some of the major details with regard to how the aerial spraying program is conducted.[65]

The aerial spraying program also has been criticized on the grounds that it is illegal and violates the Colombian constitution. Importantly, no other country in Latin America—except Colombia—

permits the spraying of herbicides from airplanes.[66] The Administrative Court in Cundinamarca determined that the aerial fumigation program is unconstitutional for several reasons. First, citizens living in Colombia have the constitutional right to public health and security, and a Colombian court ruled that the government has the obligation to provide people living within Colombia a healthy environment in which to live.[67] President Uribe refused to suspend the aerial spraying program and ignored the ruling of the court.

Alternative Development and Crop Substitution

Critics of aerial spraying argue that Plan Colombia should have allocated more money toward issues of economic development rather than to spraying the countryside with herbicides. Developmental programs could aid farmers, providing them with legitimate alternatives to growing coca, although some issues and challenges exist that must be considered when talking about alternative development strategies. Daniel Mejía argues: "It [alternative development] has been, in a lot of cases, a complete waste of money."[68] First, coca grows anywhere and is very resilient, unlike many other products, and many farmers cultivate coca in order to survive. Second, coca tends to be grown in impoverished regions.[69] Third, coca has many uses beyond being refined into cocaine. For instance, coca is chewed by people in the highlands to avoid altitude sickness. Coca also is an ingredient used to make tea and other products such as toothpaste. Fourth, coca plays an important role in indigenous rituals in the Andean countries and is exchanged between individuals as a cultural practice.[70] Vidart notes that, "the Andean Indian chews coca because that way he affirms its identity as son and owner of the land that yesterday the Spaniard took away and today the landowner keeps away from him. To chew coca is to be Indian . . . and to quietly and obstinately challenge the contemporary lords that descend from the old *encomenderos* and the old conquistadors."[71] Coca also is used by indigenous groups in various religious ceremonies.[72]

Sanho Tree argues that growing coca is a rational choice for many peasants living in the highlands because it grows everywhere, is easily produced, and acts as the primary source of income for coca farmers living in the highlands.[73] Marten Brienen, an expert on Bolivia and development, argues that coca functions like a weed. He states, "That plant is indestructible. It does not matter how you treat it, it will grow."[74] This is important to note because other legal crops cannot grow in such remote regions of Colombia where the texture of the soil is poor and not conducive to cultivation.[75] Even if a peasant wanted to grow other crops such as oranges, they will not grow in such high altitudes. Growing other products also requires expertise, which is not the case for coca.

Washington has attempted to help coca cultivators grow other legal products, such as rice, coffee, citrus fruit, grains, maize, and bananas.[76] U.S. efforts have been futile as coca growers continue to grow coca, which is more profitable. The reasons that growers cultivate coca are purely economic, yet the United States fails to understand the reality of life for *campesinos* in Peru, Bolivia, and Colombia. Mejía notes that farmers earn more money when they make coca paste or coca base as opposed to strictly cultivating the coca leaf.[77] Basic economics teaches us about the laws of supply and demand and rationality. Brienen argues, "If you look at the price of raw coca, . . . it is relatively stable."[78] Therefore, one does not need a complicated game theoretic model to understand that coca cultivators will continue to grow coca because of the earning potential despite the fact that it is illegal.

In addition, the laws of supply and demand help explain the logic and rationale for growing coca. Coca growers have a market for their goods because they play an integral part in the cocaine supply chain. As long as cocaine is in demand and profits can be earned, then coca growers will have a market to sell the coca that they cultivate. As a result of the demand, coca growers can earn more money growing and selling coca than they can from bananas or other legal products. In fact, research indicates that growers can earn between four to ten times the money growing coca than other legal alternatives, such as bananas.[79] Coca growers earn a living growing this product, and, therefore, it is a rational choice for them to want to maximize their income.[80]

Another reason coca is more profitable is that it requires less effort to maintain and to transport. In an interview, Brienen raises an important point regarding the infrastructure problems in Colombia, stating, "Coca lasts for a good long time. It [coca] can be stored away. If you grow bananas, or oranges or any kind of fruit, what people care about is what it looks like. . . ."[81] People do not want to eat a fruit that looks unappealing. He continued, "An attractive fruit can't be dented. If you are going over a bunch of not great roads through the Andes, it is hard to get fruit from one place to the other, especially at a point of export and to keep it in shape so that you can market it internationally."[82] This is not true at all for coca; the only thing that buyers care about is the total bulk weight of the coca. Thus, problems would still exist even if oranges grew in the Andes. One of the major issues with fruit like oranges is determining a way to transport the product to market without damage. Rural Colombia has major problems with infrastructure, particularly roads, and transporting oranges from the highlands to the market before the product spoils would be difficult. Ted Galen Carpenter also describes the situation for coca cultivators, stating:

> Because they operate outside the law, drug-crop growers do not have to deal with many of the obstacles that farmers of legal crops must endure. Those obstacles include poor transportation infrastructure, lack of access to credit, lack of reasonable and consistent government standards for recognizing titles to property (as well as lack of efficient enforcement of property rights), and volatile, unpredictable markets for agricultural products. Buyers for trafficking organizations merely purchase the crops, pay the growers well, and haul off the crops. Not surprisingly, a significant percentage of Latin American farmers prefer to do business that way even if it means dealing in an illegal product.[83]

Carrying baskets of oranges from the highlands to market without machinery is difficult and inefficient. Purchasing a wheelbarrow or other types of transportation requires a peasant to have money to purchase such products. A peasant may not have access to capital and cannot sign a loan for money in order to develop a productive business. Even if access to credit exists, contractual issues could arise and less developed regions of Colombia, for instance, do not have strong enforcement of property rights. Legal issues can be complicated and enforcing the law requires time, and perhaps, a lawyer to represent a client to ensure justice. Hiring a lawyer and educating oneself with regard to one's rights requires capital. This brief scenario helps demonstrate that growing legal crops and transporting them to the market is very challenging.

Another important element hindering the growth of legal goods is the security dynamic. Peasants are forced to grow coca because the armed actors, such as the FARC, could harm them if they do not grow coca. An individual residing in rural Colombia does not have the choice to grow other crops because the FARC demands that coca must be cultivated because it is an integral part of the processing of cocaine. In other words, the money from cocaine trafficking cannot be obtained if coca is not refined into cocaine. People are rational when their lives are threatened and will continue to grow coca if they are pressured by illegal armed actors who demand that they cultivate coca leaves.

Strengthening Democracy and Institutions

The United States and Colombia have both promoted improving democracy as well as the rule of law and value them as an important aspect of Plan Colombia. This is largely rhetoric because the statistics demonstrate that the United States has spent 80 percent of the money on hard components, such as the military, and only 20 percent of the money on soft programs, such as alternative development, human rights, and democracy promotion.[84] The United States reengineered Plan Colombia as a supply-side initiative designed to combat the cultivation of coca and drug production. President Clinton had a different perspective of both the problems and the solutions to the situation in Colombia. Plan Colombia is consistent with past U.S. priorities. Clearly, security always has been the primary objective in terms of U.S. foreign policy. Economics occupy the second major goal in terms of U.S. foreign policy, while human rights, democracy, and other value issues are tertiary in importance.[85]

Conclusion

The U.S. has a long tradition and history of antidrug policies and regimes. With the end of the cold war, drug trafficking, particularly from countries in the Andean region, became the major security threat for the United States. In the early 1980s, President Reagan managed to securitize the war on drugs and make it a national security issue.[86] Reagan viewed drugs as evil and believed that the United States had a major problem and more resources were needed to combat the supply.[87] Like Reagan, President George W. Bush increased aid to Latin America, particularly in the form of military and police financing. Bush implemented the Andean Regional Initiative, designed to combat cultivation and drug trafficking in the Andean region. Despite all of these efforts, drug trafficking remained constant and cultivation continued.

After three years of decertifying Colombia, Washington viewed Colombia as a major security threat. In 1994, the Republicans obtained the majority in Congress, and President Clinton felt domestic pressure and did not want to be perceived as soft on crime or the war on drugs. By 2000, the previous events led Clinton to sign into law Plan Colombia, which provided the Colombians with billions of dollars in funding. Clinton disagreed with the definition of the problem and developed a different Plan Colombia than President Pastrana initially proposed. Constructivism demonstrates that different actors have varying perceptions as well as solutions about problems.[88] Pastrana wanted to focus on peace first, then developmental issues, and finally drug trafficking.

The politicians feared extensive involven.
of Colombia and did not want to become in,
other actors. Washington thought back to th.
avoid a potential Vietnam-type situation in Colo.
combating drug production and drug trafficking th.
of Plan Colombia, and numerous experts criticized su.
amount of money for the military component.

In order to understand the formulation and evolutic.
Colombia, this chapter invoked the use of an eclectic theoretica.
work as well as what Laura Neack refers to as "levels of analys.
Realism has explanatory power, particularly in terms of explaini.
how the stronger power, the United States, used its hegemonic position to set the terms and conditions of Plan Colombia. For neorealists,
the primary goal of a state is to survive in the international system,
which is anarchical in nature.[91] The United States used its power to
reengineer Plan Colombia because it wanted to ensure its security and
remain the dominant power in the region. In other words, the United
States sought to maintain the status quo.

Neorealism, however, has many weaknesses. First, the state is
the unit of analysis for neorealists, and, therefore, this theory ignores
other non-state actors and external forces, such as the market. Drug
traffickers and organized criminal networks are illegal and defy the
laws of the state in order to earn profits. In addition, realists ignore
the forces of the market and the rules of economics, particularly the
law of supply and demand.[92] Neorealists argue that states are like
black boxes and billiard balls crashing into each other: Each state is
led by rational actors and has the same goal: to survive. One cannot
study foreign policy formation, however, without studying the internal dynamics of a country.[93] One cannot understand Plan Colombia
without invoking the tools of comparative politics and examining the
domestic factors that contributed to the formation of Plan Colombia;
the pressure Clinton felt to demonstrate that he viewed drugs as a
serious issue and that he was not soft on drug crime played a major
role in contributing to the formation of Plan Colombia.[94]

t in the internal dynamics
red with the FARC and
960s and wanted to
a.[89] Clinton made
ajor initiatives
a significant

of Plan
ame-
[90]

4

Uribe and the Fusion of the
War on Drugs with the War on Terrorism

The September 11, 2001, terrorist attacks by Muslim extremists fundamentally changed the dynamics of U.S. foreign policy. Within Colombia,
the situation changed with the election of Álvaro Uribe, who represented a fundamental shift from Pastrana. Uribe came to power and
vowed to combat the illegal armed actors operating within Colombia,
such as the *Fuerzas Armadas Revolucionarias de Colombia* (FARC).
He refused to negotiate with the FARC, signifying a major policy
change from his predecessor, Pastrana, who developed the disastrous
demilitarized zone, which became a lawless region for the FARC to
occupy and organize various operations and attacks. Connie Veillette
states, "He vowed not to negotiate with any of the armed groups until
they declared a cease-fire and disarmed. Uribe implemented new laws
giving the security forces increased power, and instituted a one-time
tax to be used to increase the troop strength and capabilities of the
Colombian military."[1] Uribe also pledged to retake control of seized
territory that the FARC occupied. In order to accomplish his goals,
Uribe needed to fundamentally alter Plan Colombia.

The events on September 11 helped Uribe successfully alter Plan
Colombia and "sell" the new changes to President Bush and his administration; the Bush administration accepted the changes, resulting in
the blurring of the lines between the guerrillas and drug traffickers
(i.e., the narco-terrorists). How did Uribe successfully alter the goals of
Plan Colombia?[2] Why did the Bush administration accept the changes to
Plan Colombia made by Uribe and his administration? Under Uribe, the
weaker power shifted the formula and the stronger country, the United
States, accepted the new conditions and agenda of Plan Colombia, defying

traditional neorealist logic. What were the goals of the reengineered version of Plan Colombia? Were these goals the same as the original version of Plan Colombia? Had either country accomplished the goals set forth? If so, how and when were these goals achieved?[3]

External Shock: September 11, 2001

One cannot understand the evolution and changes in Plan Colombia without briefly examining the impact that the external environment during this period had on U.S. foreign policy and the geostrategic interests of Washington. The attack on the World Trade Center in New York City and the Pentagon in Washington, D.C., on September 11, 2001, led to significant changes in U.S. foreign policy. The war on drugs became subordinated to the war on terrorism as the Bush administration launched the "Global War on Terror," which later became the "Global War on Terrorism." Bush vowed to combat terrorism throughout the world, stating in his address to the nation in 2001: "From this day forward, any nation that continues to harbor or support terrorism will be regarded by the United States as a hostile regime. Our nation has been put on notice, we're not immune from attack. We will take defensive measures against terrorism to protect Americans."[4] This quote demonstrates that the Bush administration's primary objective was to combat terrorism on a global scale and to prevent future attacks on the United States. Said differently, the terrorists' attacks on September 11 drastically shifted U.S. motivations and goals, which must be examined in order to understand the construction and evolution in Plan Colombia. Instead of focusing on state-to-state relations or security in the region, Bush decided to launch a global war and combat terrorism wherever it occurs.[5]

The Bush administration's global war on terrorism was highly controversial for many reasons. First, terror is a state of mind, and one cannot have a war against a state of mind. Second, terrorism is a tactic and is a weapon of the weak.[6] Third, determining who is and is not a terrorist is a social construction, and, therefore, is a constructivist issue.[7] A terrorist to one individual might be a freedom fighter to another. An Islamic extremist could argue that such tactics are used to combat Western imperialism and argue that the people that the Bush administration defines as terrorist are actually freedom fighters. During the American Revolution, for example, the British viewed the American fighters as terrorists because they used guerrilla war–style tactics and did not adhere to the conventional rules of war. Americans, however, view these individuals as heroes who acted with great valor to help found the United States.[8]

President Bush managed to securitize the war on terrorism, successfully placing the war on terrorism at the top of the security agenda and making it the primary priority of the U.S. government.[9] Barry Buzan and his colleagues at the Copenhagen School help explain the notion of securitization and how actors can securitize concepts. Security is another contested concept because it depends on what is being securitized and for whom.[10] Clearly, what one politician or individual perceives to be a major security threat may not be perceived as such to another. Buzan and his coauthors demonstrate that security can impact different levels and sectors and is a much more intricate and complicated concept than the realists proclaim it to be.[11]

President Bush managed to securitize the war on terrorism by convincing the American public that terrorism is a major threat to U.S. national security and needs to be confronted in order to prevent further attacks, particularly on U.S. soil. An examination of authoritative speech acts demonstrates Bush's efforts to securitize the war on terrorism. In a speech to the joint session of Congress on September 20, 2001, President Bush declared his war on terrorism, stating:

> On September 11th, enemies of freedom committed an act of war against our country. Americans have known wars, but for the past 136 years, they have been wars on foreign soil, except for one Sunday in 1941. Americans have known the casualties of war, but not at the center of a great city on a peaceful morning. Americans have known surprise attacks but never before on thousands of civilians. All of this was brought upon us in a single day, and night fell on a different world, a world where freedom itself is under attack . . . The terrorists practice a fringe form of Islamic extremism that has been rejected by Muslim scholars and the vast majority of Muslim clerics, a fringe movement that perverts the peaceful teachings of Islam. The terrorists' directive commands them to kill Christians and Jews, to kill all Americans, and make no distinctions among military and civilians, including women and children. . . .[12]

Bush argued that the terrorists hate Americans because of the freedom granted to individuals in the United States. He successfully marketed and sold the American public on the need to increase resources and fight terrorism. Bush also pressured other countries to cooperate in this global war, stating in a 2001 speech:

> We ask every nation to join us. We will ask, and we will need, the help of police forces, intelligence services, and

banking systems around the world. The United States is grateful that many nations and many international organizations have already responded, with sympathy and with support, nations from Latin America, to Asia, to Africa, to Europe, to the Islamic world. Perhaps the NATO Charter reflects best the attitude of the world: An attack on one is an attack on all. The civilized world is rallying to America's side. They understand that if this terror goes unpunished, their own cities, their own citizens may be next. Terror, unanswered, can not [sic] only bring down buildings, it can threaten the stability of legitimate governments. And you know what? We're not going to allow it.[13]

The events on September 11 altered U.S. foreign policy toward Colombia. Pizarro and Gaitán describe how September 11 impacted U.S. foreign policy regarding drug trafficking, stating:

The events of September 11 left the debate between the Departments of State and Defense in the dust. Because of the FARC, ELN [Ejército de Liberación Nacional], and AUC [Autodefensas Unidas de Colombia] were no longer considered insurgent or counterinsurgent forces but terrorist groups, direct or indirect, combat against them was legitimized with a simple stroke of the pen. This perspective gained credibility as the pattern of linking illegal drug traffic with terrorism grew; after all, drug trafficking is one of the principal ways terrorists groups are financed, internally and within Colombia. Debates in the U.S. Congress over new antiterrorist legislation paved the way, such as the one spearheaded by the majority leader of the House of Representatives, Dennis Haster (R–IL), in 2001, aimed at linking the fight against terrorism with the fight against drugs.[14]

Politicians within the United States began to compare the FARC in Colombia with other terrorists groups, such as Al Qaeda. Senator Bob Graham (D–FL) stated, "The FARC are doing the same thing as global-level terrorists, that is, organizing in small cells that don't have contact with each other and depend on a central command to organize attacks, in terms of logistics and financing. It is the same style of operations as Bin Laden." Other politicians agreed and continued to conflate the war on drugs with the war on terrorism and compare the FARC to other terrorist organizations.[15] For example, Mark Souder (R–IN), stated, "It is not just narcotics. It has developed into terrorism and we need to fight terrorism in our hemisphere."[16] Francis X. Taylor, the Coordinator for Counterterrorism at the State Department, echoed the sentiments by the previous two politicians, stating:

> The Revolutionary Armed Forces of Colombia (FARC), the National Liberation Army (ELN), and the United Self-Defense Force of Colombia (AUC) are on the list because they participate in terrorist activities. They will receive the same treatment as any other terrorist group in terms of our interest in pursuing them and putting an end to their terrorist activities. . . . It will include the use of all the resources in our power as well as those available to the countries in the region . . . where appropriate, as we are doing in Afghanistan, the use of military force, if that is appropriate to put an end to their activities.[17]

Uribe's Vision and Reorientation

After examining the impact that the September 11, 2001, events had on U.S. foreign policy, we now turn to analyze the internal dynamics within Colombia and see how such changes led to the shift in Plan Colombia. The failures of Pastrana and his efforts to negotiate with the FARC led to the election of Álvaro Uribe, as the "Colombians who had voted for peace in 1998 opted in 2002 for a hardline approach to dealing with guerrillas."[18] After his election in 2002, Uribe became the new president of Colombia, stating in his inaugural speech: "When a democratic State provides effective guarantees, even if it comes to do so gradually, any violence against it is terrorism. We do not accept violence as a means of attack on the government, or as a means of defense."[19] He vowed to combat illegal armed actors within Colombia and refused to negotiate with such groups that have participated in violence and have been terrorizing Colombia for decades. His hardline stance against the FARC represented a significant shift from former President Andrés Pastrana, who wanted to bring peace to the country by implementing the demilitarized zone for the FARC. This policy can only be characterized as counterproductive as the FARC moved into this zone and ran operations from this area. In essence, this area provided the FARC with a huge territory that was not under the control of the Colombian state, and the FARC, therefore, could essentially do whatever it desired in this lawless region.

The FARC responded to Uribe's statements and efforts by attempting to assassinate the president with gas cylinder bombs. The plot failed but resulted in the death of innocent bystanders. These acts led Uribe to declare a "state of internal unrest," and he ordered the military to occupy certain regions within Colombia in order to address the situation.[20] Uribe's speech changed as he conflated the war on drugs with the war on terrorism and referred to the guerrillas as narco-terrorists. Uribe reengineered Plan Colombia's goals and shifted the major initiatives toward combating the narco-terrorists rather than merely combating drug traffickers. Ramírez Lemus, Stanton, and Walsh explain the new trends Uribe implemented, stating:

> Uribe's actions, which have enjoyed the full and uncondi-
> tional support of the Bush administration, distance Plan
> Colombia even more from Pastrana's original vision. While
> counterterrorism has become another objective of U.S. policy
> in Colombia, the impact of Plan Colombia should be evalu-
> ated according to the original U.S. goals. Foreign policy
> discourse has changed, but at the end of 2003 Colombia
> was still the leading producer of cocaine in the Western
> Hemisphere, and the internal armed conflict still raging.[21]

The ability of the weaker country, Colombia, to alter the agenda and reformulate Plan Colombia defies traditional logic in international relations (IR) theory. Realists would hypothesize that the stronger country has more power and is able to set the agenda, and the weaker country must simply bandwagon or balance against the hegemonic actor. During the Pastrana administration, President Clinton constructed a different vision of the problem and solution to the situation in Colombia and reformulated the plan to focus on drug trafficking first as opposed to peace.[22] How was Uribe, the president of the weaker country, able to reorder the fundamental design of Plan Colombia? The answer is that Uribe managed to convince the stronger power, the United States, that the illegal actors in Colombia are terrorists who finance their operations through drug trafficking.[23] Determining whether the FARC and their members are terrorists is a constructivist issue that depends on the actors' perceptions.[24] Importantly, both the FARC and the ELN have been placed on the U.S. list of terrorist organizations. Is the FARC a terrorist organization or does it participate in acts of terrorism? Regardless of how one classifies the FARC, one must remember that terrorism is a tactic and the FARC wants to overthrow the Colombian government and use terrorist tactics to accomplish these objectives. Russell Crandall also notes that one should not assume that all guer-rillas participate in drug trafficking. He states:

> But guerrilla involvement in the drug trade does not—
> and did not—mean that all of the guerrillas are actually
> narco-guerrillas, in essence, indistinguishable from the drug

traffickers. In fact, while the guerrillas undoubtedly do participate in the drug trade, they maintain a distinct political and economic ideology, even if it does seem quite anachronistic now that the Cold War is over and Marxism-Leninism has been largely discredited worldwide.[25]

Uribe's new focus on combating the narco-terrorists, therefore, represented a major shift and signifies a change from the concerns of the Clinton administration, which focused on drug trafficking. As discussed, the Clinton administration, policy analysts, and the U. S. defense community feared intervening in Colombia in order to avoid becoming involved in another Vietnam-type quagmire. Bush, on the other hand, agreed with the new agenda and viewed the FARC as a terrorist organization that need to be combatted. In sum, Uribe and his reorientation of Plan Colombia demonstrated that a weaker state, indeed, can set the agenda and alter the security strategy and policies between two countries. The powerful country, however, must concede and agree with the construction of the problem. In essence, Uribe was brilliant in his ability to recognize the problem and convince the stronger power that Colombia required more U.S. assistance to combat the terrorists within the country. Uribe highlighted the relevant security issues between both countries and convinced the Bush administration that Colombia represented a worthy ally and deserved the necessary resources to combat the narco-guerrillas.

The Bush administration accepted the reorientation of Plan Colombia because it fit in with the larger agenda of Bush and the neoconservatives in his administration that helped guide his foreign policy.[26] Uribe's new vision for Plan Colombia, in essence, was brilliant because he was able to convince President Bush on the need to combat these internal actors rather than solving the internal conflict in Colombia as part of the Global War on Terrorism.[27] Like Bush, Uribe vowed to fight the narco-terrorists and wanted funding from the United States to combat terrorism. Adam Isacson describes the situation, stating: "Three years later, the mission of U.S. aid has expanded well beyond that of the war on drugs. Counter-terrorism is now the principle rationale, though policymakers are still trying to figure out what that term means in a country whose terrorists groups are armies that control territory and have tens of thousands of members. Three U.S. citizens working on a Pentagon contract have been hostages of FARC guerrillas since February 2003."[28]

The relationship between Uribe and Bush was a perfect combination: Bush and Uribe had the same fundamental principles and vision, both wanting to combat the narco-terrorists. In return for his loyal support, President Bush went further than any other president, enabling military aid to be used for other purposes besides combatting the war on drugs. Pizarro and Gaitán assert that "the most significant change in U.S. military assistance to Colombia was removal of the condition, for the first time since the end of the Cold War, that military aid to Colombia be subject to its exclusive use in the war on drugs."[29] President Bush, therefore, failed to separate or distinguish between the war on drugs and the war on terrorism, invoking the use of counterinsurgency strategies. Pizarro and Gaitán argue, "George W. Bush crossed the 'invisible line' that, formally if not always in practice, separated the counternarcotics fight from counterinsurgency programs. All Plan Colombia and the Andean Initiative funding may be used for both."[30] The blurring of the lines became apparent when President Bush submitted legislation designed to aid the Colombians against the narco-guerrillas. Pizarro and Gaitán assert that "the change was effected in the foreign aid package of President Bush submitted by Congress on February 4, 2002, which included $98 million for protection of Caño Limón–Coveñas oil pipeline in Colombia. A single sentence in the bill (H.R. 4775) gave the Colombian government authority to use Plan Colombia assistance in the war against the insurgency."[31] In sum, President Bush agreed with Uribe's reorientation of Plan Colombia and helped his newest ally by providing Uribe with the appropriate resources necessary to combat the narco-terrorists.[32]

Upon taking office, Uribe made combating terrorism the number one priority of his administration just as President Bush framed terrorism as the number one national security and foreign policy issue for the United States. He argued that Colombia did not have an internal conflict, but rather terrorists operating within the country. Uribe erased Colombia's history of having an internal conflict and framed the problem as a terrorist issue. Before Uribe, the word "terrorist" was not a major part of the Colombian vocabulary

Marc Chernick explains that "he [Uribe] basically erased this long history of conflict"[33] and made clear that people should not use the term "armed conflict" and could face repercussions for doing so. Chernick notes that "all the NGOs [(nongovernmental organizations) and] international organizations were told [they] cannot use the language of internal armed conflict."[34]

Uribe also provided the Bush administration with the opportunity to combat non-Muslim terrorist organizations, helping Bush demonstrate that he was not only at war with radical Islamic terrorists, but he was committed to fighting terrorist organizations anywhere around the globe regardless of the terrorists' religious beliefs. Bush stressed that he was not at war with the entire Muslim world, but rather he sought to combat extremists who hated the United States because of the freedom granted to its citizens. After the September 11 events, Bush found a partner in Uribe, who shared similar security interests and foreign policy objectives. Therefore, the relationship between Uribe and Bush can be defined as ideal because both leaders had the same objectives. Uribe vowed not to negotiate with the narco-terrorists and sought to increase funding to combat terrorism and violence within Colombia. In addition, Uribe became a willing partner to help Bush expand the Global War on Terrorism around the world.[35] President Bush and the elites within the United States also feared that Colombia was on the verge of becoming a failed state and something needed to be done in order to prevent Colombia from collapsing. A joint report by the National Defense University and the National War College highlighted the possibility that Colombia could collapse. The authors report: "Colombia, fragmented and wracked by violence, today teeters on the edge of implosion, raising the specter of a failed state on the U.S.'s southern flank, posing a threat to U.S. national and regional interests."[36]

The relationship between the United States and Colombia begs the question as to why should the United States care about Colombia? In other words, why is Colombia an important country in terms of U.S. geostrategic and economic interests? In terms of U.S. foreign policy, Joyce Kaufman's research indicates that the United States places certain issues as priorities in terms of importance. Again, the first priority for the United States always has been—and continues to be—security.[37] The United States wants to ensure that it survives in the international system and remains the dominant power in the Western hemisphere. The second priority for U.S. foreign policy has always been economic issues.[38] The tertiary issue comprises value issues, such as democracy and human rights. Colombia is a crucial state in terms of geostrategic interests as well as economic ties and investments for the United States. Various leading U.S. security analysts perceived Colombia as a major threat to U.S. security and "have regarded Colombia as one of the Western Hemisphere's chief security problems, greater even than Cuba, which had occupied that uncomfortable spot since 1962."[39] The Bush administration as well as other elites and policymakers feared that a failed Colombia would result in insecurity in the region and serve as a potential breeding ground for terrorist organizations

In terms of security, Colombia occupies a strategic position in the region, which has historically been the "backyard" of the United States ever since the Monroe Doctrine. Instability within Colombia not only negatively impacts Colombia but also the security of its neighbors. Colombia borders on the Panama Canal, which is a key location for the trade and the transportation of goods and services. In reality, the "Panamanian security forces are no match for well-armed guerillas and narco-traffickers that use Panamanian territory to conduct operations."[40] Ecuador also is concerned about its security as many of the FARC members are located near the borders. Reports also indicate that Venezuela "may secretly support both the FARC and the ELN, given the leftist tendencies of [former] Venezuelan president Hugo Chávez."[41] Uribe lambasted Chávez, stating: "The truth, President Chávez . . . is that we need people to help us overcome this tragedy of terrorism, but we need people who will not take advantage of the need for the humanitarian accord to invoke help for Colombia, and not come to Colombia simply to intervene there, and to pursue an expansionist project."[42] He continued:

> One cannot abuse a whole continent, or set it on fire as you do, by speaking of imperialism, when you, based on your own ambitions, are looking to set up an empire. The truth, President Chávez, is that we cannot abuse history, we cannot stain the memory of our heroes, by disfiguring them in popular demagoguery, in misleading the people. General Santander gave us the example of observance of the law. The truth, President Chávez, is that we cannot make a mockery of the law, as you do, trying to abuse General Santander, and exchange the rule of law for personal whim. The truth, President Chávez, the truth with witnesses, is that we cannot mislead the people by misinterpreting the legacy of the Liberator Bolivar (*sic*). Bolivar was an integrationist, but not an expansionist. Bolivar [brought] independence to our nations, but he did not bring them a new era of subjection. Bolivar did not spend his time trying to remove European domination from the Americans, only to impose his own terms with the power at his disposal— as you wish to do—on the people of Venezuela and on the people of Colombia.[43]

In addition, Colombia shares an unguarded border with Brazil, a rising economic power. Therefore, "Colombia's long and largely unguarded border with Brazil provides a safe-haven for the FARC and is a source of tension between the two nations."[44]

The internal problems in Colombia upon Uribe's ascension to power posed many threats to the United States, especially since Colombia is located only a couple of hours from Miami. Phil McLean echoes such sentiments, stating: "If failed states on the other side of the globe threaten U.S. interests, then Colombia, a country just two hours from Miami . . . is truly a scary prospect."[45] In September 2002, Army Brigadier General Galen Jackman of the U.S. Southern

Command declared that the FARC had begun to expand into its neighboring regions, representing a major security threat.[46] The internal situation within Colombia also creates tension between countries in the region as well as the United States because of problems with human migration. The internal dynamics within Colombia can cause refugees to flee their country, worried about their security. The neighboring countries, therefore, are concerned about a mass exodus of Colombians, which could result in increases in the number of refugees entering other countries. As a result of the high levels of violence during this period, many Colombians also began fleeing Colombia and relocating to the United States.[47]

In addition to the security dynamics, Colombia also represents an important country in terms of economic trade and investments. Some scholars argue that Colombia "is the most important market in the developing world for U.S. exports, and by 2010 total U.S. trade with Latin America will exceed U.S. trade with Europe and Asia combined."[48] U.S. citizens have significant investments in Colombia and a worsening security situation could result in problems causing Americans to withdraw investments from the country. Joseph Ganitsky states that "if you don't have security, if the government cannot guarantee security, then you do not do business. This is the reason why millions of people left the country."[49] Ganitsky argues that companies must take into account the security situation within Colombia before investing in order to maximize their return on investment. He continues, "For companies, they make a very clear assessment of their risk and take insurance for kidnapping and hire people and have policies to cover whatever may happen, so if your employee is kidnaped or killed, there will be compensation for relatives."[50]

Finally, the United States has interests in Colombia due to various value issues, such as democracy. Colombia has had a long history of democracy and represents a bastion of democratic governance in Latin America, which is a region that has experienced many authoritarian rulers. In fact, Colombia is the second oldest democracy in the Western hemisphere and has continued to hold democratic (i.e., fair and free) elections.[51] In addition, Colombia has experienced peaceful democratic transitions throughout its history. The Bush administration wanted to support Colombia and did not want one of the oldest countries in the region to become overrun by narco-terrorists. For all of the aforementioned reasons, the Bush administration recognized that Colombia was in dire need of support in order to preserve U.S. economic interests and avoid potential catastrophes within the country. Uribe understood that he needed help from the United States and sought to extend his hand to Bush, and in return he pledged his

support. Bush supported the Colombian government because it fit in
with his larger geopolitical objectives. The record between the Bush
administration and other countries deteriorated drastically over time.
By the end of his presidency, Bush had alienated many Latin American
countries and had very low approval ratings. His relationship with
Uribe, however, remained strong.[52]

New Goals of Plan Colombia

Upon taking office, Uribe vowed to continue Plan Colombia and the
fight against drug trafficking, stating:

> The agents of violence are funded by an international
> criminal business—drugs. They fight with weapons not
> made in Colombia. No democracy can stand aside from the
> sufferings of the Colombian people. We will continue with
> Plan Colombia, adding aerial interdiction and practical
> substitution programs, such as payments to small-[tract]
> farmers for the eradication of unlawful crops and care for
> the restoration of our woodlands. We will follow the path
> already opened up in the United States, knock on doors
> in Europe and Asia, and reinforce our unity of purpose
> with our neighbors. If we do not drive out drugs, drugs
> will destroy our freedoms and our ecology, and the hope of
> living in peace will be no more than an illusion. We want
> peace; not the kind of temporary reassurance that comes
> from insincerity, or an uneasy agreement or a tyrannical
> government.[53]

The Bush administration wanted Plan Colombia to be an extension
of the war on terrorism and help combat the FARC and ELN operating within Colombia. As a result of September 11, U.S. foreign policy
changed drastically and the war on drugs became subordinate and
less important for national security than the war on terrorism. Uribe
pledged to combat the narco-terrorists, who also participate in drug
trafficking. Indeed, the FARC participates in drug trafficking, and
the profits from the drug trade help finance its operations. However,
many other individuals and groups traffick drugs in Colombia. As
discussed in previous chapters, the demise of the Medellín and Cali
cartels created a vacuum and allowed smaller groups, *cartelitos*, to
traffic drugs. Uribe wanted to combat drug trafficking, but he came
to power in Colombia with the intention of combating the FARC and
other actors within Colombia, which he referred to as terrorists.[54]

Expansion of Military Operations

In 2001, President Bush sought to increase the funds provided to Colombia to combat the narco-terrorists. However, limitations existed on the number of troops that could be deployed. In 2002, the Bush administration attempted to alter the restrictions placed on the amount of military aid to Colombia and requested that Congress remove all the stipulations and restrictions with regard to military aid.[55] Ted Galen Carpenter recounts the history and rejection of the U.S. Congress with regard to this appeal:

> The House of Representatives in July of 2001 rejected the administration's bid to allow an unlimited number of civilian personnel to be in the country, which would have ended the FY 2001 cap of 300 American civilians. Instead, the House, on a voice vote, amended the administration's proposal, voting to cap the total number of military and contract personnel at 800. However, the amendment merely instructed the administration to inform Congress if and when it planned to exceed 300 civilian employees and to state the actual number it intended to send. As a practical matter, the so-called cap provided no effective limit.[56]

In effect, Congress provided the Bush administration with the metaphorical green light and enabled it to increase military personnel to Colombia in order to combat the narco-guerrillas.

Congress's approval of this policy represents a critical juncture that enabled the Bush administration to become involved in the internal dynamics of Colombia, representing a fundamental shift away from the previous Clinton administration policies, which were concerned about the United States becoming involved in another Vietnam-style conflict. Uribe's ability to fuse the war on drugs with the war on terrorism resulted in the Bush administration becoming involved in the internal dynamics of Colombia in order to help Colombia fight terrorists within the country and, therefore, adhering to Bush's promise to fight terrorism around the world. Carpenter argues that "whatever the initial intent, Plan Colombia inexorably draws the United States into Colombia's civil war. Indeed, the government in Bogotá apparently wants to draw Washington in."[57] Carpenter goes even further and questions whether the United States has become involved in nation-building in Colombia. The Bush administration pledged to support the Uribe administration and his fight against the narco-terrorists. Carpenter states, "It is likely that such cautionary sentiments will be swept aside and that the United States will expand the mission in Colombia."[58]

Critics of Plan Colombia have questioned whether it has become a nation-building exercise disguised by rhetoric or whether it is simply an initiative to combat the narco-terrorists. Analysts need not look back too far into Latin American history to realize that the United States has a terrible record with regard to nation-building in the region. Expressed differently, "but given America's miserable track record in nation-building mission through the initial post-Cold War decade, such a possibility ought to make Americans more rather than less nervous about their country's growing involvement in Colombia."[59] Until the end of his tenure, President Bush supported Colombia until he became impeded with wars in Iraq and Afghanistan.

Controlling Land Seized

President Uribe launched several other supplemental initiatives, such as the Democratic Security and Defense Policy and *Plan Patriota*, under the auspices of Plan Colombia. One must, however, recognize that Plan Colombia came before these other supplemental plans. Uribe, in essence, sought to change the thinking of Washington and, therefore, designed these plans to complement each other. The Democratic Security and Defense Policy, for instance, was a way for the Uribe administration to develop a security plan within the framework of Plan Colombia in order to help implement the strategies of Plan Colombia.

After vowing to combat the FARC and refusing to negotiate with them, Uribe implemented *Plan Patriota*. One cannot understand Uribe's success against the FARC, however, without briefly examining *Plan Patriota*, which sought to recapture territory that the FARC had seized. This represents a strong contradiction from the policies of Pastrana and the negotiations with the FARC because Uribe not only wanted to regain territory but also wanted to maintain control over the territory. In 2003, the Colombian government strengthened Plan Colombia's security components even further by instituting the Democratic Security and Defense Policy, which had very clear goals and objectives, seeking to "clear, hold, and consolidate" territory occupied by the illegal armed actors.[60] In order to recapture land seized, Uribe asserted the need to strengthen and increase the numbers of the armed forces. As a result, Colombia saw a drastic increase in the size of the police as well as the military from 279,000 in 2000 to 415,000 in 2007. In 2003, under the auspices of *Plan Patriota*, the Colombian government successfully combatted the FARC and forced it to retreat from the various areas it occupied surrounding Bogotá, which is the capital of the country. *Plan Patriota* became "the largest military operation in modern Colombian history, with the declared objective of striking a blow against the rear guard of the FARC-EP and capturing its principle leaders."[61] The Colombian government began to combat the FARC in key areas in which the organization operated, such as Guaviare, Meta, and the department of Caquetá.[62]

Plan Patriota, however, has had many challenges, particularly with regard to its execution and coordination among the security forces operating within Colombia. The FARC adapted to the Colombian government's efforts made and retreated into zones of Colombia that can be classified as rural and isolated, thus making capturing FARC operatives more difficult. The human rights commission notes, "The execution of the *Plan Patriota* revealed a lack of coordination between the security forces and the civilian institutions of the Government at national and local levels, as well as the absence of civilian State entities in these regions, which also affected the civilian population."[63] Such statements demonstrate the weakness of the Colombian state and the difficulty in asserting state control over rural and remote regions in Colombia. Ultimately, Uribe's efforts attempted to increase the capacity, or arm, of the Colombian state and combat the FARC by reclaiming land that they stole from the government. Yet, much of the territory in Colombia remains ungoverned and the Colombian state does not have the ability to control such regions. The solution is quite simple: more resources must be allocated to increase the strength of the state and its ability to govern. Money allocated for the military can help the armed forces reclaim the land, but the problem becomes how to govern and control the state after the land has been seized. A weak state will not be able to control the land within Colombia even after such territory has been reclaimed.

Despite the challenges of implementing state control over remote regions, Uribe continued to develop new strategies for combating the FARC and refused to soften his hardline policies against them. In 2004, for instance, Uribe created the Coordinating Center for Integrated Action (CCIA) to help facilitate the transportation of both civilian and military assistance to 11 major regions that had experienced serious conflicts and struggles. Throughout his presidency, Uribe battled major strongholds of the FARC, such as La Macarena, with an offensive strategy—*Plan Consolidacion*.[64]

To increase the presence of the Colombian state in rural zones, Plan Colombia allocated resources to strengthen the police forces in Colombian regions that experienced great contestation. Specifically, Plan Colombia provided $92 million from the fiscal year of 2000 to 2008 to create a Carabineros squadrons unit, which the Colombian government created to increase the presence of the state in the rural regions, as well as to help fortify and govern the areas seized from the guerrilla organizations. Reports indicate that in 2008 the Colombians had 68 Carabineros squadrons consisting of 120 individuals each. The major goal of these squadrons was to increase the presence of the state and improve stability in previously ungoverned regions. From the outset of his presidency, Uribe sought to increase the capacity and reach of the state and establish a state presence in each of the 1,099 municipalities. Prior to 2002, research indicates that 169 municipalities had no police presence.[65] Uribe boasted that the presence of the Colombian state increased during his tenure. The U.S. Embassy in Bogotá revealed that the presence of the Colombian state increased dramatically during Uribe's presidency, as each municipality had the presence of the police forces as of July 2007. The mere presence of police forces in every region did not mean that challenges vanished, however. In fact, some regions have several police officers who are required to patrol hundreds of square miles. Several police officials in a massive territory demonstrates the need for the Colombian government to strengthen the state and its ability to control and protect the entire Colombian state, as opposed to simply securing Bogotá.[66]

Equipment and Training

Counterterrorism strategies require training of military forces as well as state-of-the-art equipment. Since the implementation of Plan Colombia, the United States has provided Colombia with large infusions of cash to support the Colombian armed forces. From 2000 to 2004, the United States gave the Colombian government $2.44 billion; of which Plan Colombia allocated $1.97 billion for the military and the police forces operating within Colombia. From 2000 to 2008,[67] the U.S. Defense and State Departments have allocated approximately $4.9 billion in assistance to the military as well as the police in Colombia under the umbrella of Plan Colombia. The U.S. Defense and State Departments provided support and tactical training for the Colombian armed forces, and the number of individuals in the armed forces proliferated by 50 percent over the eight-year period from 2000 to 2008.[68] Military aid also enabled the Colombian government to develop a Joint Special Operations Command as well as mobile army units.[69]

In terms of military assistance, U.S. funds have enabled the development of brigades to assist in combating both drug trafficking and insurgency by implementing counterinsurgency tactics. "U.S. assistance to the Colombian military has focused on developing the capabilities of the Colombian Army's Aviation Brigade and the creation of an Army Counternarcotics Brigades and mobile units that focus on counternarcotics, infrastructure protection, and counterinsurgency missions."[70] Washington also has allocated financial resources to support and maintain helicopters that the Colombian army can use. From the fiscal year 2000 to 2008, Washington provided the Colombian government with $844 million for the Army Aviation Brigade, as well as training and other support. In terms of helicopters and other aircrafts, the brigade has the Plan Colombia Helicopter Program (PCHP), leasing helicopters from both the United States and Russia, and the FMS fleet. The PCHP fleet has 52 aircrafts, 17 of which are UH-1Ns, 13 are UH-60L Blackhawks, and 22 are UH-IIs.[71] The aviation units, however, have had problems that have hindered efficiency. One of the major challenges has been repairing and maintaining helicopters because the Colombian government does not have enough well-trained mechanics to maintain the equipment.[72] Like any machine, helicopters will break down and need to be repaired. Reports indicate that brigades continue to face challenges in terms of adequate staffing required to perform the necessary tasks. A Government Accountability Office report provides an excellent analysis of the problems, stating:

> We found that the Army Aviation Brigade is still understaffed. According to [the] State, as of June 2008, a total of 43 contract pilots and 87 contract mechanics were needed to operate the PCHP. U.S. officials expect that almost all of these contract personnel will be replaced with Colombian Army personnel by 2012, at which time U.S. program officials said all program support to the Army Aviation Brigade would consist of technical support. According to the commander of the Army Aviation Brigade, however, the Colombians are buying 15 additional UH-60 Blackhawks through the FMS system for delivery starting in October 2008, and in July 2008, the United States loaned 18 UH-1Ns from PCHP's inventory in Colombia.[73]

This quote demonstrates that the execution of Plan Colombia proved to be quite problematic.

Uribe Seeks to Secure Infrastructure

A major concern for Bogotá has been securing the infrastructure from terrorist attacks. Various attacks have occurred on the oil pipelines in Colombia in previous years, resulting in tremendous financial losses for oil companies. Insurgent attacks on the pipelines also have had dire economic consequences because the pipelines were forced to close for repairs. In 2001, for example, 170 attacks on the pipelines occurred, costing an estimated $500 million in economic losses.[74] Companies also are less likely to invest in Colombia due to security concerns. Potential investors logically question the security situation within Colombia and wonder whether guerrilla organizations will continue to destroy the oil pipelines. Uribe recognized that investors would not continue to invest in Colombia if they were concerned about basic safety and the feasibility of conducting routine operations. Bombings of pipelines and roads negatively impact the economic prosperity of a country by detracting investors and hindering commerce. Therefore, securing the infrastructure was a major priority for Uribe, who wanted to combat the terrorists who hindered the potential for economic prosperity in Colombia.

Increase of Resources for Interdiction

Plan Colombia has allocated money to assist the Colombians in interdiction efforts. From the fiscal year 2000 until 2008, both the U.S. Defense and the State Departments have provided the Colombian Marines and Navy with $89 million to help improve the ability of such forces to participate in interdiction efforts. The Navy plays a crucial role in interdiction efforts by stopping drugs from being trafficked. Colombian officials have credited the Marines and the Navy with seizing more than half of all of the seizures of cocaine in 2007, demonstrating that the waters play a major role in the transportation and shipment of cocaine.[75]

The Colombian Navy, however, has faced difficulties and one of its major problems has been the lack of resources necessary to conduct interdiction activities. The Navy also has faced many challenges with intelligence operations because it lacks the necessary information to help improve effectiveness in the seizure of shipments. Drug traffickers have been able to anticipate law enforcement efforts by altering the trafficking routes. Intelligence, therefore, plays a major role and can help improve the ability of the Navy to intercept shipments. The United States has been helping the Colombians to improve their intelligence capabilities. The Colombian Navy, however, does not have a great presence on the seas and needs to increase its patrolling capacities. The U.S. Southern Command officials have discussed this problem, noting the lack of resources as a continuing issue. Research indicates that "the Colombian Marines maintain a permanent presence on only about one-third of Colombia's nearly 8,000 miles of navigable rivers."[76] The ultimate goal is to increase the presence of the Navy to help improve the ability of the Colombian naval forces to interdict shipments.

Increasing the presence of the Colombian Navy and overall efforts to interdict products may appear at first glance to deter traffickers; however, minor successes in confiscation of drug shipments should not be mistaken as victories in the war on drugs. One must first briefly examine several problems with interdiction efforts. Stories in leading newspapers frequently report the successful interdiction of shipments from drug traffickers. Scholars note that marketing the notion that the war on drugs is being won to the public is easy regardless of whether interdiction efforts really result in an increase in shipments confiscated. For instance, an increase in the interdiction of drugs enabled politicians and government officials to proclaim victory and demonstrate that law enforcement efforts have worked and have resulted in large quantities of illicit substances being seized from organized criminal networks and, subsequently, not only preventing these substances from reaching the market but also causing the drug traffickers to lose money. Likewise, several months of low statistics in terms of drugs interdicted by law enforcement teams can be deemed a victory in the war on drugs because it demonstrates that fewer shipments must have been sent by drug traffickers. Such logic fails to recognize that drug traffickers constantly adapt in order to survive in this clandestine business. As a result, drug traffickers determine which regions and routes law enforcement officials are targeting and they then alter their shipping routes accordingly to avoid interdiction. Drug traffickers are experts at noticing areas that are less commonly patrolled and alter their routes to exploit such weaknesses. Therefore, neither Colombian law enforcement authorities nor various U.S. organizations have the ability to stop drugs from entering into the United States or other regions.[77]

Carpenter notes that we should think before praising the interdiction efforts and declaring victory in the war on drugs, stating, "Interdiction realities are far different from the picture painted by drug warriors. International interdiction has increased markedly over the past two decades, in part because of the improvement in radar and other detection methods."[78] He highlights that empirical evidence does not exist to show that such interdiction efforts have had a major impact on the supply of drugs. Critics are quick to point out that illicit drugs remain purer, cheaper, and more readily available than when the war on drugs began in 1971. Therefore, praising the interdiction efforts is premature.[79] However, the United States has seen a decrease in the purity of drugs and a subsequent increase in the price paid for narcotics in 2009.[80]

One must also understand the limitations of interdiction efforts. U.S. custom officials, for instance, can randomly sample large containers entering the various major ports around the country. In Miami, inspectors can select a container to inspect for drugs in an attempt to combat drug shipments from other countries. Anyone who has ever driven by the port of Miami—or any major U.S. port for that matter— knows that the containers are massive. Even a quick inspection of a container requires unpacking and inspecting some of the materials in hot and humid Miami. This is a daunting task because drug traffickers have adapted and no longer ship cargos loaded with cocaine. Instead, they intersperse the illicit substances among legal products. A random inspection of a cargo container the size of a semitruck may not be able to capture all shipments of cocaine. The United States has neither the resources nor the capacity to inspect every product entering the major ports, let alone the myriad other places that receive shipments of goods and services from other countries. Determining how many enforcement officials would be needed to inspect every cargo container entering just the port of Miami alone is nearly impossible. Carpenter explains the limitations and failures of the interdiction efforts, declaring:

> The limitations of interdiction are a long-standing reality. In the mid-1990s, the U.S. Customs [and Border Protection] admitted that only 3 percent of the nearly 9 million shipping containers entering the United States were checked by custom inspectors. To take just one example, of the 5,000 truckers entering the United States daily from Mexico, only about 200 are inspected. Most drug traffickers are perfectly willing to chance those odds.[81]

Conceptual Analysis of Alternative Development Programs

Although "soft-side" programs never represented a major component of Plan Colombia, such programs continued to receive resources. From the fiscal year 2000 to 2008, the U.S. government allocated approximately $1.3 billion under the auspices of Plan Colombia for nonmilitary programs, emphasizing judicial reform as well as programs designed to improve social as well as economic development within Colombia. The U.S. Agency for International Development (USAID) has provided the Colombians with funds exceeding $500 million for alternative development programs over an eight-year period, beginning with the 2000 fiscal year. The USAID revised its original goals and, in 2002, promoted the long-term activities as opposed to projects with short-term goals designed to help the Colombian government increase their levels of income. In other words, the 2002 objectives emphasized combating the underlying, deep-rooted alternative development issues.

Although some progress has been made, the alternative development programs continued to face many challenges.[82] One of the major challenges has been the limited geographic reach of the alternative development initiatives. Research indicates that "alternative development programs are largely focused in economic corridors in the western part of Colombia, where according to USAID officials, a greater potential exists for success due to access to markets, existing infrastructure, and state presence and security."[83] As of 2008, the eastern regions in Colombia in particular lack basic alternative development programs under the Uribe administration. Major infrastructure problems continue to stifle the potential for such programs to succeed and produce significant results. Another major problem with alternative development policies has been the "Zero Illicit" policy the Colombian government implemented during Uribe's tenure, which "prohibits alternative development assistance projects in communities where any illicit crops are being cultivated."[84] This is shocking because the regions where coca is being cultivated require the most assistance in terms of alternative development.

Results of Plan Colombia during the Uribe Administration: Successes against the FARC

Although Uribe did not have major advances in curbing drug cultivation or trafficking, he had successes against the various illegal armed actors operating within Colombia as a result of Plan Colombia and other supplemental initiatives. From the outset of his presidency, Uribe fulfilled his campaign promises and vowed to combat the FARC, refusing to negotiate and combating what he referred to as terrorists operating within Colombia. Defeating the FARC has been a daunting task and has required significant military resources in order to combat such a formidable foe. One of the major difficulties for the Colombian armed forces has been the rough terrain where the FARC operates. Combating armed groups in difficult terrain has led to critics to question whether defeating the FARC is even possible.[85] Uribe, however, rejected critics' comments and continued to combat the FARC. As of 2004, the United States provided the Colombian government with $99 million in order to help combat the guerrilla organizations, or narco-terrorists, in a crucial security region of Colombia, known as Arauca, which is where a major oil pipeline is located.[86]

Uribe's desire to combat the FARC and his subsequent increases in the resources spent resulted in significant gains for the Colombian government. Uribe successfully killed key FARC leaders, weakening

Table 4.1. U.S. Assistance under Plan Colombia and the PCCP by Program Objective—Fiscal Year Appropriations 2000 through 2008.

Program Objective/Year	2000	2001	2002	2003	2004	2005	2006	2007	2008 est.
Reduce Drugs and Improve Security	817.8 US $	$232.8	$395.9	$607.9	$617.7	$585.6	$587.3	$591.1	$423.4
Promote Social and Economic Justice	80	.5	109.9	125.7	126.5	124.7	130.4	139.7	194.4
Promote Rule of Law	121.1	.9	15.8	27	9	7.3	10.5	7.8	39.4

Source: State and Defense. This table is an adapted version from a the GAO report titled *Drug Reduction Goals were Not Fully Met, but Security has Improved; U.S. Agencies Need More Detailed Plans for Reducing Assistance,* 15.

the group. In 2008, for instance, Uribe's forces entered into Ecuador and killed Raúl Reyes, a key FARC member.[87] According to Colombian Ministry of Defense statements, the Colombian government successfully increased the territory controlled in the country by 20 percent, from 70 percent in 2003 to 90 percent in 2008. Uribe's initiatives helped decrease the financial power, numbers, and strength of the FARC, the ELN, and the paramilitaries. The U.S. Drug Enforcement Administration revealed that the FARC had been significantly weakened as a result of operations, and its membership has decreased from an estimated 17,000 forces operating in Colombia in 2001 to 8,000 in 2008. One government report notes: "According to State and embassy officials, [and] nongovernmental observers, the number of FARC combatants and its capabilities have been drastically reduced by continuous assaults on its top leadership, the capture or killing of FARC members in conflictive zones, and a large number of desertions. In 2007, the Colombian Ministry of Defense reported that it had captured or killed approximately 4,600 FARC combatants and about 2,500 had demobilized."[88]

The capturing and killing of major leaders had negative consequences in terms of Uribe's popularity among Latin American leaders. Many FARC members operated along the Ecuadorian–Colombian border. In March 2008, Colombian forces entered Ecuador in order to capture FARC leader Raúl Reyes and 16 other FARC operatives. The events that transpired in Ecuador upset many politicians throughout Latin America, who argued that such actions violated Ecuador's sovereignty. The Colombian government in turn criticized its neighbors, alleging that both Venezuela and Ecuador had linkages with the FARC. Oscar Naranjo, the Colombian national police chief, asserted, "When they mention negotiations for 50 kilos of uranium, this means that the FARC are taking big steps in the world of terrorism to become a global aggressor. We're not talking of domestic guerrillas but transnational terrorism."[89] After the raid, the diplomatic ties with Ecuador decreased. In addition, Venezuela expelled Colombian diplomats operating within the country to express its outrage over Uribe's actions. The Colombians maintain that crossing the border was necessary in order to kill FARC operatives and combat terrorism.[90]

The revenue earned per kilo of cocaine sold also decreased significantly, which is important because the Drug Enforcement Administration estimated that the FARC earned approximately 80 percent of its revenue from drug trafficking during this period. Scholars debate whether the FARC would still operate if it were not for the money from drug trafficking. As Bruce Bagley asserts, even without this revenue, it is doubtful that the FARC would cease to exist.[91] Clearly, the profits from drug trafficking help finance the FARC, but the FARC can earn money from other illegal activities, such as extortion, kidnapping, and the trafficking of women.

Uribe and his administration have praised Plan Colombia as a success because Colombia is now safer and the FARC has been weakened dramatically. However, David Mares declared in an interview that "when people talk about safety they should specify what criteria that they want to use."[92] While Uribe has obtained major successes combating the FARC, the FARC still presents a major problem for Colombia, continuing to occupy important areas in Colombia. Sandro Calvani, the director of the U.N. Office on Drugs and Crime (UNODC) Colombia Program in Bogotá from 2003 to 2007, stated that both the AUC's and the FARC's "destructive impact on [the] Colombian future has been defeated, most probably forever. Former armed group leaders' have abandoned the armed fight and they are now among the most prominent political leaders, including the mayor of Bogotá, leaders of Cali and Medellin [sic]."[93] Colombian officials have cautioned jumping to conclusions and declaring victory against the FARC, recognizing that the FARC remains a major threat to Colombian national security and continues to occupy and control various regions within the country. Colombian government representatives admit that the FARC continues "exercising control over important parts of the country, such as Meta, which serves as a key transport corridor linking many of the coca cultivation areas in the eastern part of the country with the Pacific ports used to transport cocaine out of the country."[94]

Victories against the AUC

Uribe vowed not to negotiate with the FARC, but he entered into peace accords with the paramilitaries and efforts have been made to demobilize the AUC, the major right-wing paramilitary organization operating in Colombia. The negotiations begun in 2003 have seen significant results. Over the three-year period from 2003 to 2006, experts estimate that approximately 32,000 AUC soldiers began to demobilize. Many of the leaders of the paramilitaries support the demobilization process, even though it appeared to be a major advancement for Colombia and the Uribe administration, because as Adam Isacson explains, "While the negotiations with paramilitaries look like a giant leap toward peace, the reason it could fail is also the main reason why most paramilitary leaders support it: the agreement will most likely include a mechanism to grant the leaders amnesty in both Colombia and the United States for their crimes."[95] In addition, one must note that many of the leaders of the paramilitaries supported Uribe as a candidate.

Although some of the soldiers and officers have disbanded, they have become members of other organized crime networks.[96] The new criminal networks that have resulted from the demobilization of the AUC are referred to as *Bandas Criminales* (BACRIM).[97] Soldiers often join criminal networks because their skills are easily applied to the lucrative business of organized crime and drug trafficking. The various groups that have emerged from the paramilitaries have continued to attack civilians and have been responsible for a plethora of egregious human rights violations. The BACRIM are different from the paramilitaries in several important ways. Bagley notes, "They tend to be politically much more deft and subtle in seeking political alliances inside the Colombian economic and political establishment, often hiding their political linkages through indirect and 'clean' candidates without records of paramilitary affiliations."[98] In addition, the BACRIM have expanded their activities beyond drug trafficking and into areas such as gold mining in order to diversify their portfolios and develop different sources of earning revenue to finance their operations.[99]

Different estimates exist regarding the number of individuals involved in the various groups that succeeded the paramilitaries. For instance, the Colombian National Police estimated that the groups have 3,749 members operating within Colombia as of 2010.[100] Conversely, other approximations are much higher, placing the number at 6,000 members. Rather, they are located throughout Colombia, operating in 29 of the 32 departments that exist within Colombia.[101] The State Department reports that the Colombian government has continued to train and deploy vast number of police forces throughout Colombia with the goal of increasing the "arm" of the state and implementing law and order. In 2005, the Colombian National Police deployed 9,176 police officers to rural areas throughout Colombia, a significant portion of which (8,166) secured and protected the roads in Colombia from attacks.[102]

One must understand the realities of the demobilization before determining that the process has been a success. On paper, this process seems like a major victory for Uribe and his administration in combating the armed conflict within Colombia. The previous examples, however, demonstrate that caution is needed when analyzing the demobilization efforts and understanding the potential ramifications and consequences. Importantly, some individuals believe that the AUC demobilization was a farce. Marc Chernick, for instance, argues, "The demobilization was mostly a fraud."[103] The demobilization dismantled paramilitaries. "They left the structures intact and . . . it is fiction, and it's misleading, and dangerous fiction that they are now only criminal bands and the paramilitaries is wrong . . ."[104] Critics, therefore, believe that that the paramilitaries are still much more of a threat than Uribe's proponents believe.

Weakening of the ELN

The Uribe administration also achieved success in combating one of the other major armed groups: the ELN. Colombian officials estimate that the ELN has decreased drastically from 5,000 members in 2000 to between approximately 2,200 and 3,000 members as of 2008. The same tactics used to combat the FARC have been successful in weakening the ELN and represent another indicator of the "partial victories" of the war on drugs Plan Colombia achieved under Uribe.[105]

Initial Successes Combating Corruption

Plan Colombia, as well as Uribe's Democratic Security and Defense Policy, vowed to combat Colombia's long history of corruption, which has hampered its ability to perform basic functions. During the reign of the notorious Medellín and Cali cartels, Colombia was on the verge of becoming a narco-state, or "failed state,"[106] as drug traffickers bribed many politicians and faced very few—if any—ramifications for such behavior. The accusations that President Samper had received money from the cartels caused extreme pessimism about Colombia's ability to function and cast doubt on the rule of law.

Various structural changes within Colombia also must be recognized as such reforms inevitably played a role in the decreases in corruption. In 2004, the Colombian Congress passed a law creating an accusatorial system that revolutionized criminal law in Colombia.[107] The new rules and procedures enable oral as well as public trials, placing the responsibility for prosecution on the Office of the Attorney General. The USAID's efforts enabled the creation of 35 oral trial courtrooms.[108] Another major advantage of this new system is that plea bargains are allowed, which inevitably helps increase efficiency by decreasing the time required to prosecute and, ultimately, solve criminal cases.[109]

Parapolitics Scandal

As the statistics demonstrate, Plan Colombia gave Uribe and his administration the resources necessary to combat the FARC, although some of the successes have been clouded by scandals and human rights abuses, the death squad scandal being one of the most notable.[110] In 2006, reports emerged that Uribe had close connections with right-wing paramilitary groups and even worked with the paramilitaries. The paramilitaries have perpetrated various human rights abuses, torture, and even murders of Colombians.[111] The police arrested various politicians, such as the former governor of Sucre and a former congresswoman, who were allegedly connected with the right-wing paramilitaries. Adam Isacson argues, "The paramilitaries could not have functioned without support from the politicians who held local power. Evidence, much of it from former paramilitary leaders, has brought a cascade of criminal investigations of legislators, governors, mayors, and other officials, who made common cause with the far-right warlords."[112]

Several individuals have argued that the paramilitaries controlled a large percentage of Congress and had much more power than many Colombians thought.[113] In fact, experts estimate that the paramilitaries control approximately 30 percent of the Colombian Congress. In 2009, the Colombian government investigated 43 of the 263 members of Congress elected in 2006. In addition, the Colombian courts convicted 12 members for ties to the paramilitaries, while another 13 members underwent trial proceedings in 2008.[114] A report released by a think tank in Colombia reported: "The truth could be much more overwhelming than what would appear from the recent scandals: the paramilitary phenomenon was huge . . . in addition to being a counterinsurgent military project, it was also a political project."[115] In sum, the *"parapolítico"* scandal demonstrates that corruption still exists within Colombia even among high-ranking officials. DeShazo, Primiani, and McLean describe the scandal and its impact, stating: "The recent 'parapolítico' scandals that have resulted in the arrest of dozen[s] of national legislators and other officials indicate that drug corruption and influence peddling reaches high levels. Importantly, however, the Colombian courts are going after 'big fish,' a positive sign in the struggle to combat corruption. Colombia's decentralized political system, with significant fiscal resources assigned to local governments, requires special attention in preventing corruption."[116]

Others have debated such accusations, arguing that the Uribe administration has taken initiatives to undermine the legitimacy of the Colombian court in order to ensure that the perpetrators are not prosecuted for such crimes.[117] This statement demonstrates that Uribe, indeed, has used illegal tactics in order to help defendants avoid being prosecuted. Therefore, one must recognize that Colombia still faces many challenges, particularly with regard to corruption. A decentralized state with weak institutions helps foment corruption and provide a fertile breeding ground for organized crime to flourish. In addition, the profits earned from drug trafficking provide participants with the means necessary to take advantage of a weak state and bribe law enforcement and government officials.

"False Positives" Scandal

In 2008, another major scandal, commonly referred to as the "false positives" scandal, created controversy in Colombia. Uribe wanted to combat the FARC and demonstrate that such efforts have been effective. Various security and militia forces killed thousands of civilians and subsequently dressed them in the appropriate attire the guerrillas wore. The military attracted civilians in various ways. One report states:

> Between December 2007 and August 2008, at least 16 young men disappeared under strange circumstances from the municipality of Soacha (Cundinamarca). Some of these men had informed their families that they had been offered a job . . . in Santander; others just never returned home. All of them were reported dead after having allegedly died in combat as soldiers for the Francisco de Paula Santander Batallion and the Movil 15 Brigade, both of which are entities within the Second Division of the National Military. . . . The bodies of these young men unexplainably appeared 700 kilometers from Soacha, buried without a name, in a common grave site in Ocana (North of Santander), and falsely reported by the military as delinquents, paramilitaries, and/or guerrillas killed in combat. Once these claims gained widespread notoriety, families from all over the country began to share similar stories of the disappearance and death of their loved ones, many of which revealed similar circumstances.[118]

The Prosecutor General's Office of Colombia revealed in August 2012 that this scandal was responsible for 2,997 civilian deaths.[119] The reasons for such egregious acts are that the military and security forces sought to increase their numbers in order to improve their statistics against the FARC with the ultimate goal of receiving benefits and other rewards for such successes against the guerrilla organizations.[120]

After learning about the scandal, Colombians began to protest such crimes. The "false positives" scandal has further eroded the reputation and the public's confidence in the military. In 2012, the international human rights group traveled to The Hague to the International Criminal Court to request that the leading military officials be prosecuted for such heinous acts against innocent civilians.[121]

Human Rights Abuses

Despite Uribe's accomplishments against the FARC, human rights abuses continued within Colombia during his administration, particularly as a result of the armed conflict. Under Uribe, the Colombian government failed to enforce the law and did not prosecute violators of human rights, and as a result, millions of Colombians have been displaced and forced to flee their homes. In 2006 alone, reports indicate that more than 200,000 Colombians had been displaced as a result of violence.[122] Many of the displaced individuals in Colombia are the most vulnerable populations such as the indigenous minorities and the Afro-Colombians. These two groups are particularly vulnerable to human rights abuses and have been forced to flee their lands. During his tenure, Uribe failed to assist these susceptible populations, focusing more on combating the narco-terrorists.

Another major form of human rights violations has been violence that has occurred against members of labor unions. The Uribe administration failed to address the extremely high levels of violence conducted against members who organized and formed labor unions.[123] Trade unionists in particular have been victims of human rights abuses and have even been murdered. Data gathered by one labor organization indicates that since 1991, 2,245 labor union members have been murdered in Colombia.[124] This is a staggering number and demonstrates that many Colombians are vulnerable and denied basic rights, such as the right to organize. Overall levels of violence against trade unionists, however, have decreased, although such numbers still remain high. Some argue that levels of violence against the union leaders are a result of the weakening of the FARC. DeShazo, Primiani, and McLean state, "To the limited extend [sic] that sufficient information is available to draw any presumed conclusions, there appears to be a direct relationship between greater (and lesser) levels of activity by illegal armed groups and violence against trade unionists."[125]

Some experts, however, caution that analysts must not conflate human rights abuses with Plan Colombia. Sandra Borda states that the "human rights problem is one that you will have if you have a war on drugs with or without the war on drugs."[126] In other words, Colombia would have experienced human rights abuses regardless of Plan Colombia because such abuses are the consequences of the internal armed conflict. Such comments are interesting, but it is important to remember that Plan Colombia provided the military with the necessary resources to strengthen its capabilities and overall power. Uribe clearly did not view human rights as a priority, focusing instead on combating the internal armed actors by whatever means necessary.

Uribe Desires Passage of the Free Trade Agreement in Return for His Loyalty

Another level of analysis deals with the economic dimensions that played a major role during the Uribe administration. We cannot understand the situation in Colombia during the Uribe administration without analyzing internal dynamics of the state and examining the role and impact of trade policy. One of the major domestic agendas of Uribe became the promotion of the U.S.–Colombian Trade Promotion Agreement (CTPA). Uribe wanted his ally to the north, President Bush, to approve and ratify the CTPA in order to help Colombia and promote economic development. President Bush also wanted to ratify the agreement, explaining to Congress that he intended to sign the CTPA in August 2006. Uribe placed his faith and trust in his partner to the north and hoped that the agreement would pass. For Uribe, the trade agreement would provide Colombia with access to U.S. markets and help improve the Colombian economy. Colombia has a population of 46 million and is very important to South America, particularly in terms of U.S. security interests. The Colombian economy, however, is just 1 percent of the U.S. GDP. The United States is Colombia's largest trading partner and grants Colombia access to a much bigger market. Statistically, 39 percent of Colombian exports entered the U.S. market. While the United States has economic connections with the Colombian government, the relationship is not one of complex interdependence. The passage of CTPA would promote increasing levels of interdependence between both countries. If implemented correctly, greater interdependence would enable Uribe and Colombia to obtain various concessions or leverage over the hegemonic partner.

The relationship between Colombia and the United States can be characterized as asymmetric interdependence. Colombia and the United States have various ties and linkages, but not as many linkages as the United States and other countries, such as Canada. The trade agreement would benefit Colombia much more than the United States, so Uribe continued to urge President Bush to ensure the passage of the CPTA.[127] The major components of the trade agreement deal with market access, decreasing barriers to trade, and promoting free trade. Specifically, 80 percent of the duties on exports of both industrial and consumer products would be removed with the approval of the agreement, increasing the ability for products to move between the two countries free of trade-diverting measures. Both Uribe and Bush viewed the elimination of such barriers as significant progress toward promoting trade and increasing the ties between Colombia and the United States.[128]

The trade agreement had various formidable opponents within the United States. Fears existed among certain groups, such as the American Federation of Labor and Congress of Industrial Organizations (AFL-CIO), that a trade agreement with Colombia would harm the U.S. economy and hurt U.S. workers by diverting jobs from the United States to Colombia. A Congressional Research report notes: "On the other hand, a number of other groups, such as the AFL-CIO, Public Citizen, and American Friends Service Committee, generally opposed the idea of regional trade agreements with Andean countries. These opponents generally argue that these kinds of trade agreements cost the U.S. economy jobs, erode protection for the environment and worker's rights, and improve extraneous commitments on countries. U.S. sugar producers also have voiced concern about the adverse cumulative impact the CTPA and other trade agreements would have on sugar producers."[129]

Due to the structure of the U.S. political system, groups have the ability to lobby Congress and voice their displeasures with various policies. Members of the U.S. House of Representatives are especially cognizant of the ability, opinions, and desires of voting members who reside in their congressional district. Each state in the United States also has two senators regardless of size. Therefore, a state that has sugar farmers can lobby senators about the importance of sugar to the industry in that particular state. In sum, the U.S. political system that the Founding Fathers designed helped opponents of the CPTAs mount a formidable opposition, arguing that such an agreement would hurt the economic prosperity of people who work in certain industries and reside in certain districts.

Uribe placed a tremendous amount of his political clout on his ability to convince President Bush to pass the Free Trade Agreement (FTA) in order to benefit Colombia. Uribe allied closely with President Bush and his policies and became his greatest friend in the region. Uribe focused all his attention and efforts on President Bush and a U.S. alliance. He wanted Bush to pass the FTA and compensate him and Colombia for their support for the implementation of U.S. policies, such as the war on terrorism. Bush wanted to help his strongest political ally and ratified the agreement. Bush also sought to improve his reputation and legacy in Latin America, which remained low throughout his administration.[130] However, he needed Congress to approve the bill in order for him to sign it into law. Uribe and the Colombians failed to comprehend the nature of the U.S. system and did not understand the dynamics of U.S. policymaking.[131] In fact, experts have argued that very few people within Colombia understand how U.S. policy is made, which can be can be a complicated and often ugly process that is a result of various comprises and concessions by members of Congress.[132] Uribe failed to recognize that President Bush did not have the same power that the Colombian president had in terms of law-making.

In sum, Uribe placed all his hopes in the United States and wanted a free trade agreement with the United States, which is a stark contrast from trade policies and alliance blocks in other parts of Latin America. *Mercado Común del Sur*, for instance, came into being in South America under the leadership of Brazil.[133] Other countries in the region, such as Brazil, Chile, Peru, and Argentina, were less closely aligned with the United States than ever before. Other experiments countering U.S. hegemon occurred with the *Alianza Bolivariana para los Pueblos de Nuestra América* (ALBA) countries, led by Venezuela, demonstrating that U.S. control over the hemisphere was drastically weakening.[134] Colombia, however, did not join such alliances or experiments and remained a close ally of the United States, continuing to advocate for the passage of the FTA with President Bush.

Conclusion

Plan Colombia has had partial successes, particularly in combating the illegal armed actors operating within Colombia. Uribe came to power and had a completely different vision and social construction of how to achieve victory in Colombia.[135] Uribe disapproved of Pastrana's demilitarized zone and refused to negotiate with the FARC. Uribe also made an important distinction, arguing that Colombia did not have an internal armed conflict but a terrorist problem.[136] Uribe successfully altered Plan Colombia and made the primary goal combating the narco-terrorists. Indeed, revenue obtained from drug trafficking enterprises has helped finance the FARC, but one can debate whether the FARC should be labeled a terrorist organization. In reality, the FARC use terrorist tactics in order to intimidate Colombians and achieve their goals.

Uribe shifted the goals of Plan Colombia, defying realist logic. According to neorealism, the weaker power will be required to adhere to the rules set forth by the hegemonic actor. In other words, the weaker actor will be required to oblige the stronger actor and comply with the rules in order to receive foreign aid and the money necessary to combat drug trafficking.[137] The events of September 11, 2001, resulted in the United States waging a Global War on Terrorism in order to combat terrorism around the world and prevent future attacks on U.S. territory. Uribe successfully sold and marketed Plan Colombia as an initiative to combat the narco-terrorists, and President Bush agreed with the new shifts in the agenda and goals of Plan Colombia because they went along with U.S. national interests and priorities. In addition, Uribe's Colombia provided Bush with non-Muslim terrorists, enabling him to defend his policies and argue that the war on terrorism was against any terrorists regardless of religious affiliations or ethnic identity. Uribe's ability to frame the internal conflict in Colombia as part of the larger war on terrorism, in essence, was quite successful.[138] The new version of Plan Colombia provided him with the necessary resources to combat the illegal armed actors, which is something that the Clinton administration wanted to avoid. Unlike Bush, the Clinton administration, as well as many government officials, politicians, and policy analysts, feared becoming involved in the internal dynamics of Colombia, wishing to avoid becoming bogged down in another Vietnam-type situation.[139]

From the outset, Uribe and Bush had a strong relationship because they had the same social constructions and solutions to the major problems in Colombia. Uribe's alliance was an unexpected benefit for the Bush administration because he vowed to combat the terrorists and helped Bush implement his larger vision in Latin America. Uribe enabled the United States to place bases in Colombia, which angered his neighbors. By the end of their respective administrations, both Bush and Uribe did not have much soft power nor did they have many political allies or "friends" in Latin America.[140] In 2005, Uribe stated: "Let me say this. First, I want to repeat, on behalf of all Colombians, our gratitude because of the help we receive from the United States. It is very important, from your people, from your Congress, from your government, and, of course, from President Bush. We consider your country, your government, your people a great ally of Colombia. Second, to defeat terrorism, we need political will, persistent democracy and social cohesion."[141]

The close alliance between the Bush and Uribe administrations enabled President Bush to institutionalize the model of security cooperation in Colombia. The implementation of Plan Colombia required the institutionalization of the plan. The two presidents made efforts to establish a permanent institutional framework to facilitate security cooperation as well as to provide a mechanism for channeling the billions of dollars in U.S. aid that Plan Colombia provided the Uribe administration. The result of the institutionalization meant an increasing U.S. presence in Colombia. In addition, the close friendship between Bush and Uribe enabled President Bush to increase the role of important U.S. actors in Colombia, such as the ambassador.[142] Ultimately, Uribe remained the only ally and supporter of the Bush administration according to the statistics and perceptions among Latin American governments.[143] In 2009, Bush awarded Uribe with the

Presidential Medal of Freedom for his valiant efforts. In the award ceremony, Bush stated: "For President Uribe, the great demands of office continue. Today the United States honors all Colombians by honoring the man they have chosen to lead them. By refusing to allow the land he loves to be destroyed by the enemy within, by proving that terror can be opposed and defeated, President Uribe has reawakened the hopes of his countrymen and shown a model of leadership to a watching world. Colombia remains a nation with challenges. But the future will always be bright in a country that produces men such as President Alvaro [sic] Uribe."[144]

Critics argue that the award sends the wrong message because President Bush acknowledged the leader of a country who failed to produce changes to address human rights abuses. During his tenure, Uribe continued to ignore the major human rights abuses that occurred throughout Colombia and that have outraged human rights activists and members of civil society. After Bush recognized Uribe at the White House, Human Rights Watch released the following statement: "U.S. President George W. Bush's decision to award the Presidential Medal of Freedom to President Álvaro Uribe of Colombia is a disturbing example of the Bush administration's disregard for serious human rights concerns out of zeal to show unconditional support to governments that it views as strategic allies, seven leading nongovernmental organizations said today."[145]

Uribe promised to combat the FARC upon obtaining office. By the end of his tenure, violence in Colombia had decreased and Uribe had not only successfully combatted the FARC by forcing them to retreat but also made advances in terms of the professionalism of the military. Sandra Borda states, "Before Plan Colombia, armed forces in this country . . . were inefficient, [without] intelligence, [and] . . . were not getting results."[146] Uribe managed to strengthen the armed forces in Colombia and make them more effective, and as a result, Uribe increased security within Colombia.

These partial victories represent significant strides for Colombia in terms of increasing security, however, Plan Colombia failed to address many underlying issues.[147] In particular, Plan Colombia failed to allocate significant resources to strengthen democracy, promote the rule of law, and help strengthen existing institutions. In terms of long-term strategy, a country with weak institutions fosters corruption and foments organized crime. Colombia has never had strong institutions and Uribe's reorientation of Plan Colombia failed to address these deep-rooted issues. Pizarro and Gaitán echo such sentiments declaring, "Fundamental to any country's real achievement of the rule of law and respect for human rights is a state that is capable of guaranteeing a minimum of democratic order."[148] Colombia, therefore, will continue to face hardships if it does not have a state that is capable of carrying out the rule of law and decreasing corruption. Colombia has made significant strides from the days of Pablo Escobar when Colombia was on the verge of collapse and becoming a narco-state. Having democratic order requires that the state "must be capable of legislating and enforcing laws, and second, power must be exercised by duly elected officials who are willing to be held accountable for their actions."[149] The Colombian state, therefore, must strengthen its institutions to combat organized crime and corruption.

During this period examined, Plan Colombia has been a failure in terms of stemming the trafficking of drugs. Plan Colombia allocated billions of dollars for aerial spraying of herbicides. Despite spending large amounts of money, coca cultivation actually increased in some areas of Colombia. The next chapter addresses the failures of Plan Colombia to decrease drug cultivation and narco-trafficking, the plan's initial goal.[150]

5

Beyond Plan Colombia and Desecuritization

Toward the end of the decade, President Bush (2009) and President Uribe (2010) ended their respective presidential terms. By the end of the Bush administration and the beginning of the Obama administration, the United States reduced aid to Colombia. How did the Colombians perceive and evaluate Plan Colombia in terms of its successes and failures? Were the initial goals of the United States and the Colombians achieved? If so, how were these goals achieved? Why did the policies change from Uribe to Santos?

This chapter first examines the goals of Plan Colombia during this period, and then, after examining the goals for both the United States and Colombia, evalulates whether Plan Colombia achieved these goals. A significant transition occurs in 2010 with the departure of Uribe and the inauguration of President Santos. President Santos has made significant statements and implemented new policies departing from those of Uribe. Santos has recognized that the war on drugs has been a failure and is more open to dialogue, arguing:

> Sometimes we all feel that we have been pedaling on a stationary bicycle. We look to our right and our left and we still see the same landscape. There has been an important decrease in the world's coca crops, mainly due to the great efforts we have made in Colombia, but the market is still huge and the business is highly profitable. My proposal is very simple: we need to start an in-depth discussion, led by scientists and experts, about the "war" against drugs.

> We have to determine whether we are doing the best we
> can, or whether there are better options.[1]

The chapter ends with a discussion of the change in rhetoric and
policy that has occurred with Santos's inauguration, and his policies
and stances are contrasted with those of Uribe.

Determining what constitutes a success or failure is a constructivist issue.[2] Examining whether Plan Colombia has been successful and
achieved its goals requires one to compare the goals and outcomes. As
previously discussed, the original goals have shifted over time. In 2000,
President Clinton signed into law Plan Colombia, making combating
drug trafficking the number one priority. Has Plan Colombia achieved
the original goal of reducing coca cultivation and drug trafficking set
forth by the Clinton administration? The answer is no, and the subsequent sections provide an extensive analysis.

As discussed in chapter 4, the goals of Plan Colombia shifted
drastically after the events of September 11, 2001. Uribe assumed
the presidency and vowed to combat the terrorists such as the FARC
and other armed actors. The narco-terrorists, as the name implies,
earned a tremendous amount of money and financed their operations
from the proceeds of drug trafficking. Uribe successfully convinced
President Bush that Colombia had a terrorist problem. However, one
cannot assume that the cultivation and trafficking of drugs no longer
mattered for Uribe and for the Bush administration. Uribe wanted to
stop drug trafficking, but his number one priority became combating
the FARC.[3] David Mares states, "I don't believe it was ever the intent
of the Colombians to use this to destroy the drug trade."[4] Chapter 4
demonstrates that Uribe made very important strides in Colombia,
particularly with regard to the FARC. Plan Colombia, therefore, has
had some successes with regard to the war against the narco-terrorists,
resulting in decreases in the levels of violence. The large decreases in
the level of violence such as kidnappings and murders indicate that
Uribe's policies and initiatives to combat illegal armed actors helped
stabilize security within the country. However, even though kidnappings
in Colombia decreased dramatically, Colombia continues to rank as the
country with the highest kidnapping rate despite Uribe's valiant efforts.[5]

Uribe would argue that Plan Colombia has been a success because
his administration combatted the narco-terrorists, making Colombia
safer. Uribe's efforts have resulted in substantial decreases in the
number of FARC members. However, the FARC has not been defeated
and continues to constitute a major security concern for Colombia.[6]
Although the FARC has been weakened under Uribe, the organization
remains a formidable adversary. The FARC have been forced to retreat

and leave the neighboring cities and towns in Colombia, but they continue to operate within rural Colombia. It is therefore shortsighted to believe that Uribe's successes represent a victory over the FARC.[7] This organization has the ability to rearm and regain strength and continue to fight the government. The Colombian state continues to face challenges with regard to its inherent weaknesses and inability to maintain control over many of the rural regions throughout the country.

The next portion of this chapter analyzes the failure of Plan Colombia to reduce coca cultivation and drug trafficking. Some experts argue that Plan Colombia was never an initiative to reduce the drug trade. From the beginning, Plan Colombia clearly states that it seeks to reduce coca cultivation, drug production, and trafficking by 50 percent. While the lines between the war on drugs and the war on terrorism became blurred after September 11, Plan Colombia has failed with regard to its drug goals. The next section empirically evaluates the results of the drug trafficking initiatives.[8]

One cannot discuss Plan Colombia and the drug war without examining aerial herbicide spraying because this strategy constituted one of the major initiatives of Plan Colombia. Determining whether aerial spraying initiatives have been successful can be measured empirically by examining the statistical results produced by various agencies. One has to be careful with statistics and view them with some skepticism because organizations have different methodologies and ways to calculate results.[9] Although one must be cautious when evaluating statistics and not view them as an exact number or a science, statistics, indeed, are valuable because they provide researchers with a baseline or estimate of progress.[10] One cannot argue that the aerial spraying initiatives have been successful when the number of hectares of coca being cultivated has actually increased over time. The balance sheet reveals that aerial spraying has not only been unproductive but also counterproductive because of the environmental damages and health problems it created. Bush administration officials would counterargue that Plan Colombia achieved its goals because the airplanes sprayed the correct number of targets the Bush administration set forth. Therefore, determining what is a success is a constructivist issue and is subjective to those being asked.[11]

Despite spending billions of dollars, the area under cultivation increased in certain regions and drug trafficking continued. Plan Colombia failed to achieve its goal of decreasing coca cultivation by 50 percent. The area under cultivation decreased from 2001 until 2003, but then proliferated despite the eradication efforts. In 2001, Colombia cultivated 211,100 hectares of coca. In 2003, Colombia recorded 153,800 hectares of coca.[12] However, coca cultivation continued to increase after 2003 despite the fact that the United States sprayed hundreds of thousands of hectares of coca being cultivated.[13]

In 2002, for instance, the United States sprayed 130,364 hectares of coca fields according to a report on Colombia by the U.N. Office on Drugs and Crime (UNODC). The number of hectares sprayed increased dramatically over the years.[14] In 2006, the United States recorded spraying 172,025 hectares of coca. The number of hectares sprayed began to decrease in 2007 as a shift occurred toward manual eradication. In 2009, the number of hectares sprayed had decreased to 101,940.[15] The 2008 Government Accountability Report indicates that the area of coca being cultivated increased by approximately 15 percent in 2006 from 2000; in 2006, farmers cultivated 157,000 hectares. U.S. officials noted that increases may result from different calculation methods. From 2005 to 2007, for instance, more regions received surveys regarding coca under cultivation. In 2008, the area under coca cultivation in rural Colombia increased by 27 percent.[16]

Cultivating coca and selling it to drug trafficking organizations is an illegal business and requires that farmers adapt to the changing circumstances, including aerial spraying initiatives. Increases in law enforcement led to shifts in coca being cultivated in other areas. Farmers intermix coca with other plants and legal substances, making detection from airplanes or satellites much more difficult. Farmers can also grow coca in smaller plots of land in order to avoid detection.[17] Profits from coca cultivation are the primary means of income for coca cultivators, and, therefore, they learn from past interdiction efforts. Even after plants are sprayed, growers can clean the plants or spray products to ensure that the coca does not die. Ramírez Lemus, Stanton, and Walsh assert, "Though large-scale producers are known to fragment their coca fields in order to avoid detection, most small coca plots are cultivated by individual farmers for their own subsistence."[18]

In addition to aerial spraying, Plan Colombia allocated money for manual eradication and other programs such as crop substitution. As of May 2008, Colombian government officials revealed that manual eradication initiatives resulted in the eradication of 28,000 hectares,[19]

Table 5.1. Coca Cultivation in the Andean Region 1998–2008 (in hectares)

2000	2001	2002	2003	2004	2005	2006	2007	2008
163,000	145,000	102,000	86,000	80,000	86,000	78,000	99,000	81,000

Information adapted from *Coca Cultivation Survey* (Bogotá, Colombia: UNODC, 2009).

Table 5.2.

National Parks	2007	2008	Percentage Change
Catatumbo-Bari	38	477	+1,155%
Paramillo	420	464	+10%
Sierra Nevada	94	170	+81
Munchique	55	96	+75
Utria	12	44	+267

Information adapted from *Coca Cultivation Survey* (Bogotá, Colombia: UNODC, 2009).

but it presents several challenges, one of which is protecting participants in the program from the guerrilla organizations that earn profits
from coca cultivation and that can threaten the lives of individuals
participating in such programs. It becomes a logical choice for a coca
cultivator to grow coca not only to earn more profits per yield of coca
than other products, but also to stay alive and avoid persecution by
the guerrillas as well as other drug trafficking organizations. Many
of the regions where coca is cultivated are located in contested areas
inundated with FARC operatives. Despite various initiatives designed
to protect participants in manual eradication programs, reports indicate
that violence still occurs against manual eradicators by various means,
including fire from snipers as well as improvised explosive devises and
minefields. By the end of August 2008, 23 manual eradicators died as a
result of actions taken against them by the groups that stand to profit
from coca cultivation. Reports indicate that 118 individuals died from
participating in the manual eradication program over the three-year
period from 2005 to 2008.[20] Manual eradication initiatives occur in
some of the most dangerous regions of FARC-controlled Colombia,
and, as a result, the Colombian government must provide security for
the participants in the manual eradication program to prevent them
from being killed. For these reasons, manual eradication efforts have
not been successful in decreasing coca production.

Internal Displacement

Another major consequence of the aerial spraying initiatives has been
the displacement of many individuals who live in those regions. Poor,
small-tract farmers, in particular, have been harmed as a result of
aerial spraying and have been forced to relocate to other regions.
Organizations such as the Council for Human Rights and Displacement
in Colombia estimate that 75,000 people were displaced in 2001 and

2002 as a result of aerial spraying. These displaced farmers, many of whom live near the border of Ecuador, are not eligible for the same government benefits provided to individuals displaced as a result of the internal conflict.[21]

One can read news reports about seizures of drug shipments or the capture of drug traffickers, yet, one should be skeptical of the overall trends. Capturing one drug dealer and seizing several shipments does not change the fact that the United States has spent billions of dollars fighting the war on drugs in Colombia. The overall empirical measures demonstrate that drugs remained readily available during this period. Youngers and Rosin note that contrary to the evidence, U.S. officials continue to view counterdrug programs as effective, stating:

> A significant gap exists in the U.S. drug control programs between expansive goals and limited achievements. U.S. officials routinely assert that international counterdrug programs are successful. Short-term tactical successes are indeed evidence[d]—coca crops are eradicated, traffickers are arrested, and shipments are intercepted. . . . There is no evidence demonstrating a significant reduction in the supply of illicit drugs on the U.S. city streets. To the contrary, the stability of price and purity levels of drugs point to their continued accessibility. Winning the drug war is as elusive today as it was when the effort was first launched.[22]

Uribe's Departure from Power

In 2010, President Uribe departed from power after the Colombian courts ruled on the referendum, denying him the opportunity to run for a third term. Some have hailed the ruling as a victory for Colombian democracy. He accomplished a tremendous amount in terms of decreasing violence in Colombia and combatting the terrorists, but by the end of his tenure, he was unpopular with many leaders in Latin America. He remained the only ally of the Bush administration in the region, however, and continued to support Bush's vision with regard to the Global War on Terrorism.[23] Uribe allowed the United States to create bases in Colombia, irritating his neighboring countries, which certainly neither improved his relations with Colombia's neighbors, nor did he devote any effort to promote cooperation between Colombia and other countries. Uribe declared that two of Colombia's neighbors, Ecuador and Venezuela, both allowed the FARC as well as the ELN to relocate near their shared borders.[24] Additionally, Uribe "publicly accused Venezuela and Ecuador of acquiescing or tolerating the presence of FARC and ELN on their territory and even aiding and financing them."[25] Such accusations did not sit well with the leaders in Caracas and Quito and resulted in tense—actually, cantankerous—relations between Colombia and its neighbors. By the end of his presidency, Uribe had lost a tremendous amount of soft power with other countries in the region, and he had not a friend in the region after alienating and subordinating diplomatic relations to winning the war against the narco-terrorists.[26]

Uribe's major accomplishment was weakening the FARC. Uribe argued that his administration dealt a crushing blow to the FARC, and Colombia was on the verge of achieving a new stage in its history: the postconflict stage. Indeed, the Uribe administration forced the FARC into retreat, but it and the other actors not only still operate within Colombia, but they also have the capability to rearm and strengthen their power.[27]

After eight years, Uribe left the presidency in Colombia with an abysmal record on human rights. One of the most controversial scandals was the "false positives" scandal, where members of the Colombian military dressed civilians in FARC attire in order to inflate the statistics with regard to the number of FARC members killed. Increased statistics would mean increased monetary bonuses. Under Uribe, the military also violated international humanitarian law with such tactics. Ultimately, Uribe's legacy has been one of mixed reviews because many of his accomplishments have been tainted by the accompanying human rights abuses. The "Uribe legacy, consequently, is mixed, since violent conflict has become more diffuse, with a broader range of criminal and armed groups operating and interacting in both rural and urban areas."[28]

Election of Juan Manuel Santos

Uribe's former defense minister, Juan Manuel Santos, defeated Green Party member Antanas Mockus in a landslide victory, winning 69 percent of the votes in the June 20, 2010, presidential runoff.[29] Santos's ascension to the presidency represents a critical juncture because he made many changes in terms of policy, the most fundamental of which was his recognition that Colombia indeed had a raging internal armed conflict. This is a fundamental shift from Uribe, who denied the internal armed conflict, stating instead that Colombia simply had terrorists. Experts, however, have never denied that Colombia had an internal armed conflict because it has been ongoing for decades.

Uribe has responded publicly to President Santos's discussion of the internal "armed conflict." Santos, Uribe's right-hand man, talked about an internal conflict, in essence challenging Uribe's perception of the situation. Using the words "armed conflict" implies civil war, whereas Uribe stressed that Colombia had a terrorist problem. Hannah Stone writes, "This was met with a furious response by his predecessor and one-time mentor, Álvaro Uribe, who insists that the country faces not an internal conflict, but a terrorist threat.[30] The former president fired off numerous Tweets, complaining that the country's armed groups are terrorists fighting against a legitimate state, do not deserve the status of belligerents, and should not be given political recognition."[31]

Santos Seeks to Assist Marginalized Communities

Certain groups in particular, such as the indigenous communities and the Afro-Colombians, are prone to maltreatment by the armed conflict. In 1990, Colombia passed laws that enabled the Afro-Colombian communities to gain the title to the land they occupied for many years. Afro-Colombians faced extreme violence, particularly from the paramilitaries, because the Afro-Colombians are located in land that can be used to produce the coca later processed into cocaine. The Colombian state has not ensured the security of the Afro-Colombian communities in rural Colombia, and, therefore, many individuals have experienced violence and or even have been killed. Amnesty International describes the lack of security and precarious situation that the Afro-Colombians must endure, stating:

> Over recent years, Afro-descendant communities living in departments bordering the Pacific coast of Colombia have faced repeated death threats, killings and forced displacement at the hands of the paramilitary, either acting alone or with the collusion of the security forces, who accuse them of being guerrilla collaborators. These human rights violations are often motivated by efforts to secure control over lands rich in mineral resources or with other economic potential. Many of these lands are legally owned by Afro-descendant communities who hold collective land titles. Repeatedly, paramilitaries have threatened and killed members of these communities just in advance of or after they have been granted these land rights. Guerrilla forces have also killed and threatened members of these communities accusing them of siding with the security forces or with paramilitary groups.[32]

This statement demonstrates that the Afro-Colombians have experienced many hardships, and Uribe's Colombia failed to provide these vulnerable communities with security and basic rights. Many politicians have ignored marginalized groups, such as the Afro-Colombians, but President Santos has taken steps to address the grievances of such vulnerable populations. Despite Uribe's efforts to improve the security of these groups, the murder rates continue to increase.[33] The Santos administration must provide further protection for these groups because they are still subjected to great violence. The "protective measures defined by the government for Afro-Colombian and indigenous communities, their organizations, and leaders are insufficient."[34] Critics complain that the Colombian state has not taken into considerations the opinions and suggestions of the marginalized communities when creating policies. Such policies have not "advanced in the creation of effective protective measures that are consulted with the affected communities and take into account the specificities of their ethnicity and the collective nature of their communities."[35] In addition, the Santos administration has failed to ensure the security of these groups despite constant threats.

The Victims and Land Restitution Law

President Santos did not wait long before addressing issues that had been largely ignored under the Uribe administration. Uribe sought to combat the guerrillas using the necessary force required and ignored the repercussions of such policies such as human rights abuses. In 2009 alone, 177 crimes occurred and were recorded in Colombia against human rights activists; quite possibly many more occurred under Uribe's administration. Of the 177 documented crimes, the paramilitaries were responsible for approximately 47 percent. Various state agencies also participated in such crimes and abuses of human rights, accounting for an estimated 9 percent of the recorded crimes.[36]

From the beginning, Santos vowed to address human rights abuses and has attempted to separate his administration from the past scandals and abuses. Just three months into his presidency, Santos proposed and submitted two important laws to the Colombian Congress that sought to address human rights violations and compensate individuals who have experienced hardships as a result of the internal conflict within Colombia. The Colombian Congress combined the two pieces of legislation Santos proposed into one law: The Victims and Land Restitution Law (Victims Law). The law, which Congress officially passed on June 10, 2011, sought to compensate victims of the internal armed conflict in Colombia from 1985 until 2011.[37] Uribe had rejected this legislation because he neither believed nor acknowledged that Colombia had an internal conflict, opting instead to spend resources combating the various internal armed actors, resulting in a continued decrease in violence in Colombia.

The Victims Law begins with the Colombian government accepting—and acknowledging—that the internal armed conflict in Colombia continues. The law is partly symbolic, but it also clearly identifies the armed conflict and concedes that the plethora of victims forced to flee their homes as a result of such large-scale violence must be compensated.[38] The Victims Law recognizes that individuals who suffered hardships have rights, one of which is the right to reparations for their hardships. The law symbolizes a fundamental shift from Uribe and a step in the right direction in addressing human rights abuses. Various challenges still exist with regard to the implementation of the law. Critics have censured the Colombian government for not consulting with human rights organizations and addressing their concerns and incorporating their recommendations into the law. A report by the Washington Office on Latin America (WOLA) states, "We hope that the government meets the obligations stated in the law and that it guarantees the participation of victims and civil society in the different phases and implementation."[39]

The Colombian government also has faced challenges with regard to people wanting restitution as a result of human rights abuses. Leaders of communities that have been displaced as a result of the Colombian armed conflict have been murdered as they sought reparations from the Colombian state. Reports state that various leaders requested protection from the Colombian state because they had received threats. Yet, the Colombian state has failed to protect the leaders of these groups, who were later murdered for their attempts to regain their lands. WOLA notes, "It is a great concern that the law does not sufficiently guarantee a protection program for the victims, witnesses and public servants that assures the life and integrity of the persons and families reclaiming their land rights."[40] Clearly, WOLA feels that the Colombian government has the responsibility to protect individuals who have suffered from such hardships and ensure that they do not experience more violations of their human rights as a result of their attempts to reclaim their land. The WOLA report continues, "It is broadly demonstrated that current protection programs do not respond to the security needs of the displaced population and victims. As they stand, these programs cannot guarantee the protection of communities that wish to return to their lands in their places of origin."[41] Overall, the reparations policies represent a step in the right direction, but the Colombian state suffers from traditional weaknesses and has not demonstrated the ability to protect citizens who are sup-posed to benefit from this program. The murder of 18 leaders of such communities despite some requesting protection from the government is embarrassing. Efforts must be made to protect many of the most vulnerable populations in Colombia.[42]

Colombian Minister of Agriculture, Jan Camilo Restrepo, announced in October 2010 the creation of the Pilot Project for the Restitution and Formalization of Lands and Territory. The project has several goals, including increasing the territories that belong to various marginalized populations in Colombia, such as the Afro-Colombians. The project also seeks to provide farmers with the rights to the land that they have farmed for more than five years by granting them an official title indicating ownership of the property. The program has witnessed some results, particularly with regard to granting farm-ers land ownership. Despite these initial results, the lack of security continues to hinder further progress with regard to restitution initia-tives. The project has enabled some farmers to receive the official title to their property, but problems have arisen as a result of various security factors.[43]

Addressing Internal Displacement

Upon assuming the presidency, Santos also sought to address Colombia's internal displacement problem caused by the internal armed conflict. Millions of Colombians have been forced to flee their homes fearing for their lives and as a result of violence in their communities. Colombia remains the world's leader with the largest number of individuals dis-placed, surpassing other war-torn countries such as Iraq, Sudan, and Afghanistan. In fact, Colombia produces the greatest number of refugees in Latin America.[44] Research indicates that approximately 117,000 Colombians are documented refugees and have obtained official refugee status. This number, however, does not include the number of people who live in other countries illegally and who have not officially received refugee status. One must also note that the refugees have relocated to more than 20 countries,[45] straining the social services in many of the other countries that cannot afford to continue accepting large inflows of refugees every year due to the current economic recession. Santos's Victims Law is an effort to address the internal displacement as a result of the internal conflict, but the weakness of the Colombian state continues to hinder progress. The number of displacements continues to increase because the Colombian government lacks the appropriate capacity and strength to address such problems.[46]

The refugees remain susceptible to attacks by the guerrilla organizations. In particular, "The refugee population that resides in the areas along the border with Colombia continues to be victimized by attacks perpetrated by Colombian illegal armed groups. Women and girls are particularly vulnerable to sexual violence and recruitment into trafficking networks."[47] The National Development Plan (PND) for 2010–2014 is the official program developed to help displaced persons. However, the PND "does not include any concrete measures of prevention of displacement nor protection of this population during its displacement, return, or reintegration."[48] Although Santos faces various challenges and minimal progress has been made, such advances still represent a drastic change from Uribe.

Addressing Impunity

Colombia has had a long history of impunity in which violators of human rights are not held accountable for their egregious actions. The Santos administration also has made changes in order to prosecute violators of human rights, representing yet another fundamental shift away from the Uribe administration. The Uribe administration actually assisted human rights abusers to avoid prosecution by undermining the legitimate efforts of the courts. Both human rights advocates and key witnesses in human rights cases have received threats and have even been murdered, thereby prohibiting justice. Such threats deter potential witnesses from discussing violations with law enforcement officials because the Colombian state has clearly demonstrated that it has not been capable of protecting these witnesses from the violators of human rights. Importantly, witnesses and human rights activists have not been the only groups that have been threatened or even killed; lawyers and judges also have been murdered.[49]

A new Prosecutor General was appointed in Colombia in December 2010, representing a positive step because until this point the position had been empty. The Prosecutor General has attempted to use the judicial system to prosecute human rights violators. Despite valiant efforts, Colombia still records an astonishing 90 percent impunity rate. The new leader of the criminal justice system faces many challenges, particularly with regard to the prosecution of human rights violators. Critics argue: "The administration of justice in cases of violations against human rights defenders remains tragic. The majority of investigations remain in the preliminary phase."[50] The prosecution also has been slow because the cases are investigated in a decentralized manner,[51] and the Prosecutor General lacks appropriate resources necessary to administer justice.

Peace Talks

In June 2012, the Congress in Colombia passed a law that paved the way for peace talks with the guerrilla organizations, representing a fundamental shift from Uribe, who came to power vowing to combat the FARC and refusing to negotiate. In part, the Colombians elected Uribe for his hardline stances against the FARC and his refusal to negotiate with such "terrorist" organizations. Voters remembered the disastrous negotiations that occurred between the FARC and the Colombian government during the Pastrana administration, where Pastrana's demilitarized zone provided the FARC with territory the size of Switzerland, enabling the organization to reorganize and centralize its operations in this lawless territory. The negotiations failed and, in essence, provided the FARC with its own state where it could operate free from intervention by the Colombian state.

Santos's new policy to negotiate with the Marxist rebels has provoked controversy because many Colombians remember the Pastrana administration's failed negotiations. In 2012, the Colombian Senate passed the Legal Framework for Peace, which proposed less stringent sentences for FARC leaders if the Colombian state and the FARC could reach a peace agreement. The logic is that the Colombian government is willing to negotiate reduced sentences in order to promote peace because Colombians have become tired of dealing with the decades-old armed conflict.[52] Santos hopes to move forward and obtain peace within Colombia despite the various challenges. Millions of Colombians have been victims as a result of the armed conflict, and Santos, therefore, has distinguished himself from Uribe as being willing to initiate new policies to achieve the goals.

Santos and the War on Drugs

Santos has recognized that the war on drugs has been an utter failure in Colombia and has argued that a serious debate regarding drug policy is necessary to change the current situation. In an interview, Santos stated:

> I would talk about legalising marijuana and more than just marijuana. If the world thinks that this is the correct approach, because for example in our case we used to be exporters, but we were replaced by producers in California. And there even was a referendum in California to legalise it and they lost it but they could have won it. I ask myself how would you explain marijuana being legalised in California

and cocaine consumption being penalised in Idaho? It's a contradiction. So it's a difficult problem where you set the limits. It's a difficult decision. For example, I would never legalise very hard drugs like morphine or heroin because in fact they are suicidal drugs. I might consider legalising cocaine if there is a world consensus because this drug has affected us most here in Colombia. I don't know what is more harmful, cocaine or marijuana. That's a health discussion. But again, only if there is a consensus.[54]

Santos's comments reveal that he is open to a serious discussion about the legalization of drugs, implying that he welcomes a discussion based on sound scientific evidence with regard to the health impacts of illicit drugs. It appears that Santos has a different social construction of the war on drugs as well as the potential solutions. Indeed, his perceptions are quite different than his predecessors, and some might even criticize him as being radical.

Santos understands that the U.S.–led war on drugs has caused a tremendous amount of bloodshed and violence. The Colombians are tired of experiencing the hardships that have resulted from the war on drugs, and Santos's statements symbolize his willingness to move in a new direction with regard to drug policies and the war on drugs and represent a fundamental shift in policy from Uribe, who wanted to combat coca cultivation because the production and trafficking of drugs helped fuel the guerrilla organizations. Uribe refused to listen to critics about the negative repercussions of aerial spraying of herbicides. As previously discussed, many studies have demonstrated that the aerial spraying program in Colombia has had disastrous health and environmental effects. Uribe never talked about legalization or decriminalization of drugs. He had a different social construction[55] and focused on supply-side initiatives, attempting to simultaneously combat the cultivation, production, and trafficking of drugs in Colombia.

Some scholars, such as Daniel Mejía, have criticized Santos, arguing, "As time goes by, what I have seen is pure rhetoric. 'Yeah, let's open a debate and it is welcome but I [Santos] will not push it.'"[56] Mejía contends that the debate for legalization must start in Colombia or Mexico because those countries have suffered greatly from the war on drugs. Mejía questions whether a country not so affected by drug trafficking would begin the debate regarding the war on drugs if Colombia or Mexico fail to do so.[57]

Santos recognizes that the war on drugs has been a failure and many people have suffered in Colombia as a result of such policies—or the lack thereof. Santos is open to addressing a new agenda and promoting new policies. Indeed, Santos remains an ally of the United

States, but Colombia wants more relative autonomy to make its decisions. Under Santos, the Colombian government no longer wants to be subordinate to the United States and is diversifying its partners, seeking trade relations with China.[58] Such actions defy realist logic, which argues that a country can either balance or bandwagon. Santos is maintaining amiable relations with the United States, but he is not putting all his hopes or political clout into the United States. Instead, he has diversified his partners in order to increase the relative autonomy of Colombia, which is in stark contrast to Uribe who placed all his faith in the Bush administration.[59]

Conclusion

Plan Colombia has had some partial victories in terms of decreasing violence and combatting the FARC.[60] However, Plan Colombia has not achieved its goals in terms of drugs. In many respects, aspects of Plan Colombia—like the aerial spraying initiatives—have been counterproductive as they have destroyed the Colombian countryside. Despite the failures of aerial spraying, the United States continued this activity for many years, and more recently it has supported manual eradication programs. The aerial spraying initiatives in Colombia have been both ineffective and counterproductive. Mejía states, "What we've seen is that aerial spraying does not work as a strategy,"[61] and maintains that rigorous studies using quasi-natural experiments, structural models, and economic strategies prove that aerial spraying does not work. He continues, "It does not reduce coca cultivation in the medium, or short-term, or long-run. What it does is create incentives so that farmers, in the presence of aerial spraying . . . plant more coca."[62]

Coca cultivators, then, adapt to external conditions to survive. For instance, molasses can be sprayed on the plants in order to protect it from the herbicides. The United States has financed aerial spraying, which has had many negative consequences in terms of health and environmental effects, but continues to argue that aerial spraying is safe. Washington counters critics by defining the accuracy of the spraying, arguing that pilots control for wind, but research demonstrates that spray drift has been a major issue.[63]

Despite spending a tremendous amount of money on spraying coca cultivated in Colombia, drug cultivation increased over time. The program, then, cannot be deemed a success if the number of hectares being sprayed led to increases in cultivation, or barely impacted the percentage of coca being cultivated. While accurate reporting of the impacts of aerial spraying is difficult, one must note that agencies have different mechanisms for calculating coca, and, therefore report different results. Washington calculated that the area under cultivation decreased by 7 percent since 1999. On the other hand, U.N. research resulted in a much different number, reporting that the aerial spraying initiatives since 1999 resulted in a 50 percent decrease in the area being cultivated in Colombia, which suggests that the aerial spraying programs have been effective, whereas the 7 percent decrease the United States reports implies a much less effective program. This also raises another important issue in terms of how agencies measure coca being cultivated and the difficulty in finding such information.[64]

Uribe placed all his faith in the Bush administration for support and rewarded the Bush administration for the aid to Colombia. By the end of Uribe's presidency, he had few allies in the region, having alienated most with his desire to combat the guerrillas. The border crossing to capture Raúl Reyes in Ecuador created substantial tension between the two countries. Uribe also accused both Ecuador and Venezuela of assisting the ELN and the FARC. In sum, Uribe's presidency neither improved Colombia's soft power, nor did it help promote cooperation between Colombia and other Latin American countries.[65]

In addition to angering his neighbors, Uribe upset many human rights advocates around the world for his failure to address the grave human rights abuses within Colombia. Extremely high levels of impunity continued under Uribe for violators of human rights.[66] The former president even meddled in the internal affairs of the Colombian court and successfully undermined cases to prosecute violators of human rights. Uribe became so focused on combating the narco-terrorists that he ignored any of the repercussions or collateral damage. He failed to help address the displacement of a plethora of Colombians, who were forced to flee their homes as a result of the violence. Uribe did not seek to accommodate victims, but merely continued combating the FARC and forcing them to retreat, ignoring the millions of displaced Colombians. Uribe also failed to ensure basic security for many vulnerable members of the population living within Colombia.[67]

After the court's decision to not allow Uribe to run for a third term, Juan Manuel Santos was elected president. Santos, the former Defense Minister under the Uribe administration, made some drastic changes. Santos and Uribe had fundamentally different social constructions of the problems as well as the solutions within Colombia.[68] Santos came to power and recognized the importance of human rights and the need to prosecute human rights violators as a result of the internal armed conflict. The new president also vowed to compensate victims for their hardships as a result of the internal conflict within Colombia. The recognition that an internal armed conflict did indeed exist within Colombia represented a major milestone in Colombia since

Uribe refused to recognize Colombia's internal conflict, insisting that the strife was due to terrorists.

Another major shift happened when President Santos said that he would be willing to negotiate with the guerrilla organizations; Uribe, conversely, refused to negotiate with the FARC. Many Colombians voted for Uribe as a hardline candidate who would be tough against the FARC and combat them unlike Pastrana, who negotiated with them and created the demilitarized zone. Uribe prepared for the postconflict stage at the end of his presidency, and he wrongly believed the FARC no longer presented a threat for Colombia and would cease to exist. Indeed, Uribe dealt striking blows to the organization, but the FARC not only continues to operate, but also has the capital to rearm and strengthen its capabilities.[69]

Santos has attempted to implement the appropriate changes in order to prosecute violators, and although many challenges still exist, his efforts are a step in the right direction and represent a drastic change from Uribe. Under Uribe, impunity remained a major problem and the Colombian judiciary system failed to prosecute many individuals who participated in egregious acts and violated Colombians' human rights. Uribe even interfered with the judiciary system in order to ensure that the court did not prosecute human rights violators.

The final major difference between Santos and Uribe has to do with their perspectives on drug trafficking. For Uribe, the drugs provided the "terrorists" with the revenue necessary to finance their operations, and he viewed drugs as a major problem and sought to increase aerial spraying programs.[70] He refused to recognize the futility of the aerial spraying programs despite empirical evidence that coca cultivation actually increased during his presidency. Contrary to Uribe, President Santos recognized that the war on drugs has failed, and he has publicly stated that he is open to discussion regarding legalization and decriminalization for some drugs based on sound research and international consensus. Uribe's former right-hand man has sought to undo many of Uribe's policies and move Colombia forward in a different direction, inviting a discussion of alternatives rather than repeating the mistakes of the past.

6

Desecuritizing Plan Colombia

In the aftermath of the transition between Bush and Obama, President Obama pledged to support Colombia. In reality, he sought to desecuritize Colombia as a major security issue and priority for the U.S. government. Why did the United States cut funding to Plan Colombia and attempt to desecuritize Colombia? How have efforts been made to desecuritize Colombia? Has Obama successfully desecuritized Colombia? In terms of methodology, analyzing the authoritative speech acts and the financial resources will help demonstrate whether Colombia has successfully been desecuritized.

This chapter examines the notion of desecuritization. Barry Buzan and his colleagues at the Copenhagen School provide scholars with a methodology for analyzing how something can be securitized, although they fail to examine in depth how an issue can become desecuritized.[1] This chapter argues that President Obama sought to desecuritize Colombia as a result of other more pressing priorities that he inherited from President Bush. In reality, the desecuritization process initially began when the Democrats were elected to Congress during the Bush administration and reduced U.S. assistance to the country.[2] It is important to note that desecuritization is a process that does not happen quickly. Obama inherited two wars from President Bush as well as a dire economic situation, which experts hail as the worst financial recession since the Great Depression. Mexico also began to explode with violence as a result of the various drug cartels battling for control of turf and drug routes.[3] Voices emerged that sought to desecuritize the war on drugs and shift the foreign policy goals in Colombia during the end of the Bush administration. This chapter, then, traces the beginning of the desecuritization effort in Colombia.[4]

97

Additionally, this chapter examines speech acts and analyzes the allocation of resources for Plan Colombia to prove that President Obama sought to desecuritize the drug war in Colombia. Authoritative speech acts enable scholars to track the discourse of key figures with regard to security matters in a country. One can say whatever he or she wants, but this does not mean that the goals are accomplished. Speech acts alone, therefore, do not suffice; politicians can speak about a topic and attempt to change the discourse on the subject, but this does not mean that such efforts will succeed. Therefore, scholars need to determine whether resources have been allocated to support what the politician, or authoritative actor, is attempting to securitize or desecuritize.

Examining the allocation of resources is the best way to determine if something has been successful because politicians and members of the epistemic community can discuss issues in public, but this does not mean that their goals have been achieved. Many scholars and policy analysts who constitute the epistemic community have talked about the need for Washington to have a serious debate about drug policies and change the course of U.S. foreign policy. People such as Bruce Bagley and Ethan Nadelmann have argued for years that the war on drugs should be desecuritized, and drugs should be treated as a health issue rather than as a security issue.[5] Yet, just because academicians have written about the failed war on drugs and the need for change does not mean that Washington has listened.[6] This can be proven when one examines the finances and allocation of resources to Colombia through programs such as Plan Colombia. The speech acts of authoritative figures are important and provide useful insight into the discourse of the subject, but alone they are insufficient. Politicians and key figures can try to change the discourse and perceptions of the public. Examining the allocation of resources is vitally important, and is what I have termed "the show me the money" phenomenon.[7] To prove that something has been successfully securitized or desecuritized, scholars must follow the money trail to determine whether a security issue has successfully been securitized—or even desecuritized. Proving the desecuritization (or partial desecuritization) of the war on drugs in Colombia requires an examination of the allocation of U.S.-provided resources.

Plan Colombia II

Before delving into President Obama's efforts to desecuritize the war on drugs in Colombia, we need to understand the significant altera-tions made to change the direction of Plan Colombia starting before the beginning of the Obama administration. In 2007, the National

Planning Department (NDP) and Department of Justice and Security (DJS) produce the report "Colombia's Strategy for Strengthening Democracy and Promoting Social Development (2007–2013)." This report outlines a plan often referred to as Plan Colombia II. Plan Colombia II promoted a rethinking of past efforts and an inversion of Plan Colombia. Plan Colombia II proposed focusing on developmental issues. According to the *Miami Herald*, "58 percent of the money would go toward economic and social projects, including strengthening human rights and the justice system, long thought to be weak points in the Colombian government."[8]

Several Colombian agencies developed Plan Colombia II with ten major goals in mind. The report states, "the Strategy presented by the national government for consideration by the international community has the main goal of consolidating achievements and advancing still further on the main goals of: strengthening democracy, overcoming threats to democratic stability, promoting human rights, promoting economic development and social development, and fighting poverty."[9] Steven Dudley estimated that the plan would cost $43 billion. The authors of Plan Colombia II recognized the successes against the *Fuerzas Armadas Revolucionarias de Colombia* (FARC) under the Uribe administration, but they emphasized the fact that Colombia needs aid to promote "soft issues," such as human rights, strengthening democracy, and alternative development. In no particular order, the ten major goals of Plan Colombia II are:

1. Promote alternative development and provide Colombians with other legal alternatives. In addition, the plan seeks to promote environmental awareness and conservation.

2. Consolidate the current accomplishments against the various narco-terrorist organizations.

3. Consolidate territorial control, especially in regions that have experienced extreme levels of violence and conflict.

4. Promote flexibility and cooperation.

5. Promote the efforts to demobilize actors and members in the armed groups.

6. Improve policies against human rights violators.

7. Fight impunity.

8. Improve the economy.

9. Develop and improve social policies.

10. Help individuals displaced as a result of internal conflict and the war on drugs.[10]

Plan Colombia II represents a critical juncture because it initiated the dialogue regarding the need for a new strategy to combat drug trafficking and address the internal armed conflict. Plan Colombia II failed to make progress and was implemented by neither the United States nor Colombia. For the remainder of his tenure, Uribe sought to combat the narco-terrorists, and he continued to ignore issues such as human rights violations and alternative development. As discussed in the previous chapters, Santos addressed some of the challenges and proposals made in Plan Colombia II. Ultimately, while Plan Colombia II never came to fruition, it represents a critical juncture because it promoted rethinking Plan Colombia and implementing new policies.

Why Obama Would Want to Cut Plan Colombia

One needs to examine briefly why Obama would want to defund Plan Colombia after the United States has provided the Colombian government with billions of dollars over several years to fight the drug war. The first major reason is that President Obama inherited many problems from the previous administration and sought to reorient U.S. foreign policies and priorities. Obama inherited two very costly and unpopular wars in Iraq and Afghanistan. While President Obama did not support the war in Iraq, he assumed responsibility for the decisions and policies of the Bush administration once he became the U.S. commander-in-chief. Over time, popularity for the Iraq war began to wane and the American public became weary of losing American lives. A February 2008 Pew Research Center survey regarding the war in Iraq found that 54 percent of Americans believed that the United States made the wrong choice to intervene in Iraq, vastly outnumbering the number of individuals that believed that President Bush made the correct decision to intervene.[11]

Additionally, President Obama has different perceptions of the world as demonstrated by the fact that he desecuritized the war on terrorism by focusing more on state-to-state relations and regional security as opposed to acting as the world's police force and seeking to fight a Global War on Terrorism. During his presidency, Obama has mentioned neither the Global War on Terrorism nor the war on terror and eventually began withdrawing the troops in Iraq. He could easily point to Colombia and show that his administration vowed to combat all forms of terrorism. Colombia, therefore, fit within President Bush's worldview and his construction of the situation as well as his perception of how to solve the problem.[12] President Obama vowed to end the war in Iraq and fulfill his campaign promises. The Pew Research Center survey discovered that 52 percent of Americans supported the policy to withdraw troops from Iraq as soon as possible. In addition, a June 2007 poll revealed that 56 percent of the American population supported removing the troops from Iraq and bringing them home.[13]

In August 2010, President Obama officially stated that the combat mission in Iraq had ended.[14] After praising the troops, Obama proclaimed that the United States had to move on, declaring, "Through this remarkable chapter in the history of the United States and Iraq, we have met our responsibility. Now it's time to turn the page."[15] The exiting of troops from Iraq, however, did not ease the minds of Americans because Obama still had to address the increases in violence in Afghanistan and the resurgence of the Taliban. Clearly, Colombia became less of a priority as Obama sought to address the looming war in Iraq and address the problems of the increasing violence in Afghanistan. Fighting two wars during a devastating recession has preoccupied Obama, and, therefore, he made Colombia less of a U.S. priority.[16]

Events in the Middle East have continued to occupy the attention of the Obama administration. The "Arab Spring" resulted in regime change in Egypt and led to conflict in Libya, as Gadhafi refused to step down from power and promised to travel door-to-door and extinguish "the rats" within his country.[17] Obama then became preoccupied with the situation in Libya. Obama remains concerned about the Middle East as events in Syria continue to worsen. The situation in Iran regarding nuclear weapons also continues to occupy President Obama's time and distract him from other foreign policy issues.[18]

Mexico, Not Colombia

As of 2013, Colombia no longer appears to be the major drug trafficking epicenter in the war on drugs during the Obama administration. The routes began to shift toward Mexico and the various cartels began to battle for territory as well as control of the drug trade, leading to extreme levels of violence. Mexico, not Colombia, became the priority for several reasons. First, Mexico and the United States share a vast border and have many interconnections. The ease with which Mexican cartels can infiltrate the United States and impact the security of American lives caused many politicians to call for more protection along the border and resources to combat drug trafficking in Mexico. Governor Rick Perry of Texas called for Obama to place the National Guard on the border to help secure the border region and decrease the large levels of violence.[19] Mexican cartels have successfully penetrated the U.S. border as elements of Mexican cartels operate in more than 230 U.S. cities.[20] Americans are concerned about the extreme levels of violence and their security, particularly those living in the states that border Mexico. Nearly every day one can read or hear a news report about the extreme levels of violence in Mexico as a result of the war on drugs and war among various organizations. As of 2012, more than 50,000 Mexicans have died as a result of the war on drugs.[21] Violence has spilled over the border and dead bodies have appeared on the U.S. side of the border. As a result, the United States has become very concerned about the extreme levels of violence within Mexico. The U.S. border is porous and organized criminal networks have been able to penetrate the border. Today, Mexico has become the Colombia of the 1990s. Drug trafficking and organized crime has appeared in Mexico leading U.S. politicians and the American public to pay less attention to Colombia and focus on the violence resulting from the drug war occurring in Mexico.

The Recession

Another major element that cannot be ignored is the economic recession that President Obama inherited from President Bush as a result of the subprime mortgage crisis on Wall Street. The recession has been deemed the worst economic situation since the Great Depression and has resulted in hardships for millions of Americans. Over the course of his administration, Obama has attempted to stimulate the economy and promote job creation. The economic recession has led many experts and critics to argue that the United States must reduce its budget because it cannot afford to police the world. During Obama's tenure, weary Americans question why the United States has continued to fight wars abroad when millions of Americans are struggling at home. These wars have cost a tremendous amount of money that could have been spent creating jobs or bolstering education. Joseph Stiglitz, a Noble Prize–winning economist, estimated the total cost of the wars in Iraq and Afghanistan in excess of $3 trillion.[22] Therefore, we can easily understand why popularity for the spending abroad has made many skeptical. Average Americans are concerned with their personal budget issues, such as where their next meal is coming from or how to pay for their mortgage or their children's college tuition. The Tea Party, for instance, has called for the United States to take control of the budget and stop excessive spending. The Tea Party does not want the United States to police the world and has urged U.S. leadership to focus on pressing domestic issues. The economic recession and movements at home are another contributing factor to President Obama's desire to desecuritize Colombia as a major U.S. foreign policy issue. Given the billions of dollars the United States has already spent on Colombia's drug war, increasing the money allocated for Colombia to combat the war on drugs while budgeting for other foreign policy issues as well as the accounting for the fallout from the financial crisis would be difficult for Obama. President Obama wants the Colombians to finance their own war on drugs and has shifted resources away from Plan Colombia.[23]

We also need to use comparative politics tools once again to examine election politics in order to understand why President Obama has tried to desecuritize drug trafficking in Colombia. When Obama ran for reelection in November 2012, people voted with their wallets, deciding whether they were better off financially before Obama assumed office or four years later, in essence evaluating Obama's performance based on the economy's performance. As a result, Obama had little motivation to spend billions of dollars helping the Colombian government fight the war on drugs as he was more interested in demonstrating that the economy had improved and jobs had been created.

The Republican opponent, Mitt Romney, argued that Obama had neither created jobs nor improved the U.S. economy. From the outset of his presidency, Obama has taken initiatives to improve the economy and help millions of struggling Americans by passing the stimulus package. As the election cycle approached, the economy and President Obama's economic report card received a great deal of attention and the previous national security issue in Colombia remained less of a priority.[24]

Speech Acts

This next section examines President Obama's authoritative speech acts regarding drug trafficking, Colombia, and Plan Colombia to demonstrate that Obama has sought to change the discourse with regard to drug trafficking in Colombia: Obama has not portrayed Colombia as a major threat to national security. Before delving into the speech acts, however, one needs to analyze briefly what analysts can reasonably expect President Obama to say in such speech acts. Perhaps one should momentarily think back to the speech acts of President Bush when he attempted to securitize the war on terrorism or the war in Iraq. He painted terrorism as the major threat to U.S. national security and vowed to combat terrorism around the globe. He explained the capabilities of groups such as the Taliban and Al Qaeda and argued that they must be defeated. An analysis of President Bush's speech acts revealed that he perceived the terrorists as a major threat and attempted to convince the American public that the terrorists must be combatted at whatever costs in order to avoid another catastrophe such as the terrorist attacks on September 11, 2001.[25] Bush argued that terrorists hate Americans because of their freedoms and way of life, and he wrongly linked Saddam Hussein with the attacks on September 11, despite the fact that Saddam had no connections to Al Qaeda. President Bush used language that painted Iraq as the most dangerous country in the world and Saddam Hussein as a terrible dictator who needed to be ousted because he harbored weapons of mass destruction and because such a ruthless dictator could not be trusted. One can see in this example of President Bush's rhetoric that language is a powerful—and useful—tool when an actor attempts to securitize an issue.[26] The language is dire because the actor must portray a particular issue or region as a major security threat that must be addressed.[27]

What can we expect to hear from President Obama, who wanted to desecuritize the war on drugs in Colombia? What would be appropriate for Obama to say? Will the language be as dire as an actor trying to securitize a particular issue? President Obama is a politician and must remain diplomatic in his language. Therefore, we cannot assume that he will outright say that Colombia is not a U.S. security priority. This chapter predicts that the speech acts will contain language explaining the interconnectedness and need for equal responsibility with regard to drug trafficking. The hypothesis is that President Obama will vow to help the Colombian government and support them, but he will emphasize cooperation and coordination in combatting drug trafficking. Experts would expect Obama neither to make statements about the need for increases in funding to combat drug trafficking nor to characterize Colombia as a major national security objective that could threaten security within the United States and the region. Obviously, Obama cannot explicitly say that Colombia is no longer a U.S. priority with regard to national security issues. Instead, we should expect Obama to recognize the achievements of Colombia with regard to increasing security and decreasing violence. We can also hypothesize that Obama will acknowledge Colombia as a thriving democracy.

In the Summit of the Americas in Cartagena, Colombia, a joint conference that occurred in October 2012, President Obama praised Colombia for the improvements in security declaring, "As I said to my fellow leaders yesterday, there was a time not so long ago when few could have imagined holding a summit like this in Colombia. That we have and that the summit was such a success is a tribute to the remarkable transformation that's occurred in this nation."[28] Such praise implies that Colombia has made great strides in terms of security and is no longer teetering on the verge of becoming a failed state. Obama continued to praise Colombia stating, "There's a level of security that's not been seen in decades. Citizens are reclaiming their communities."[29] Analysis of these brief statements indicates that Obama is pleased with Colombia and the improvements in security, and feels that the country is more secure today than ever before. Obama is suggesting that Colombia is no longer a major security threat, and he portrays Colombia as having a bright future. His speech continues: "Democratic institutions are being strengthened. In Colombia today, there's hope."[30] These words are in stark contrast to those said when Colombia was a major national security threat to the United States.

In his remarks made at the joint conference, President Obama pledged support for Colombia and continued cooperation between the two countries, stating, "Today, I pledged to President Santos that as Colombia forges its future Colombia will continue to have a strong partner in the United States."[31] Obama emphasized the need for cooperation in his speech at the Summit of the Americas, stating:

> So there are a number of areas where I think cooperation is proceeding. Sometimes it's not flashy. I think that oftentimes in the press the attention in summits like this ends up focusing on where are the controversies. Sometimes those controversies date back to before I was born. [*laughter*] And sometimes I feel as if in some of these discussions or at least [in] the press reports we're caught in a time warp, going back to the 1950s and gunboat diplomacy and Yanquis and the Cold War, and this and that and the other. That's not the world we live in today.[32]

In his speech at the summit, President Obama made an interesting point when he discussed the notion of equal partnership, as opposed to one where the United States sets the agenda, declaring, "When we met for the first time two years ago, we agreed to take the partnership between our two countries to a new level. This is part of my broader commitment in the Americas to seek partnerships of equality that are based on mutual interest and mutual respect."[33] Such rhetoric might sound innocuous, but behind such statements is a deeper meaning: it suggests that President Obama wants an equal partnership. Many Colombians have viewed the United States as the hegemonic actor that has implanted policies that it has viewed desirable without the consent of Colombia. We can recall the Clinton administration's

180-degree shift in the formula of President Pastrana and his version of Plan Colombia. Pastrana had one construction of Plan Colombia, while the United States had a different perception of the problem in addition to a different social construction of the solution. The United States has a long and troubled history in Latin America where Washington intervened in the affairs and policies of "backward countries," believing it has the obligation to help such countries, and it used its hegemonic position to intervene in the internal dynamics of states within the region.[34] An equal partnership is a step in the right direction. Colombia wants to be treated as a serious ally and equal partner as opposed to having the United States use its hegemonic power to dictate the terms and conditions.

An equal partnership, however, is exactly what the term implies: equal. Equal means that the Colombian government must share the burdens and responsibilities of combating drug trafficking. President Obama's comments, therefore, imply that the Colombian government must meet these challenges and take more responsibility in fighting the drug war in Colombia. The Colombian leadership, therefore, cannot simply rely on the United States for billions of dollars in aid because President Obama has other important domestic issues that he must address. In sum, such statements by President Obama might appear to be merely rhetoric, but, in reality, they have a deeper, more profound meaning for the relationship between the United States and Colombia. An equal partnership has more advantages because the Colombians have more leverage in terms of designing the initiatives and policies to combat drug trafficking if they are not receiving billions of dollars from the United States, but this in turn requires Bogotá to finance the war on drugs.

President Obama's notion of equal partnership extends to more than just drug trafficking. During his remarks, President Obama commented on the economic partnership between the two countries. He stated, "President Santos and I reviewed our progress and, I'm pleased to say, reached agreement on several new initiatives."[35] Obama praised the approval of the Free Trade Agreement (FTA) between Colombia and the United States, arguing that this agreement would benefit both countries. He stated, "As I said before, this agreement is a win for both our countries. It's a win for the United States by increasing our exports by more than $1 billion, supporting thousands of U.S. jobs and helping to achieve my goal of doubling U.S. exports."[36] Despite the fact that Colombia only accounts for a small percentage of U.S. trade, President Obama's statement demonstrates that Colombians indeed are an important trading partner. Such assertions reveal that Obama wants more integration between the United States and Colombia, and that the FTA is a step in the right direction toward helping increasing cooperation and integration between these two important partners. Obama argued that the FTA also would benefit Colombia, stating "it's a win for Colombia by giving you even greater access to the largest market for your exports—the United States of America."[37]

President Obama also has made statements regarding the partnership with Colombia on security issues, declaring, "I reaffirmed to President Santos that the United States will continue to stand with Colombia shoulder to shoulder as you work to end this conflict and build a just and lasting peace. And that includes supporting President Santos's very ambitious reform agenda, including reparations for victims and land reform."[38] Obviously, President Obama wants to reaffirm to the Colombian government that he supports its efforts to combat the FARC and other internal actors.[39] However, an analysis of the finances indicates that President Obama supports the Colombian government, but he is not willing to spend billions of dollars and does not view the internal conflict in Colombia as a major U.S. security threat. President Obama's support for Santos's efforts to help marginalized communities and address the consequences that have occurred as a result of the internal conflict indicate that he supports Santos's attention to human rights abuses and other value issues. Obama's support of Colombia and his recognition of its accomplishments are important because Colombia is a functioning democracy, and Washington wants to promote free and fair elections in the democratic process in Latin America.

The previous sections analyzed the speech acts of President Obama with regard to Colombia and cooperation. We now turn to Obama's rhetoric on the war on drugs within Colombia and analyze his statements to see if they confirm or disprove the hypotheses made at the beginning of this chapter. With regard to drug trafficking, President Obama remarked: "And so whether it's working with President Santos or supporting the courageous work that President Calderón is doing in Mexico, I, personally, and my administration and I think the American people understand that the toll of narco-trafficking on the societies of Central America, Caribbean, and parts of South America are brutal, and undermining the capacity of those countries to protect their citizens, and eroding institutions and corrupting institutions in ways that are ultimately bad for everybody."[40] Here Obama demonstrates that he recognizes the negative impact that the drug trafficking has on societies. While President Obama supports President Santos and the war on drugs, the budgetary allocations of the money—as will be examined later—demonstrate that Mexico, not Colombia, has become the priority for Washington. Indeed, Obama supports strengthening institutions within Colombia and improving the capacity of the state.

Obama has recognized that the United States needs to be an equal partner in combatting drug trafficking and organized crime and address demand reduction. This is a shift in policy because the United States has historically focused on decreasing the supply of drugs and has allocated much less money to demand reduction.

Obama has made other comments indicating that the United States wants to be a partner and ally of Colombia, explaining, "This is one of the reasons why we have continued to invest in programs like Plan Colombia, but also now are working with Colombia, given their best practices around issues of citizen security, to have not just the United States but Colombia provide technical assistance and training to countries in Central America and the Caribbean in finding ways that they can duplicate some of the success that we've seen in Colombia."[41] Such statements reveal that President Obama wants the Colombian government to assume more responsibility as an equal partner. Obviously, he cannot outright say that the United States does not want to support Colombia, but he can use rhetoric to urge the Colombian government to be more active in combatting drug trafficking and organized crime.

In sum, a brief analysis of several important comments President Obama made demonstrate that he has attempted to change the rhetoric on Colombia and, in effect, has sought to desecuritize Plan Colombia and the war on drugs in Colombia. Yet, desecuritization is a process that does not happen overnight but rather in stages. President Obama's statements did not depict Colombia as in dire need of U.S. assistance. Instead, he made assertions that implied that the situation in Colombia has improved greatly: Colombia has made significant progress and is no longer a major U.S. security priority. President Obama's statements confirm the hypotheses made in the beginning of this chapter: Obama wants to be diplomatic and cannot say outright that he is desecuritizing Colombia because Colombia no longer represents a major priority for the United States in terms of national security interests. As expected, President Obama made comments about the need for a more equal relationship with Colombia, which means that the Colombian government must incur more of the responsibility, including the financing of, its own war on drugs.

Speech acts by authoritative figures are important to analyze, but rhetoric alone cannot prove that something has been successfully desecuritized. The successful desecuritization of Plan Colombia and the war on drugs in Colombia, hence, would require the United States to provide the Colombian government with fewer resources and, in essence, defund the war on drugs. A politician can say whatever he or she desires, but this does not mean that such efforts to change the dialogue, securitize, or desecuritize an issue or region will be successful. In order to prove that President Obama successfully desecuritized the war on drugs, one must follow the money trail and track which programs received less funding.[42] An examination of the budgetary allocations and funding for Plan Colombia will help prove empirically whether President Obama has successfully desecuritized the war on drugs.

The first place to examine in terms of resource allocations is the money used to finance Plan Colombia. In 2011, President Obama's budget proposal included a sharp decrease in spending for Plan Colombia, reducing the aid allocated for the plan by $50 million. Uribe, the Colombian president at the time, expressed concern about this decrease in funding, asserting, "This reduction in money to Plan Colombia . . . worries us."[43] He continued to voice his concern, declaring, "Luckily we signed the cooperation agreement [with the United States], which guarantees a continuation of the same conditions as under Plan Colombia."[44]

The budget proposal for the State Department for 2012 shows that President Obama proposed cutting the money allocated for Plan Colombia by 15 percent. In the 2012 budget, the United States allocated $400 million to the Colombian government to help combat drug trafficking, representing a sharp decrease in the resources that Washington had provided in the past.[45] Rodrigo Rivera, the Colombian Defense Minister in 2011, flew to Washington, D.C., for an official visit to voice his trepidation with Washington's desire to cut resources for the Colombian war on drugs, declaring, "It is an issue of concern that Colombia continues to receive the help of the United States, which has been absolutely essential over the past years."[46] His statements demonstrate Bogotá's concern as to whether they can combat coca cultivation and drug trafficking within the country without significant U.S. aid. One could question whether the Colombian government has the capacity to combat drug trafficking and extend the presence of the state without significant U.S. assistance. The equal partnership rhetoric implies that the Colombian government must accept responsibility and play more of a role if Colombia wants to be an equal partner with the United States.

In February 2011, reports revealed that the 2011 budget President Obama proposed to Congress did not even mention Plan Colombia. Although this did not signal that Colombia would not receive any U.S. aid—the United States would not abruptly stop all aid—it did propose, however, that Colombia would receive 20 percent less funding—military and economic—than in 2009. *Colombia Reports* states, "According to justf.org, Colombian military aid will be 20 percent down to $228 million, 20 percent less than it received in 2009. Economic aid will be slightly diminished and it's proposed to be worth $239 million."[47]

These statistics reveal that President Obama has sought to decrease funding for Plan Colombia. However, one needs to examine the statistics regarding what the Colombians spent. The United States wants to shift the financial burden to the Colombians. In other words, Washington wants the Colombian government to pay for its own war on drugs. To see if this is happening, one needs to determine the money the Colombian government spent. As expected, U.S. aid to Colombia increased from 2002 to 2008 during the Bush administration from $388,550,141 to $433,664,757. The Colombian defense budget, however, has increased drastically from 2002 to 2008 when President Obama was elected. In fact, the numbers are quite astounding with the Colombian government spending $U.S. 4,186,135,410 in 2002 and $12,328,723,355 in 2008. These statistics demonstrate that the Colombian government must spend more money to finance its own war on drugs and improve security within the country.[48]

Conclusion

Colombia is no longer a major U.S. security threat. In part, the desecuritization of Colombia is a result of what happens when a country deems its efforts as successful. Jennifer Holmes echoes such sentiments, stating, "Maybe U.S. aid is less crucial now then it was."[49] President Obama cannot continue to provide Colombia with billions of dollars because he must address other major issues. He inherited the worst economic situation since the Great Depression as a result of the subprime mortgage crisis on Wall Street[50] and has been preoccupied with the U.S. financial situation, concerned about the millions of Americans struggling to find jobs. Groups such as the Tea Party have emerged and called for Obama and Washington to stop excessive spending and focus on domestic issues rather than financing foreign missions.

Additionally, Obama has had other foreign policy priorities that have superseded Colombia, such as the end of the U.S. operation in Iraq as well as the increasing levels of violence in Afghanistan. In addition, Obama continues to deal with the Iran situation and try to avoid a potential war in the Middle East, although some neoconservatives are in favor of doing "whatever necessary" to protect Israel and to ensure that Iran does not develop nuclear weapons.[51] Along with the Middle East foreign policy issue, Obama and Washington have become more concerned with the extreme levels of violence in Mexico as a result of the drug trade. Mexico—not Colombia—has become the main focus for the United States because of the long border and spillover effects. The United States remains shortsighted and focused on the most current or pressing security issues.[52]

This chapter analyzed President Obama's speech acts regarding the war on drugs in Colombia. Obama has stressed the need for a more equal partnership between Colombia and the United States. While Obama has emphasized the importance of maintaining good relations with Colombia, he wants the Colombian government to play a greater role in solving its own problems. Obama's speech acts demonstrate that he has sought to change the discourse and challenge the Colombian government to assume more responsibility, thereby becoming true equal partners. An equal partnership requires the Colombians to take responsibility and stop relying on large amounts of U.S. aid.

This chapter also examined the finances and demonstrated that efforts have been made to defund Plan Colombia. President Obama's proposed 2011 budget did not include funding for Plan Colombia, thereby sending a message to the Colombian government to assume responsibility and finance its war on drugs. Understandably, some Colombians feel that the United States has given up on the war on drugs and forgotten about Colombia. Although Obama advocates an equal partnership, one should be skeptical about whether the Colombian government has the state capacity and resources necessary to fight the war on drugs itself.

Conversely, advocates of Plan Colombia who believe that it has accomplished its job argue that the war on drugs should be desecuritized because Plan Colombia resulted in many great successes. Although Plan Colombia did not decrease drug cultivation or trafficking, it did have success, particularly under Uribe, in increasing the presence of the state in remote regions of Colombia and regaining formerly FARC-controlled territories. Uribe successfully combatted the FARC and forced them to retreat, which ultimately led to a decrease in violence in Colombia. As a result of the Plan Colombia successes, Colombia is no longer on the brink of becoming a failed state and currently is not a major priority for the United States in terms of national security.[53]

Plan Colombia's partial victories have increased security and decreased violence in Colombia, resulting in President Obama decreasing resources to Colombia, in essence desecuritizing Colombia as a major U.S. priority.[54] The situation in Colombia could regress, however, and instability within the country could increase. Smaller organizations such as *Bandas Criminales* (BACRIM) have emerged and could increase instability in Colombia. Some experts note that suggesting Colombia is now a success, free of problems is both wrong and premature. Marc Chernick even goes as far as to say that Colombia is not safer and still faces many problems, noting that the FARC has not been defeated by any means: "What I see is a reconfigured battlefield. If you are a social movement leader, human rights defender and academic, you are still threatened. . . . Do we have a more stable Colombia? No! No!"[55] Such statements demonstrate that the conflict in Colombia continues and the FARC will strengthen if it has not already. In an interview, Jennifer Holmes stated, "Things can always get worse" when asked if the FARC could resecuritize and become a major security threat.[56] Holmes argues that the FARC's history demonstrates that such a scenario is quite possible.[57] Thus, the possibility exists that drug trafficking in Colombia could become securitized and efforts might be made to provide the Colombian government with the necessary resources to combat such organizations. While no one can predict the future, Colombia quite possibly will become resecuritized. Inevitably, only time will tell.

7

Social Constructions of Colombia's Anti-Drug Campaign

An Analysis of Speech Acts from 1998 to 2009

This chapter examines speech acts made by important figures from 1998 to 2009 by examining two leading newspapers, the *Washington Post* and *Semana*, to analyze the social constructions that are behind Plan Colombia's implementation. This chapter stands alone because it examines the core perceptions and social constructions of the various presidents and key actors of both Colombia and the United States, which are vital for understanding Plan Colombia's implementation and evolution. This chapter, therefore, is not the study of the reality of Plan Colombia, but rather is an examination of what various key actors perceived the reality to be and should be understood in this vein.[1] Therefore, this chapter analyzes the perceptions rather than examining the outcomes that resulted in the formulation, implementation, and evolution of Plan Colombia over its various phases,[2] and analyzes the discourse made by important individuals in order to trace the evolution of Plan Colombia during various critical junctures. Readers should note, however, that this is not an exhaustive effort, but rather the chapter highlights certain periods and is a collection of statements made by decisionmakers. Analyzing authoritative speech acts helps bolster the arguments made throughout the previous chapters.

The place to begin the analysis is in 1998 when the former drug czar, Barry McCaffrey, helped influence the thinking and policy of the Clinton administration. McCaffrey was quoted in the *Washington Post* in 1998 stating that Peru had obtained "remarkable success in its coca reduction program." However, he argued that the progress in Bolivia represented a sign of encouragement and complimented the government of President Hugo Banzer for making a "'promising start' toward the goal of eradicating illegal coca production within five years."[3] Such statements demonstrate that McCaffrey believed that the problem in the Andean countries had to do with the production of drugs; he viewed the problem as one of supply as opposed to a demand problem and focused on the need to combat the illicit cultivation of coca.

During this period in U.S.–Colombian relations, the Clinton administration had a harsh view toward Ernesto Samper's administration. In February 2, 1998, the *Washington Post* ran an interesting quote from Secretary of State Madeline Albright about the reason for the United States lifting the sanctions. She stated that "the sanctions waiver was issued in recognition that Colombian anti-drug forces 'have conducted an effective eradication and interdiction effort.'" Albright continued, "But the current government has not demonstrated full political support for counter-narcotics efforts."[4] While the Clinton administration did not fully support the Samper administration, Albright recognized that lifting the sanctions signified an attempt to improve bilateral relations. She declared, "Coming on the eve of that country's congressional and presidential elections, the waiver decision is intended to lay the groundwork for increased cooperation and to support those in Colombia who are striving to strengthen the rule of law and buttress their embattled democracy."[5]

Despite Albright's statements, the Clinton administration clearly never had respect for Ernesto Samper and never viewed him as an equal partner.

Samper argued, "All the topics are related. You can talk of drug trafficking and of human rights. That is our main concern in discussing military aid. . . . You cannot ask the guy who is shooting you [from] downstairs, 'Look, are you a guerrilla, are you a narco-trafficker, because I cannot use this helicopter against you.'" While Samper might have wanted more support from the United States, this work has proven that McCaffrey knew that it would be unpopular and unwise for the United States to become drawn into a Vietnam-type quagmire despite Samper correctly stating that drug trafficking fuels the guerrillas. He was quoted in the *Washington Post* arguing, "There is a common element for all forms of violence . . . [in] Colombia. Drug trafficking is financing the guerrillas in the south. Drug trafficking is financing the paramilitary groups on the Atlantic coast. Drug trafficking is financing the insecurity." He added, "So for us . . . the fight against drug trafficking is fundamental."[6]

While the Clinton administration refused to become involved in the drug conflict, clearly Bogotá needed help. Armando Montenegro, president of the National Association of Financial Institutions, went on record saying that the Colombian armed forces were ineffective. He told the *Washington Post*, "The most common quality of military people is incompetence. . . . So what you should do is remove the irresponsible ones and put in new ones."

Montenegro went further, not only criticizing the Colombian armed forces but also the Colombian leadership: "It's another symptom of the Colombian crisis," Montenegro said. "There's no political order, there's no leadership in the country. We cannot rule out a very serious problem like institutional collapse in a few years if this thing gets worse."[7] While the United States did not want to become involved in the conflict, it did increase the military aid provided to the Colombian government to combat the supply of drugs. On March 28, 1998, a senior national security official declared, "We continue to have a counternarcotics focus but are sensitive to the fact there's a connection . . ." between insurgents and drug traffickers. He continued, "But we are still not ready to join the military side . . . in a way that is unconnected to counternarcotics."[8]

The increased assistance, however, did not immediately prove to be a panacea to the problem as the Colombian armed forces still had many problems. On April 10, 1998, Charles Wilhelm asserted during a congressional hearing: "The primary vulnerability of the Colombian armed forces is their inability to see threats, followed closely by their lack of competence in assessing and engaging them." In an April 6, 1998, letter to the Colombian military commander Manuel José Bonett, Wilhelm stated, "At this time the Colombian armed forces are not up to the task of confronting and defeating the insurgents. . . . Colombia is the most threatened in the area under the Southern Command's responsibility, and it is in urgent need of our support."[9]

While the United States provided training to the Colombian armed forces to help them improve their effectiveness, concerns remained about human rights abuses. On May 25, 1998, Senator Patrick J. Leahy (D–VT), a champion of human rights, was quoted in the *Washington Post* stating, "From Colombia to Indonesia, our Special Forces have trained foreign troops without regard for who they are or whether they turn around and torture and shoot pro-democracy students."[10]

The Election of Pastrana

Pastrana represented the opportunity for improved U.S.–Colombia relations. On June 23, 1998, Andrés Pastrana was quoted in the *Washington Post* stating, "I hope that relations with the U.S. will open up the agenda. The agenda with the U.S. cannot just be drugs,"

Pastrana said at a news conference. "We have to open it to include peace, human rights and commercial themes."[11] The United States made a conscious effort to improve the relationship between the two countries.

The year 1998 represents important period because Pastrana began to negotiate with the *Fuerzas Armadas Revolucionarias de Colombia* (FARC), gave it a demilitarized zone the size of Switzerland, and aroused fear among U.S. leaders. Douglas Farah was cited in the *Washington Post* on December 27, 1998, describing U.S. concerns, stating: "Washington's fears that the corruption-ridden Colombian military may be losing a war to Marxist rebels who receive much of their income from drug traffickers has caused the United States to step up its involvement with the Colombian armed forces, despite their history of human rights abuses. . . . After working closely with the Colombian military in the late 1980s and early '90s, the United States largely cut off direct aid, citing human rights abuses. While the Special Forces training has continued, the bulk of U.S. money to fight drug trafficking has been steered to the country's national police force."[12]

Throughout this period, McCaffrey continued to play a crucial role, focusing on the supply of drugs in Colombia. On February 22, 1999, Barry McCaffrey was quoted in the *Washington Post*: "The drop in price made the drug more affordable, and the rise in purity—Colombian heroin is about 80 percent pure when it hits U.S. streets, compared to 7 percent for Southeast Asian heroin—meant the drug does not have to be injected, but can be smoked or inhaled. The combination of low price and high quality has helped drive the estimated number of heroin users in the United States from 600,000 to 810,000 in the past three years, according to Barry McCaffrey, the Clinton administration's drug policy director."[13] The General Accounting Office echoed the increasing U.S. role in the counternarcotic strategies in Colombia. "U.S. Embassy officials have decided to routinely provide intelligence information related to the insurgents to Colombian units under control of the joint [military and police] task force," said a report on Colombia released last week by the General Accounting Office.[14] "According to these officials, the information is being used to plan counternarcotics operations in the area controlled by insurgents; however, they do not have a system to ensure that it is not being used for other than counternarcotics purposes."[15]

In 1999, the Colombian government recognized the need for U.S. assistance to help them combat drug trafficking. Ambassador Luis Alberto Moreno understood this and continued to fight on behalf of Colombia. On July 29, 1999, he was quoted in the *Washington Post*, declaring: "The crisis facing Colombia is drug related but cannot be understood solely in those terms. The challenge is to end nearly a half-century of violence and to offer hope and opportunity to parts of the nation that have been bypassed by progress and growth. We shall continue to fight the war on drugs, but our primary task is to achieve peace."[16]

On August 5, 1999, the *Washington Post* reported Bernard Aronson's comments emphasizing the increasing need for U.S. assistance. He asserted, "Last week the Clinton administration's national drug coordinator, retired Gen. Barry McCaffrey, called the latest upsurge in guerrilla violence in Colombia an 'emergency' and a 'regional crisis.' The president said events in Colombia—where 90 percent of the cocaine and nearly half the heroin that reaches the United States originate—affect U.S. 'national security.' And prominent members of Congress warned Colombia could become a 'narco-guerrilla state.'"[17]

Gen. Charles Wilhelm of the U.S. Southern Command, however, believed that separating the guerrillas from the drug war was possible, countering the arguments of others who believed this was not possible. On August 11, 1999, the General was quoted in *Semana* stating, "It is easy to distinguish between a counternarcotics and a counterinsurgency operation. If its [sic] counternarcotics, it is aimed to destroy a lab, crops, a landing strip and any armed personnel that defends them. If it is whatever else, it is counterinsurgency and is forbidden."[18]

Plan Colombia

The year 1999 is significant because it is when President Pastrana first developed his version of Plan Colombia. A high-ranking White House official told *Semana* on December 13, 1999, that the solution to the problem "is to have both parties sit and conspire to augment spending but agreeing not to disclose who proposed it first. It is the only way."[19] Other countries in the region supported Pastrana's version of Plan Colombia, and on March 24, 2000, the *Washington Post* wrote, "Ecuador supports Colombian President Andrés Pastrana's development proposal called Plan Colombia, he said, but warned that it will not accept it if it means pushing the problem of drug traffic and cultivation south across the border into Ecuador." The Ecuadorian president stated, "We don't have borders with Colombia, we have a front line with narco-traffic and FARC." He also emphasized that they "can't stop it alone."[20]

Obviously, the Americans had a different construction of Plan Colombia as demonstrated by the comments made by Jaime Ruiz, a Colombian official in charge of the overall implementation of Plan Colombia. On April 10, 2000, he said: "In American terms, they want to see the problems of Colombia through the prism of El Salvador, or human rights, or guerrillas, or left versus right. Or through the prism of drugs—that the guerrillas are narco-traffickers and the problem is drugs."[21]

On August 5, 2000, President Clinton announced that he would travel to Colombia to speak with Pastrana, saying in a prepared statement: "I am pleased to announce I will travel on August 30 to Colombia to meet with President Andrés Pastrana and to personally underscore America's support for Colombia's efforts to seek peace, fight illicit drugs, build its economy and deepen democracy."[22] Rhetoric is one thing, but clearly Clinton's actions demonstrate that he was more concerned about the supply and did not want to become involved in the internal armed conflict.

The Plan Colombia that emerged out of the Clinton administration indeed received criticism from many individuals. On August 23, 2000, Diego Perez, head of the Center for Investigation and Popular Education, was quoted in the *Washington Post*, stating, "This plan is just going to make the war worse." He argued that the United States ignored the underlying internal armed conflict, asserting, "By militarizing this conflict, you're not going to resolve the guerrilla or the drug problem. . . . Anything that sounds like Plan Colombia is going to become a military target. . . . We see this as one big package, in which you can't differentiate the military from the social part."[23]

On August 30, 2000, Bill Clinton emphasized that he did not believe that the conflict had a military solution, saying, "Please do not misunderstand our purpose. We have no military objective. We do not believe your conflict has a military solution. We support the peace process. Our approach is both pro-peace and anti-drug."[24] Clinton also wanted to reassure the U.S. public that he did not want to become involved in Colombia's internal conflict. At a joint news conference with Pastrana on August 31, 2000, Clinton declared, "There won't be American involvement in a shooting war, because they don't want it and we don't want it. . . . This is not Vietnam. Neither is it Yankee imperialism."[25]

The international community, however, did not approve of Clinton's reengineering of Plan Colombia. On October 19, 2000, Arianne da Costa de Moraes, Austria's ambassador to Colombia, said, "The military aid [in the plan] has been like putting a blue stocking in the wash with white clothes—everything comes out blue." The ambassador continued, "It will be very difficult for [Europe] to say we support Plan Colombia because of the psychology involved."[26]

Barry McCaffrey went on the offensive, trying to bolster support for Plan Colombia. On November 21, 2000, McCaffrey said, "There will be no change in the long-term U.S. commitment for Plan Colombia."

He continued, "This is not North Korea. This is a democracy three hours from Miami. We simply have no choice but to understand that our interests are wrapped up in the success of Venezuela, Colombia and other regional partners."[27]

Leadership Transition

Both the United States (2000) and Colombia (2002) experienced changes in leadership with two new presidents: Bush and Uribe. Upon entering office, Bush received requests from the Colombian government for more support. On February 16, 2001, President Andrés Pastrana stated, "We are a poor country." He argued that Colombia was "spending $1 billion a year of our money to keep drugs off the streets of Washington and New York. We need more help. This is a long-term plan, maybe 15 to 20 years."[28] George Bush responded to such requests, declaring:

> . . . I look forward to meeting with President Pastrana. I'm looking forward to the briefing that he'll be bringing from Colombia. And I, too, am worried about ever committing the United States military to an engagement in that part of the world. I know we're training, and that's fine, but the mission ought to be limited to just that. And so I share the concern of those who are worried that at some point in time the United States might become militarily engaged. Now, in terms of the success of the mission, the president is going to bring me his first-hand account of what's taking place in the country. I am concerned about the amount of acreage in cultivation for the growth of cocoa leaves. We've got to do a better job of working with the Colombia government on its eradication program.[29]

Some continued to question the allocation of resources and objectives of Plan Colombia. William M. LeoGrande and Kenneth Sharpe were quoted in the *Washington Post* on April 1, 2001, asking:

> But what exactly is the objective of U.S. policy in Colombia? Is it to reduce the flow of drugs into the United States? That's how former drug czar Barry McCaffrey defended the increase in military aid and advisers under Plan Colombia. Or is it to help the Colombian armed forces win their decades-long war against leftist guerrillas, as some U.S. military officials have intimated? U.S. policymakers have yet to clarify which of these very different aims is paramount.

Some policymakers want to fight drugs, and some want to fight guerrillas. To satisfy both, Plan Colombia calls for fighting drugs in areas controlled by guerrillas, even though that is not a sensible approach to either problem.[30]

Pastrana made several trips trying to market the softer elements of Plan Colombia. Scott Wilson of the *Washington Post* Foreign Service stated on May 22, 2001:

Since it began, Plan Colombia's aerial spraying has wiped out what the government says is 60,000 acres of coca in the south, or about 6 percent of the country's total. By reducing supply, it has driven up the price by roughly 30 percent and coaxed new farmers into the business while prompting others who lost crops to preserve coca seedlings and wait for a safer time to replant. The social development portion of the plan was supposed to arrive far sooner to help soften the blow of the lost coca crop and prevent the emergence of new growers. Subsidies to encourage farmers to pull up coca that were scheduled to begin at the beginning of the year have yet to arrive in many areas. The amount of the promised subsidies, supported in part by $81 million in U.S. aid, has shrunk by more than half.[31]

The U.S. Congress, however, provided several roadblocks when the House of Representatives rejected President Bush's requests for more funding for Colombia.

Critics of Plan Colombia continued to argue that the money could have been better allocated. On October 17, 2001, Judy Mann criticized the funding of Plan Colombia, declaring: "But the reality is that the military aid is reinforcing Colombia's army in its attempt to battle internal insurgency, and the United States is at risk of getting drawn into Colombia's 40–year-old civil war. The reality also is that defoliation has hurt farmers growing legal crops such as yucca and has forced them off their land. And the reality, which U.S. officials admit, is that Plan Colombia has yet to affect cocaine prices since it was launched late last year."[32]

The Drugs and Terror Nexus

This work has focused a great deal on the shift in the U.S. grand strategy after the events of September 11, 2001. Now, we must analyze what important figures said during this period. On December 24, 2001, Marc Grossman discussed the connection between drugs and terrorism. The *Washington Post* quoted him: "The results? We have delivered 80 helicopters to Colombia and trained more than 2,000 members of a counter-narcotics brigade. We have destroyed more than 700 cocaine labs, sprayed more than 90,000 hectares of coca and 1,800 hectares of poppy, signed more than 36,000 families to manual eradication pacts and trained more than 3,000 judges to improve the judicial system. Colombia extradited 23 drug lords to U.S. courts—an unprecedented level of cooperation."[33]

Dennis Jett also made significant comments on January 12, 2002, regarding the drug war. He argued that the war on terrorism has overlapped with the war on drugs, declaring: "The war on terrorism is like the war on drugs in at least two ways. In neither struggle will there ever be a final victory. Yet in both cases, the damage that would result from failing to combat the problem would be far worse than the cost of waging a struggle without end. Whatever qualms people have about the drug war, we must strive for effective, not random, enforcement. And unless we decide to legalize drugs, we cannot abandon that enforcement effort."[34]

President Bush reiterated such sentiments on February 12, 2002, asserting, "It's important for Americans to know that the traffic in drugs finances the work of terror, sustaining terrorists, that terrorists use drug profits to fund their cells to commit acts of murder. . . . If you quit drugs, you join the fight against terror in America."[35]

On June 10, 2002, Hernando Gomez, wrote an opinion column analyzing why the United States should become involved in the internal dynamics of Colombia. He wrote, "The USA has had three reasons to get into our 'internal' war. The first one, in the times of the USSR, was to face the communist menace. The second and—by far—the most important, is to destroy drug trafficking. The third, now more akin to Bush, is to defeat terrorism."[36]

Rhetoric also began to appear about the possibility of Colombia collapsing. Lt. Gen. James T. Hill said, "It would be a terrible loss if democracy failed in Colombia."[37] President Bush continued to echo support for Colombia not only because it is a democracy, but also because he wanted to combat terrorism wherever it appeared. On September 26, 2002, the *Washington Post* wrote: "Bush made a connection between terrorism and drug trafficking when he cited the unsealing of federal charges Tuesday against Carlos Castaño, head of a violent right-wing Colombian paramilitary group, who is accused of bringing 17 tons of cocaine into the United States and Europe since 1997." Bush classified the indicted individual as a terrorist, stating that "the guy who got indicted yesterday made a decision to be a terrorist."[38]

Bush asserted, "We made a decision to hold him to account, and we will continue to do that."[39]

During this period, Scott Wilson of the *Washington Post* Foreign Service questioned the expanding U.S. role in Colombia. Marcela Sanchez echoed the concern about the deepening U.S. involvement, declaring, "If the budget President Bush proposed this week is any indication, his administration appears to be moving boldly toward establishing an outright and unabridged military relationship with Colombia—exactly the kind Washington sought so long to avoid."[40]

Álvaro Uribe countered such notions, stating that Colombia did not need the U.S. military to fight its war. On May 5, 2003, he stated, "We don't need american [*sic*] troops. Our troops are growing and will be suffice [*sic*] to defeat the terrorists in Colombia. But we need planes, satellites, radars and trucks."[41] Minister of Defense Jorge Alberto Uribe echoed these sentiments, asserting, "It is not just the money, the aid goes further and it is not just from the United States but from other countries too. Nowadays Colombia, without international economic, logistic, and political cooperation, cannot move forward and face its very grave problems."[42]

Throughout his tenure, President Bush vowed to support Uribe. On November 23, 2004, Bush pledged his support stating, "I'm proud to be with my friend, President Uribe. El es mi amigo." He continued, "President Uribe and the Colombian people are dedicated to the triumph of democracy and the rule of law against the forces of violence. And the United States stands with you."[43]

Assistant Secretary of State Roger F. Noriega maintained that the Colombian government made tremendous progress as a result of Uribe's efforts and U.S. support. On February 25, 2005, he declared: "No one is claiming victory in Colombia, but to deny that the momentum on the battlefield has shifted under Mr. Uribe is wrong. Heroin and cocaine production are down, as are terrorist attacks, murders and kidnappings. Several key terrorists have been captured, and a number of major narco-traffickers have been arrested and, in some cases, extradited to the United States. The United States remains committed to working with Mr. Uribe to create a secure and peaceful Colombia."[44]

However, not everyone always has been so complimentary of the events that have transpired under the Uribe administration. Patrick Leahy (D–VT) declared, "The demobilization process has been as much about avoiding justice and consolidating ill-gotten gains as it has been about disarming the paramilitaries. . . . The government needs to stop appeasing the leaders of these outlaw militias and listen more to their victims."[45]

In an interview with *Semana* on March 9, 2007, Uribe discussed the situation in Colombia, stating: "Ok, the truth is this: The U.S.

have [sic] given Colombia a practical help to eradicate the drugs. A help that amounts to around $600 million USD a year. I think that there are positive results. We are winning, although we have not won yet. There is a great effort in spraying, a great effort in manual eradication. Colombia is making a huge effort on the forest [park] rangers; there is a great effort on alternative crops. But there [are] still a lot of drugs."[46]

Clearly, both the United States and the United Nations failed to learn the lessons from history. Coca continued to be cultivated because it is a rational choice for Colombian peasants. As discussed in previous chapters, many underlying development and security issues explain why coca is cultivated. The laws of economics and supply and demand are strong drivers of this business. Coca is grown because drug traffickers must produce cocaine to meet the demand of drug users. Duncan Smith-Rohrberg Maru echoed such sentiments about the large waste of resources used in combatting drug production and trafficking. The *Washington Post* quoted him on November 24, 2008, stating, "The primary lesson for the new administration to take from Plan Colombia's failures is something that many economists have been saying for years: Efforts to decrease the supply of drugs in America without major efforts to curb demand for them will only increase the profits of drug dealers and the associated crime rates."[47]

Drug policy experts and academics were not the only critics of the U.S. approach during this period. A March 14, 2009, *Washington Post* article, "Brazil's President to Seek a Change in U.S. Approach," quotes Foreign Minister Celso Amorim stating, "We would hope that the United States and the Obama administration would not look to Latin America and South America under the prism of drug trafficking. Drug trafficking is one problem, it's a serious problem, but the relation is much broader and otherwise it will be contaminated from the beginning. . . . If there is a message we would like to give, that would be [the] one."[48]

Not only did the U.S.-led war on drugs anger leaders in Latin America, but the decision to allow the United States access to bases in Colombia also annoyed many people. On August 8, 2009, the *Washington Post* reported that "a senior State Department official, speaking on the condition of anonymity, said by phone from Washington on Friday that the plan would give the United States access to Colombian bases from which to carry out vital counter-drug surveillance flights over the Pacific, a conduit for cocaine smuggled to Mexico and on to the United States." The State Department official said, "Our ability to have broad coverage in that area was important."[49]

The willingness of the Colombian government to grant bases to the United States demonstrated that the partnership between Uribe and Bush remained strong. Rep. Steny Hoyer (D–MD) echoed the strong relationship between the two countries and was quoted in a *Semana* article on January 16, 2009, stating, "Colombia is a valued partner to the United States on many different issues, including the fight against drugs, and will continue to be so in the years to come."[50] He continued: "The U.S. is committed to our allies around the world and does not go back on its word. The Bush Administration signed the trade agreement, not Congress. Unfortunately the Bush Administration chose not to follow standard protocol when submitting a trade agreement to Congress."[51]

Conclusion

This chapter provided insight into the sentiments of key actors during the various critical periods of Plan Colombia, although an exhaustive analysis of every statement ever made is clearly not possible. This chapter also revealed how different actors define the problems and solutions to various issues. The statements do not necessarily reflect reality, but rather help shed light on the social constructions of various key actors. In addition, the statements highlight the difference between the social constructions and the realities.

8

Analytic Conclusions and
Policy Lessons from Plan Colombia

This chapter is divided into two sections: analytical conclusions and policy lessons that can be drawn from Plan Colombia, which answers the "So what?" question. Analyzing Plan Colombia alone is insufficient, and the chapter seeks to bridge the gap between academia and the real world by answering the "So what?" question. Far too often, some academics, particularly political scientists, avoid delving into the policy world and simply engage in what remains an intellectual exercise.[1] Some scholars have criticized the field of political science for being obsessed with imitating the rigor of economics and invoking the use of methodologically sophisticated techniques.[2] This work seeks to move beyond a sheer intellectual enterprise and answer these questions: What does Plan Colombia teach us? Does Plan Colombia have any valuable lessons? Why does Plan Colombia matter?

In terms of analytical conclusions, Plan Colombia teaches scholars fundamental lessons in international relations (IR) theory. This section analyzes which IR theories are useful for explaining Colombia's behavior and its relations with the United States. How does Colombia help scholars understand various IR concepts such as alliance politics? What does the Colombia case suggest for IR scholars and policy experts regarding the relations between hegemonic powers and weaker actors?

Before delving into the theoretical arguments, one must examine why the United States cares so much about Colombia, and why Washington allocated $8 billion to Plan Colombia over its duration.[3] First, the United States has many security concerns regarding the stability and the future of Colombia. A major concern for Washington is that drug trafficking in Colombia can traverse borders and penetrate other countries in the region. Second, the United States supported Colombia for many years because Colombia is a bastion of democracy, and the United States supports democracies throughout the region. While Uribe had victories in terms of combatting the *Fuerzas Armadas Revolucionarias de Colombia* (FARC) and the internal armed actors, the FARC and internal armed groups still operate in Colombia.[4] These groups have the potential to hinder Colombia's ability to strengthen democracy and institutions. Third, the United States is concerned about the stability and the future of Colombia as the internal armed conflict, drug trafficking, and organized crime can impact trade and security throughout the region. The FARC is regaining power and may quite possibly, along with the *Ejército de Liberación Nacional* (ELN), launch strikes against crucial infrastructure and strategic locations like the Panama Canal. In addition, the FARC could potentially target key oil producing centers, located in neighboring countries such as Brazil.

For all of these reasons, the United States has security interests in Colombia and viewed Plan Colombia as a crucial policy to help the Colombian government combat its security threats. Realism is one of the IR theories that helps explain how the United States was able to change the formula and shift the design of Plan Colombia by a complete reversal. Realism fails to understand how and why a country, such as Colombia, can challenge a stronger hegemonic power and enhance its bargaining leverage vis-à-vis the dominant country. Colombia simply does not have two options as realist logic indicates: to balance or bandwagon.[5]

Before delving into the weaknesses of realism, we need to examine its analytical capacity. The relationship between Colombia and the United States is by no means equal because the Colombian government depends on the United States for aid and resources. During the Clinton administration, Pastrana proposed a version of Plan Colombia, but the United States failed to accept it because Washington feared becoming involved in a Vietnam-type situation.[6] Under President Clinton, the United States used its power to set the agenda for Plan Colombia. During Uribe's tenure, however, he demonstrated that smaller powers can have the ability to set the agenda. As discussed in previous chapters, Uribe came to power with the goal of combating the FARC and other illegal armed actors operating in Colombia. He made significant policy changes from his predecessor, refusing to negotiate with the FARC and vowing to bring peace to Colombia. The events of September 11, 2001, fundamentally changed the course of U.S. foreign policy, and the primary focus for the Bush administration became combating global terrorism, thereby declaring a Global War on Terrorism. Uribe described the internal armed actors in Colombia as narco-terrorists, providing a fusion for the war on drugs with the war on terrorism. Uribe, therefore, convinced President Bush and his administration that Colombia was an ally deserving of U.S. aid and that fit perfectly into the global vision and grand strategy of the United States.

Uribe's ability to shift the nature of Plan Colombia to focus on narco-terrorism provides an important lesson in IR theory. According to realism, greater powers, such as the United States, have the ability to set the agenda and use their power, whether economic or military, to implement strategies that fit within their global vision and security initiatives.[7] Under Uribe, Colombia, the weaker power, set the agenda thereby demonstrating that weaker powers need not always simply follow orders from greater powers. The Bush administration approved Uribe's new objectives and accepted the reorientation of Plan Colombia because it fit within the goals and objectives of the U.S.

Without a doubt, Uribe remained a "true" ally of the United States and the Bush administration, supporting Bush's global vision. The relationship between Bush and Uribe remained strong throughout both of their tenures in office. By the end of the Bush administration, Uribe was the only ally or "friend" that President Bush had in the entire region. Although Uribe pledged his support for Bush, he was able to pursue his own domestic priorities despite U.S. dominance.[8] The strong relationship and alliance between Colombia and the United States enabled Colombia to achieve major successes during Uribe's tenure by his being able to reorient the direction and focus of Plan Colombia, which is a significant lesson for leaders of small states and IR theorists.

President Santos also has made several policy maneuvers that suggest something about the politics of bandwagoning.[9] Santos has not simply bandwagoned[10] with the United States during his tenure, but he has sought to build alliances with other countries, such as China. Li Changchun, a government representative of China, traveled to Colombia in April 2012 to demonstrate that Colombia and China want to increase linkages between the two countries. In May 2012, President Santos traveled to China with the goal of initiating a trade agreement between the two countries. Santos is seeking to extend his options and build relationships with other countries so that Colombia no longer has to rely on the United States for everything. Santos, unlike Uribe, does not want to make everything dependent on the United States. Instead, Santos wants relations with other countries that will help strengthen Colombia not only in economic terms but also provide it with more leverage and negotiating power.[11]

President Santos appears to be conscious of the new limitations that the growing distance between the security interests of the United States and Colombia in the second decade of the twenty-first century. As a result, a trade-off exists for Colombia between closely aligning with the United States or being able to develop its own foreign policy without the influence of Washington. In analytical terms, therefore, the realist approach fails to capture the nuances in its interpretation of the foreign policy autonomy that closely aligned subordinated countries, such as Colombia, can achieve against stronger powers. On the contrary, a country that is no longer closely aligned with the greater power will be less likely to exercise the same degree of leverage and exert its relative autonomy in its foreign policy.

This work also demonstrates that realism alone is insufficient because it cannot account for the economic linkages between the two countries. Liberalism reveals that national security is not the only consideration for the United States and economic linkages focus on explaining and understanding how economic interconnections impact the relationship between the United States and Colombia.[12] The United States, for instance, provided substantial aid through Plan Colombia with the goal of increasing security in Colombia.[13] The Colombian government sought the approval of the free trade agreement known as the TLC (*Tratado de Libre Comercio entre Colombia y Estados Unidos*), and the United States was interested in the TLC because the approval of this agreement would benefit both countries economically. The transition from Uribe to Santos resulted in a change in the discourse toward key issues such as human rights and democracy and is another important factor that helps explain why the United States eventually passed the TLC. The TLC also provides a justification for the United States in further reducing the aid granted to Colombia under the auspices of Plan Colombia without damaging the Colombian economy. In sum, liberalism's emphasis on the economic relationships, although minor for Washington, helps explain U.S.–Colombian bilateral relations during this period.[14]

Constructivism is the final theoretical approach covered in this work and helps explain the perspectives and social constructions. Constructivism also sheds light on the role of leaders and the importance of leadership.[15] From the outset of Plan Colombia, Clinton and Pastrana had different social constructions of the problems and solutions; the differences in perceptions help policy analysts understand why the final version of Plan Colombia differed drastically from Pastrana's initial vision and proposal. Constructivism also explains the perceptions and consensus between Uribe and Bush and how Uribe successfully convinced Bush that Colombia was a vital country for the United States and its geostrategic interests.[16] The constructivist approach explains Uribe's proactive leadership, convincing President Bush and the United States that the new version of Plan Colombia was in the national interest of the United States, In conclusion, liberalism adds a component but is unable to explain everything because it neglects the role of leadership. Constructivism, therefore, acts as a useful analytical tool and fills the void left by the other two theories. Scholars and policy analysts studying relations between the United States and other Latin American countries or those throughout the developing world cannot truly understand foreign policy without taking an eclectic theoretical approach to understand the additional bargaining vis-à-vis the United States that the less powerful country can attain.

Desecuritization

The United States has sought to desecuritize[17] the war on drugs in Colombia for various reasons. First, the United States is in the midst of a recession, and Washington does not have the resources to continue providing Bogotá with billions of dollars in assistance through Plan Colombia. Second, drug trafficking has shifted routes and Mexico is receiving more attention from the United States because both countries share a large border, and violence and bloodshed have spilled over the border. Advocates of Plan Colombia argue that it has been a success and should be considered a model and used in other countries such as Mexico. Santos counters such arguments stating that the war on drugs in Colombia has been a failure, having witnessed 40 years of bloodshed and violence.[18] In addition to the vast number of Colombians who have suffered from the war on drugs and its consequences, Colombia has forgone and sacrificed economic earnings because of organized crime and the internal conflict. Santos argues for the need for alternative paradigms. Santos's rhetoric presents the possibility of a structural gap between the United States and Colombia in terms of interests as well as the perceptions of the problem. Santos wants an alternative paradigm that will not cause such extreme levels of violence.

Desecuritization, therefore, can occur in one country, as it has in the United States; the United States has tried to desecuritize the war on drugs in Colombia as a major U.S. security concern. On the other hand, U.S. policy can result in Colombians interpreting the desecuritization process as the United States giving up on the war on drugs. The United States has precipitously declared victory in the war on drugs in Colombia, yet the empirical results and analytical analysis demonstrates that Colombia still has a drug problem as well as an internal armed conflict. While this work is a single case study, similar problems have occurred with desecuritization in other countries, such as Iraq and Afghanistan.

The desecuritization process, therefore, is not as easy as the securitization process during a crisis because it requires the development of alternative strategies, paradigms, and social constructions both in the United States and the other country in the bilateral relationship. Realism fails to account for the importance of perceptions.[19] Like realists, liberals also fail to account for the role perceptions play, although they recognize the importance of economic interdependence. Desecuritization can have important economic consequences for Colombia because the economic issues are much smaller than the military aid provided under Plan Colombia.

Policy Contributions of Plan Colombia

The United States has been quick to praise Plan Colombia as a success, although this is debatable. Indeed, Uribe successfully combatted the FARC and the guerrillas, but the country still has an internal armed conflict and Uribe by no means has eliminated the various internal armed actors. Colombia continues to confront drug trafficking and organized crime has returned to the country as a result of the changing trafficking routes. As a result, U.S.-led policies have had negative consequences for Colombia as the routes shifted from Colombia to Mexico and now back to Colombia.[20] Simply shifting coca cultivation and drug routes away from Colombia and toward other countries does not make Plan Colombia a success. It is, then, premature for the Colombian government to claim victory in the war on drugs when in reality the overall landscape has not changed but rather countries continue to volley the drug problem back and forth between each other; the overall framework remains the same and drugs continue to be produced and trafficked in the region.[21]

Military Spending

Plan Colombia demonstrates that military aid alone cannot solve the problem. Eighty percent of Plan Colombia funds were at one time earmarked for the military. Indeed, Colombia was able to contain the FARC but it did not eliminate the FARC. Focusing on the military alone ignores other issues such as the capacity of the state.[22] A key question is when the United States desecuritizes a state, does it have the institutional capacity to control its own territory and maintain security? The FARC has adapted and continues to earn profits from drug trafficking, and, therefore, remains a formidable threat to Colombian security. Ultimately, eliminating the guerrillas without addressing issues such as alternative development is not possible. The FARC are able to recruit young people by promising them friendship, brotherhood, food, and other enticements that young people who live in extremely poor areas do not have; many of the recruits live in regions mired in poverty, and they lack basic education, skills, and the opportunity to improve themselves. Therefore, Colombia cannot solve its internal conflict without addressing issues such as alternative development, and the need for assistance to socially excluded areas. President Santos has proved willing to negotiate with the internal armed actors to produce peace. If the negotiations fail, Colombia will have to increase its military action but the underlying social and developmental issues will still remain. Most importantly, the United States will not provide Bogotá with the same support as in the past. Instead, the Colombian government will need to fight this battle themselves and cannot rely on the hegemonic power to the north to provide these resources.[23]

Aerial Spraying

Aerial spraying has been counterproductive, and Colombian peasants continue to grow coca, interspersing the illicit crops with licit ones so they are not as easily detected from the air. The peasants also cultivate coca in the jungle and under canopies, which also stymies detection. The aerial spraying initiatives have simply caused coca cultivation to shift and expand to other regions.[24]

A brief discussion of the statistical analysis of the U.N. Office on Drugs and Crime (UNODC) reports demonstrate that aerial spraying has been ineffective, and Colombia still has major problems with coca cultivation. The UNODC reports are some of the best reports because they explain their methodology and take many measures to provide accurate results.[25] Whether Colombia produces 61,000 hectares or 62,000 hectares of coca is not crucial because drug production and trafficking is an illegal business and is not a science.[26] The statistics provide analysts with a range of estimates but should not be viewed as exact. Daniel Mejía, one of the leading experts on this subject, argues that "what shouldn't be believed is the figures produced by the State Department in the U.S. Why? Because they have never been clear about their methodology. They have never explained to anyone—not even the U.N.—about how they do the survey."[27] The main substance of concern is cocaine. Peru, Colombia, and Bolivia account for nearly 100 percent of the production of coca in the world.[28] The hectares of coca being cultivated can be measured over time, enabling scholars and policy analyst to analyze Plan Colombia's effectiveness with regard to decreasing the cultivation of coca. Again, we need to be mindful that agencies have different measures for calculating coca cultivation. Calculating the area of coca being cultivated is not scientific and should be viewed as an estimate rather than an exact number. Although the numbers are not exact, the data provides analysts with a benchmark as to how well Colombia has done in terms of combating coca cultivation.[29]

In 1999, Colombia produced 160,100 hectares, whereas in 2002 Colombia witnessed a significant decrease in the yields of coca, recording 102,000 hectares of coca cultivated according to the 2011 UNODC report. The total acreage in Colombia decreased rapidly from 86,000 hectares in 2003 to 78,000 hectares in 2006. In 2010, the total acreage of coca being cultivated in Colombia decreased by an estimated 15 percent. Some regions in Colombia, however, continued to cultivate large quantities of coca. The 2011 UNODC report notes that the Pacific region cultivated an estimated 42 percent of the coca in Colombia in 2010. In 2009 and 2010, an interesting evolution occurred in the methodology for calculating coca cultivation. Coca farmers in Colombia began cultivating coca in smaller plots of land, making detection of such small amounts of coca difficult for satellites.[30] To address this problem, the UNODC began to calculate and include smaller plots of coca being cultivated throughout Colombia. The 2009 unadjusted number reported for coca cultivation in Colombia is 68,000 hectares. After considering the small fields under cultivation, the 2009 hectares under cultivation increase to 73,000. The unadjusted figure reported for 2010 is 57,000 hectares, and the adjusted figure is 62,000 hectares.[31]

Rural Colombia has witnessed increases in coca cultivation. According to the country report by the UNODC for 2011, coca cultivation in Putumayo increased dramatically to 9,951 hectares in December 2011 from 4,785 hectares in December 2010, or a 108 percent increase. Another region in Colombia that has witnessed a dramatic increase in cultivation is Norte de Santander, which in December 2010 recorded 1,889 hectares of coca being cultivated, increasing 85 percent in December 2011 to 3,490 hectares. Guaviare saw a 20 percent increase in the hectares under cultivation from 5,701 hectares in December 2010 to 6,839 hectares in December 2011.[32] Other regions in Colombia have experienced decreases in the net change of coca cultivated from December 2010 to December 2011. Cordoba, for instance, recorded a 72 percent decrease from 3,889 hectares in December 2010 to 1,088 hectares in December 2011; Amazonas recorded a 64 percent decrease from 338 hectares to 122 hectares during that same period.[33] That said, we need to recognize that the decreases may appear large but the overall hectares produced in regions such as the Amazonas are much smaller than the total hectares cultivated in other locations such as Putumayo. The amazon, for instance, accounts for only 1.1 percent of the total hectares cultivated in Colombia from 2005 to 2011. On the other hand, the Pacific region of Colombia historically has produced the most number of coca fields. The 2011 Colombia report by the UNODC reveals that from 2005 to 2011, the Pacific region in Colombia accounted for 42 percent of the total hectares cultivated in Colombia, whereas Putumayo-Caquetá accounted for 20.8 percent of the coca produced between 2005 and 2011.[34]

Statistics reveal that Colombia has made progress in decreasing the overall acreage of coca cultivated within its borders. Before claiming victory, however, we need to analyze the recent trends in coca cultivation in the two other coca cultivating countries: Peru and Bolivia. An analysis of the data reveals that cocaine production in Peru has been increasing since 2005. In 2005, Peru cultivated approximately 48,200 hectares of coca. By 2007, Peru recorded 53,700 hectares of coca under cultivation, which rapidly increased to 61,200 hectares in 2010.[35]

Like Peru, Bolivia has witness a proliferation in coca cultivated within the country. Bolivia had 21,800 hectares under cultivation in 1999, which dropped dramatically to 14,600 hectares in 2000. From 2000 to 2004, coca cultivation in Bolivia increased, and then decreased from 27,700 hectares in 2004 to 25,400 hectares in 2005, but it has continued to increase over time. By 2009, the total area of coca cultivated reached 30,900 hectares.[36]

The data reveals several key trends. While Colombia experienced an overall decrease in the acreage of coca cultivation, Peru and Bolivia have experienced increases over the past several years, which is a prime example of the balloon effect. The balloon effect is one of the best studied phenomenons by drug trafficking scholars;[37] it is similar to a law like the theory of relativity because it can be proved empirically. When a balloon is squeezed, the air is displaced to another part of the balloon, but it does not go away. Likewise, the balloon effect in coca cultivation occurs when the routes shift

Table 8.1. Coca Fields in Colombia

Department	Dec.-2010	Dec.-2011	Change % 2010–2011
Putumayo	4,785	9,951	+ 108%
Guaviare	5,701	6,839	+20%
Antioquia	5,350	3,104	−42%
Vichada	2,743	2,264	−17%
Magdalena	121	46	−62%
Valle del Cauca	665	981	+48%

Information adapted from *Coca Cultivation Survey* (Bogotá, Colombia: UNODC, 2011), 10.

Table 8.2. Coca Cultivation Variation Per Region

Net area under coca cultivation (thousands)	2010 62,000 hectares	Variation 3%	2011 64,000 hectares
Pacific region	25,682	4%	26,789
Central region	15,308	−31%	10,641
Meta-Guaviare region	8.709	13%	9,879
Putumayo-Caquetá region	7,363	80%	13,278
Amazon region	1,505	−52%	717

Information adapted from *Coca Cultivation Survey* (Bogotá, Colombia: UNODC, 2011), 7.

to another region as a result of increases in law enforcement and interdiction efforts in one region. Enforcement activities, therefore, merely cause coca cultivation to shift to other regions. Individuals who grow coca can easily move their crops to areas of the forest that are hard to spot from an airplane and that are difficult to detect from a satellite. Individuals who cultivate coca also can replant the crop after it has been sprayed with herbicides, spreading—ballooning out—it to regions that are harder to spray.[38]

Marten Brienen argues that "the demand for the product is inelastic. There is a certain demand for this product. . . . The more you hamper the availability of this product, the higher the price is, the more attractive it becomes for people to grow it."[39] Therefore, coca will continue to be grown because of the profits for farmers. Brienen declares, "If you manage to eradicate 80 percent of the total acreage, you would have raised the price to the point where every farmer will want to switch to this particular crop. . . . It provides you with a constant income throughout the year."[40] With the support of the U.S. government, Colombia has received billions of dollars to help combat drug trafficking and has witnessed some decreases in coca cultivation. Because Colombia has been the epicenter of the war on drugs in South America for decades, Peru and Bolivia have received less attention in terms of coca cultivation; therefore, both countries have witnessed a proliferation in coca cultivation.[41]

Determining whether Plan Colombia has been a success and whether the U.S. and Colombian governments have succeeded in combating drug trafficking does not result in a definitive answer and depends on one's social constructions and perceptions.[42] When asked whether the U.S. and Colombian governments have succeeded in combating drug trafficking, Sandro Calvani, the UNODC Director of Colombia Program in Bogotá from 2003 to 2007, writes: "The Colombian Govt [sic] made sincere and intellectually honest efforts to focus on farmers at least with the same intensity than what was done against drug traffickers. More than 80,000 families of coca farmers . . . were reached by various programmes which . . . convinced them to stay out of illicit crops."[43] While Calvani praised the Colombian government's efforts, he also questioned the success of Plan Colombia. Critics of Plan Colombia would agree and argue that Plan Colombia has been an utter failure in terms of reducing drugs because they are more readily available today than ever before. Therefore, arguing that Plan Colombia accomplished its goals in terms of reducing cultivation, production, and the trafficking of drugs is difficult.

Plan Colombia teaches analysts an important lesson in terms of supply-side policies and combating drug trafficking. While Plan Colombia has resulted in significant improvements in security within Colombia, drug cultivation, production, and trafficking remain major issues. Supply-side initiatives alone are not enough, and countries must address demand. The United States is the largest consumer of cocaine in the world and provides the Colombian drug traffickers with a vast market for such products. The United States must be an effective partner with Colombia in order to curb demand for such substances.[44] The law of supply-and-demand demonstrates that drug traffickers will continue to traffic drugs as long as a market exists for such products. More emphasis, therefore, must be placed on reducing demand. Countries must become equal partners in combatting drug trafficking by addressing the demand rather than merely stopping supply. Decreasing demand for drugs requires more money to be spent on education, prevention, rehabilitation, and treatment so that addicts can become productive members of society and overcome their addiction to drugs.[45]

Is Plan Colombia a Model?

One of the major questions that has emerged is whether Plan Colombia should be used as a model, and the answer depends on whether one feels that Plan Colombia accomplished its goals. Plan Colombia, indeed, had successes against the FARC and other organizations.[46] Officials and policymakers in Washington are quick to praise Plan Colombia as a great success. Others concur, asking that if Plan Colombia is not a model, then what is? As the statistics regarding kidnapping and murders demonstrate, Colombia has reached a significant turning point and is much safer today.[47]

As a result, some policymakers have argued that Plan Colombia should be used as a model and implemented in other regions of the world that experience high levels of violence and problems related to drug trafficking. President Clinton, for instance, visited Mexico and called for a "Plan Mexico," in order to help Mexico make the strides and advancements in security that Colombia has made. Other government officials have suggested using the same model in Afghanistan. Joint Chiefs of Staff Chairman Adm. Mike Mullen traveled to Colombia in June 2010 and proclaimed, "I see the same kinds of challenges in Afghanistan, and I also see them in Mexico,"[48] which suggests that both Afghanistan and Mexico could benefit from an initiative designed to combat drug production and increase security.

Another major question is whether the Colombian model is exportable. Colombia and Mexico are countries with different issues. Colombia has an internal armed conflict, whereas Mexico does not. Both countries have different histories, geographies, and political systems. The comparison and question of whether Plan Colombia is a model for Afghanistan becomes an even more daunting proposition. Afghanistan, for instance, has tribal societies that have more loyalty to their clans than to the state, and one can argue that Afghanistan has never had a functioning state.

When questioning whether Plan Colombia should be considered a model, one needs to recognize that trade-offs exist between security and other issues, such as human rights. The United States has often neglected human rights issues and abuses, particularly against the indigenous and Afro-Colombian populations in Colombia. The most important thing for the United States remains security. Policy analysts can question how effective the United States was in helping Colombia consolidate democracy by strengthening institutions and protecting human and civil rights over the long term. The situation in Colombia teaches policy experts that trade-offs exist, have major implications, and can lead to "blowback" or unintended consequences.[49] Critics of Plan Colombia caution that this policy cannot simply be exported to other countries without modifications.

Critics of Plan Colombia argue that it should not be used as a model because Colombia is no safer today than before. Not only has the FARC not been defeated, but Colombia has also witnessed a reorientation of the battle ground.[50] The demobilization of the *Autodefensas Unidas de Colombia* (AUC) has been a farce because many of them joined *Bandas Criminales* (BACRIM) and applied their skills to drug trafficking. While those living in Bogotá or other major cities can easily argue that Colombia is much safer, those in the rural areas know the war rages on in full force. Sanho Tree of the Institute for Policy Studies argues that the perception of success is quite different if one does not leave the major metropolitan area. Tree states, "It is like living on two different planets. If you are in Bogotá, the conflict and the bad stuff is like something that you watch on TV."[51] The armed conflict in Colombia continues and rural towns have witnessed extreme levels of violence. Marc Chernick argues that Colombia is quite dangerous for certain professions, such as human rights defenders.[52]

Plan Colombia has achieved some security gains, but they have come at high costs. Adam Isacson also believes that Plan Colombia should not be a model. He writes, "looked at more closely . . . though, **Colombia's security gains are partial, possibly reversible, and weighed down by 'collateral damage.'"**[53] Collateral damage includes a plethora of human rights abuses and lost lives as a result of the war on drugs in Colombia. In an interview, Lisa Haugaard of the Latin American Working Group questioned how one could call Plan Colombia a model, arguing that the costs in terms of human lives as a result of human rights abuses have been far too grave to consider exporting Plan Colombia as a model. She notes that from 2004 to 2008, members of the Colombian army recruited young men convincing them that they would be working as brick layers or at other day jobs, but later murdered them in order to falsify the results against the armed groups. She continues, "I have seen a huge increase in direct violations of human rights . . ." because more than 3,000 people have been killed in extrajudicial executions (far more as a result of the war; in excess of 3,000 just in extrajudicial executions allegedly by members of the army) and more than 3 million people displaced during Plan Colombia.[54] Haugaard also emphasized the Uribe administration's role in protecting human rights abusers. She points out that the Administrative Department of Security (DAS), an intelligence service operating in Colombia, often functioned more as the secret police.[55] The first director, Jorge Noguera, reportedly had linkages with the paramilitaries and even provided the AUC with information about Colombia's military operations. Noguera provided the AUC with secret information about names of human rights defenders as well as leaders of labor organizations.[56] Isacson agrees with Haugaard, stating that approximately 21,000 police, soldiers, paramilitaries, and guerrillas have been killed as a result of Plan Colombia and the attempt to bring peace to the country. Experts estimate that 14,000 civilians also have been killed since 2010.[57] The increases in security, therefore, have cost a tremendous amount in terms of blood and treasure.

Plan Colombia demonstrates that a country such as Colombia can comply with the United States and make improvements and progress with regard to coca cultivation, but this does not mean that the country has become more democratic or has more robust institutions. Eighty percent of the money for Plan Colombia assisted the military and other "hard components."[58] Plan Colombia demonstrates that military aid and supply-side policies alone cannot solve the problem. Indeed, the Colombian government was able to contain the FARC but it did not eliminate the threat. Focusing on the military aspect alone ignores other key issues such as the capacity of the state. The FARC has adapted and continues to earn profits from drug trafficking.

Therefore, Colombia cannot solve its internal conflict without addressing issues such as alternative development, and the need for assistance to socially remote areas. President Santos has proved willing to negotiate with the internal armed actors to produce peace.[59] If the negotiations fail, Colombia will have to increase its military action but the underlying social and developmental issues will still remain. Most importantly, the United States will not provide the Colombian government with the same support as it has in the past. Instead, the Colombian leadership will need to fight this battle themselves and cannot rely on Washington to provide these resources. Colombia has traditionally had a very weak state and has not been able to exert control over much of the territory.[60] Uribe made some progress in terms of state presence but Colombia still has a weak state that has been prone to corruption and abuses. In addition, the institutions in Colombia remain weak and must be strengthened. While Santos has sought to address this problem, Colombia still faces many challenges with impunity and prosecuting violators of the law, particularly human rights abusers.

The United States has rushed to praise Plan Colombia as a success, which is questionable. Indeed, Uribe successfully combatted the FARC and the guerrillas, but Colombia still has an internal armed conflict and by no means has Uribe eliminated the various actors. Colombia also continues to confront drug trafficking and organized crime that have returned to the country as a result of the shifting routes. As a result, U.S.-led policies have had negative consequences for Colombia as the routes shifted from Colombia to Mexico and now back to Colombia.[61]

The United States perceives the security threat in Colombia as fading and the realist[62] proposition that countries have interests as opposed to friends will occur. Colombia cannot expect that the United States will remain a close ally when Washington believes that the security threat has diminished. This is the reality that Santos faces as he diversifies his friends throughout the region. Santos, therefore, has sought to improve Colombia's relations with other countries in the Americas, such as Brazil and Canada, as well as European countries, and, finally, Asian countries, particularly China. The United States may quite possibly distance itself from Colombia if problems occur as a result of drug trafficking, organized crime, and the internal armed conflict; the United States will not be willing or equipped to reengage Colombia. As a result, the Colombian government will have to fight its own war on drugs and solve its own problems within the country without U.S. assistance.[63]

Conclusion

This chapter has examined the analytical conclusions and policy lessons from Plan Colombia. Indeed, Plan Colombia, particularly under Uribe, has had some successes and increased security in Colombia. However, in terms of reducing cultivation, production, and trafficking, Plan Colombia has been a failure. While the total hectares of coca being cultivated in Colombia have decreased over time, Peru and Bolivia have witnessed corresponding increases in coca cultivation.[64] The United States has failed to learn from the lessons of history, which demonstrate that coca cultivation can shift and adapt. Increasing aerial spraying programs in Colombia merely shifts coca cultivation to the neighboring countries, which is what has happened despite spending billions of dollars trying to spray the countryside in Colombia. Another cost that needs to be factored into the balance sheet of Plan Colombia is the negative repercussions and cost of the environmental damages. Estimating the cost of the environmental damages to Colombia from the aerial spraying program is difficult.[65] Flora and fauna, however, have not been the only things damaged by the herbicides; aerial spraying initiatives have had devastating effects on the water in the rich ecosystem of Colombia. In sum, the aerial spraying initiatives have not only failed to reduce coca cultivation, but also have had negative environmental consequences as well as health consequences for Colombians. Consequently, such initiatives have created much damage and, in turn, have been counterproductive. Ramírez Lemus, Stanton, and Walsh provide an excellent summary of the negative repercussions of aerial spraying initiatives, stating:

> The fumigation strategy in Colombia is not merely ineffective; it is also counterproductive. It has destroyed the livelihood of thousands of peasant farmers who lack viable economic alternatives to producing illicit crops, also endangering their health and the environment. The implementation of the fumigation program in disregard of Colombian legal principles, and against the will of local and regional elected officials, has undermined the rule of law and government authority. And as coca cultivation has dispersed in response to the fumigation, the illegal armed actors have followed the new production, further extending the reach of the internal armed conflict.[66]

Despite the failure of Plan Colombia to reduce cultivation and drug trafficking in Colombia, many advocates praise Plan Colombia and argue that it should be used as a model. The United States has been too hasty to praise Colombia for its success and has sought to desecuritize the issue. The Colombians still have an internal armed conflict and drug trafficking organizations operating within the country. Many officials in Washington have praised Plan Colombia as a success, applauded, and moved on to other important foreign policy issues. The future of the Colombian government's security looks quite bleak as the Colombians will now have to combat drug trafficking and organized crime and address the internal armed conflict without U.S. assistance. However, policy experts and politicians may quite possibly try to resecuritize Colombia in the near future if the situation worsens.

9

Back to the Future

The Unintended Consequences of the
Partial Successes of the War on Drugs

While President Álvaro Uribe proclaimed victory against the narco-terrorists, the reality is that Colombia still faces many challenges and
still has an internal armed conflict. This chapter briefly examines the
major security challenges that Colombia faces over the next decade by
reviewing the peace process and the various criminal organizations that
have emerged in Colombia and represent a real danger to peace and
stability within the country. In essence, this chapter serves as more
of a postscript because this book has not been about the peace process
or the internal armed conflict. The point, however, is that we cannot
discuss drug trafficking in Colombia and examine the results of Plan
Colombia without briefly analyzing the consequences of Plan Colombia
and where the peace process is today as the FARC and various actors
finance themselves through drug trafficking and other illegal activities.[1]

The FARC: A Menacing Threat

As discussed throughout the book, Uribe came to power and refused
to negotiate with the *Fuerzas Armadas Revolucionarias de Colombia*
(FARC), calling it a terrorist organization.[2] Uribe's ability to convince
the Bush administration that Colombia was a deserving ally of the
United States and fit into the Global War on Terrorism was brilliant.[3]
Uribe had successes against the FARC because he used U.S. assistance
to beat back this group and cause them to suffer major defeats.[4] The

reality, however, is that the FARC has neither been defeated nor eliminated.[5] In fact, the FARC is regaining power and continues to finance itself through drug trafficking.

Like Uribe, the Santos administration (2010–2014) launched attacks against the FARC and has killed top leaders such as Vince Julio Suárez among others. June S. Beittel explains the actions of the Santos administration, writing:

> Following the August 2010 inauguration of President Juan Manuel Santos, who had pledged in his electoral campaign to continue the aggressive security policies of his predecessor, the campaign against the FARC leadership (as well as mid-level commanders) continued. The Colombian government dealt a significant blow to the guerrilla group by killing the FARC's top military commander, Vince Julio Suárez (better known as "Mono Jojoy") in September 2010 in a raid on his compound in central Colombia. A year later, in November 2011, the Colombian military located and killed the FARC's top leader, Alfonso Cano, who had replaced founder Manuel Marulanda in 2008.[6]

Even though the Santos administration was successful against the FARC, interestingly, many people living in Colombia actually believe that the overall security situation within the country has worsened during this administration.[7]

Santos, however, differed from his predecessor who refused to negotiate with the FARC. On the contrary and much to the dismay of Uribe, President Santos is willing to negotiate with the FARC in order for Colombia to have peace since the conflict has carried on for decades and resulted in much suffering for Colombians.[8] Santos's logic is that this internal armed conflict has cost too much in terms of lives lost and people affected, and, therefore, he wants peace by whatever means necessary. In August 2012, Santos revealed that his government secretly had begun peace talks with the FARC in Cuba. Both parties in the negotiations agreed on and signed five major points that would be discussed. These points included both land and rural development because the concept of land reform has been a major cause of conflict in Colombia, as well as the reparations for victims of the conflict. The agreed upon points for negotiation also dealt with the FARC's political role and participation in the Colombian government as well as drug trafficking. And, finally, both parties in Cuba agreed to discuss how to end the armed conflict.[9]

President Santos emphasized that his administration was committed to peace, having learned from the past to avoid making the same mistakes during such talks.[10] The exploratory talks in Cuba represented the beginning, and the Santos administration continued the talks between the FARC representatives and the government in Norway in October 2012. The parties agreed that after Norway the talks would continue again in Cuba, and Santos has indicated that he wants a timeline for the negotiations so the talks do not carry on indefinitely. Santos has declared that he foresees the discussions coming to a close by November 2013 even though the FARC has refused to accept a deadline for the negotiations, yet the talks continue into 2014. Importantly, Santos is being strategic about the deadline because the next presidential elections will occur in May 2014.[11] If President Santos is successful in the negotiations, then history will remember him as a champion of peace, and he could win the Nobel Peace Prize for ending such a long conflict.[12]

The Consequences of the Demobilization of the AUC

While the FARC has entered into peace discussions, the situation in Colombia is complicated by the other groups involved in the internal armed conflict. One of Uribe's major success stories—at least according to him—has been the demobilization of the paramilitaries, particularly the *Autodefensas Unidas de Colombia* (AUC).[13] The reality is that AUC soldiers demobilized into various criminal bands, often referred to as *Bandas Criminales* (BACRIM), that participate in drug trafficking and other criminal activities. As a result, the demobilization could be described as a partial demobilization at best and a total farce at worst.[14] The Legal Framework for Peace declared that BACRIM members are criminals, which is an important distinction because they are not recognized as key actors in the decades-old internal armed struggle in Colombia. Members of the armed conflict had more incentive to negotiate under the aforementioned framework because they could receive lighter prison terms in return for their willingness to stop fighting, turn themselves in, and face their punishments.[15] Experts have argued that the exclusion of these criminal networks "from the Framework has been largely uncontested, mostly due to the fears that anything resembling negotiations with the BACRIM would echo the government's flawed demobilization of the BACRIM's predecessors, paramilitary groups of the . . . AUC."[16] In reality, the BACRIM play a crucial role in the internal armed conflict of Colombia and are responsible for grave human rights abuses throughout the country.[17] Ultimately, the demobilization on paper might appear to be a major success for the Uribe administration and Colombia, but the reality is that the demobilization was a farce and has not improved the security situation in Colombia.

The BACRIM represent a major security challenge to Colombia and the stability of the country because of their propensity for violence and ability to penetrate and corrupt many aspects of society. June S. Beittel argues, "The *Bacrim*, which are involved in many types of violent crime including drug trafficking, are considered by many observers and the Colombian government to be the biggest security threat to Colombia today. Some contend that these powerful groups, successors to the paramilitaries, are tolerated by corrupt officials, and prosecution of their crimes has proceeded slowly."[18] One of the major BACRIM groups is *Los Rastrojos*, which emerged from a drug trafficking organization in the Norte del Valle and constitutes a major security threat to the stability of Colombia. Drug trafficking provides the main source of income for this group, and it is heavily involved in the cocaine trade, exporting the product to Central America and Mexico. *Los Rastrojos* have developed strategic alliances with other major actors in Colombia such as the FARC, in order to help them have access to the coca base used to make cocaine.[19] In addition to drug trafficking, *Los Rastrojos* participate in various other criminal activities such as kidnapping and extortion.[20]

This group uses its power and influence to recruit various militia members who operate in both urban and rural areas throughout Colombia, which helps maintain control of its territory. In addition, this organization has used its power and influence to infiltrate the police as well as the Colombian army.

A Changed Battlefield

The previous discussions demonstrate that Colombia faces many challenges in the second decade of the twenty-first century. While Uribe proclaimed victory in the war on drugs and against the narco-guerrillas, such claims are premature because Colombia still wrestles with an internal armed conflict that threatens the security and well-being of many Colombians, particularly those living in rural regions. The reality is that the conflict in Colombia has morphed, or as Marc Chernick describes it, the battlefield has changed.[21] The actors are different, yet the activities and violence remains the same.

Conclusion

As a result of Plan Colombia, Colombia has witnessed partial successes as security levels increased under Uribe. While Uribe successfully

beat back the FARC, he by no means defeated them.[22] Despite costing $8 billion for 2000 to 2012, Plan Colombia failed to decrease drug
production and simply shifted coca cultivation to Peru and Bolivia.[23]
Colombia, however, continues to be a major player in drug trafficking.
Before claiming victory from the partial successes of Plan Colombia,
one needs to recognize that Colombia faces many security challenges
as various groups continue to traffic drugs and participate in other
criminal activities.[24]

The emergence of the groups that together are referred to as the
BACRIM represent a major security challenge for Colombia. These
groups participate in drug trafficking and use their power and influence to corrode the institutions and various actors in Colombia, such
as the police and military. These groups, along with an increasingly
more powerful FARC, demonstrate that Colombia has not escaped the
violence of the past, but rather continues to be plagued by violence
and organized crime. The power of the various internal armed actors
in Colombia is frightening. As the title of this chapter indicates, the
reality is that Colombia could return to the same levels of violence
and drug activity, which contradicts Uribe, who believes that Colombia has reached a critical time period and is not going to go back but
only forward toward a more secure and peaceful future. The reality,
however, appears to be the opposite because the internal situation
can always worsen.

Much of Colombia's future depends on the success of Santos and
the peace process.[25] Differing opinions exist about the prospects for
peace, but it is a daunting task at the very least. FARC members have
been waging this war against the Colombian government for decades,
and they will not be defeated so easily. The reintegration of former
combatants into society is not an easy task: they are professional
criminals and armed combatants, many of whom come from poor and
undeveloped regions of Colombia and lacked the same opportunities
for legal work as other Colombians. Consequently, the FARC is easily
able to recruit poor and vulnerable youth and adults and indoctrinate
them into its causes. Once a FARC member has been trained as a
drug trafficker and combatant, he has great difficulty in relinquishing
his arms and becoming a productive member of society.[26] Although
Colombia has a better chance than in the past of achieving peace,
major obstacles could thwart the progress.

What happens if the Santos administration cannot reach a peace
agreement with the FARC? The reality is that Santos is willing to
become a war president and continue to combat the FARC in order
to weaken the organization. What role will the United States play if
the situation in Colombia worsens?[27] Will Washington come to the
aid of Colombia and help the next president, whoever that may be,
combat the internal armed actors and drug trafficking? As previously

discussed, the Obama administration has sought to desecuritize Colombia as a major security issue. In fact, Obama did not even mention Plan Colombia in the 2011 budget proposal. The potential exists for the situation in Colombia to be resecuritized, but the Obama administration currently has many more pressing issues on its foreign policy agenda. Therefore, Colombia will most likely not be the recipient of billions of dollars in aid anytime soon, despite the fact that Colombia was the third largest recipient of U.S. aid in the past.[28]

In conclusion, President Santos faces many challenges not only with the peace process but with his reelection. After countrywide strikes, Santos's approval decreased to 21 percent in September 2013.[29] Santos is willing to become a wartime president if the peace negotiations fail.[30] Judging the success of the peace talks and assessing the internal dynamics within Colombia will be difficult in the short-run. The reality is that we will only be able to analyze the success or failures over the next decade or so. Colombia faces many challenges and any party claiming victory in the war on drugs or praising many of these achievements must acknowledge the reality and grave security challenges that Colombia faces in 2014 and for the foreseeable future.

Notes

Chapter 1. Introduction

1. Russell Crandall, *Driven by Drugs: U.S. Policy toward Colombia* (Boulder, CO: Rienner, 2002), 193; Russell Crandall, "Clinton, Bush and Plan Colombia," *Survival* 44, no. 1 (2002): 159; Russell Crandall, "Explicit Narcotization: U.S. Policy toward Colombia during the Samper Administration," *Latin American Politics and Society* 43, no. 3 (Fall 2001): 95–120.

2. Government Accountability Office, *Drug Reduction Goals Were Not Fully Met, But Security Has Improved; U.S. Agencies Need More Detailed Plans for Reducing Assistance* (Washington, DC: Government Accountability Office, 2008).

3. See an interview with Bruce Bagley on the war on drugs: Bruce Bagley, interview with Steve Paikin, *The Agenda*, TVO-TV, YouTube video, Feb. 23, 2010, http://www.youtube.com/watch?v=WwGZtFyaVyo.

4. Washington estimated that Plan Colombia would cost $7.5 billion. Of the $7.5 billion, the United States would provide $4 billion and the international community would contribute the remaining $3.5 billion. In terms of financing, Plan Colombia allocated 80 percent of the money toward "hard components," such as military spending, while only 20 percent of the money was allocated for "soft" programs, such as crop substitution and other development programs.

5. Crandall, *Driven by Drugs*, 193; Crandall, "Clinton, Bush and Plan Colombia," 159; Crandall, "Explicit Narcotization," 95–120; Eduardo Gamarra, *Entre La Droga y La Democraci* (La Paz, Bolivia: Ildis, 1994).

6. Crandall, "Explicit Narcotization," 95–120; Ivo H. Daalder, *America Unbound: The Bush Revolution in Foreign Policy* (Washington, DC: Brookings Institution, 2003), 246.

7. *Human Rights during the Juan Manuel Santos Administration's First Year in Office* (USOC; Washington, DC: Washington Office on Latin Affairs, 2011).

8. "Desecuritization" is the opposite of "securitization." In other words, how does an issue change from being a security threat to being perceived as less of a threat? Various scholars have called for the desecuritization of the war on drugs. See Ethan A. Nadelmann, "Thinking Seriously about Alternatives to Drug Prohibition," *Daedalus* 121, no. 31 (Summer 1992): 85. In addition to

being a framework or approach, security also is a methodology. Scholars can trace how an issue becomes securitized by analyzing authoritative speech acts. Analyzing the speech of epistemic communities, policymakers, and politicians enables one to follow how an issue becomes securitized. Actors can attempt to securitize a topic and give speeches that demonstrate that a certain issue is an imminent threat and must be securitized. The founders of the Copenhagen School distinguish between two types of actors: functional actors and securitizing actors. Although the Copenhagen School explains in great detail how an issue becomes securitized, the authors fail to discuss the concept of desecuritization in detail. For more in the Copenhagen School and securitization, see Barry Buzan, Ole Weaver, and Jaap de Wilde, *Security: A New Framework for Analysis* (Boulder, CO: Rienner, 1997). My book makes a contribution to the literature by discussing the role of desecuritization. This work examines how an issue can shift from being a major security issue to something that is less securitized. One logical explanation is to invoke the use of reverse engineering to desecuritize an issue. In other words, actors can work backward in order to change the perceptions of what was perceived as a major security threat.

9. Johan Galtung, "Diachronic Correlation, Process Analysis and Causal Analysis," *Quality and Quantity* 4, no. 1 (1970): 55–94.

10. David Marsh and Gerry Stoker, eds., *Theory and Methods in Political Science* (Basingstoke, UK: Palgrave Macmillan, 1997), 392; Gary King, Roberto O. Keohane, Sidney Verba, *Scientific Inference in Qualitative Research*, (Princeton, NJ: Princeton University Press), 245.

11. For more on constructivism, see Barry Buzan, Ole Weaver, and Jaap de Wilde, *Security: A New Framework for Analysis* (Boulder, CO: Rienner, 1997), 239; Alexander Wendt, "Anarchy Is What States Make of It: The Social Construction of Power Politics," *International Organization* 46, no. 2 (1992): 391.

12. I received approval to conduct these interviews by the Institutional Review Board of the University of Miami.

13. The "snowball technique" requires one to gather names from experts. Experts will continue to list the same people that you should interview.

14. Buzan, Weaver and de Wilde, *Security;* Wendt, "Anarchy," 391.

15. Laura Neack, *The New Foreign Policy: Power Seeking in a Globalized Era* (Lanham, MD: Rowman and Littlefield, 2008).

16. For more on realism, see Kenneth N. Waltz, *Theory of International Politics*, 2nd ed. (1979; Long Grove, IL: Waveland Press, 2010). For more on liberalism, see Michael Doyle, *Ways of War and Peace* (New York: Norton, 1997). For more on soft constructivism, see Wendt, *Social Theory of International Politics*, 199.

17. Crandall, *Driven by Drugs*, 193; Crandall, "Clinton, Bush and Plan Colombia," 159; Crandall, "Explicit Narcotization," 95–120.

18. Neack, *New Foreign Policy*; Andre Lecours, *New Institutionalism: Theory and Analysis* (Toronto, ON: University of Toronto Press, 2005), 380.

19. John J. Mearsheimer, *Tragedy of Great Power Politics* (New York: Norton, 2001), 8.

20. Ibid., 10.

21. Ibid. I argue this point based on Mearsheimer's case selection. It appears that he chooses cases that will justify or explain his theory.

22. "Robert Pape: The Strategic Logic of Suicide Terrorism," *Conversations with History*, YouTube video, Feb. 16, 2006, http://www.youtube.com/watch?v=mHXLdwuFi7Q (accessed Feb. 18, 2012).

23. Waltz, *Theory of International Politics*; Kenneth N. Waltz, *Man, the State and War* (New York: Columbia University Press, 1959); Christopher Layne, *The Peace of Illusions: American Grand Strategy from 1940 to Present* (Ithaca, NY: Cornell University Press, 2006), 290.

24. See p. 17 of Bruce M. Bagley and Juan G. Tokatlian, "Dope and Dogma: Explaining the Failure of U.S.–Latin American Drug Policies," in *The United States of Latin America in the 1990s: Beyond the Cold War*, eds. Jonathan Hartlyn, Lars Schoultzs, and Augusto Varas, 214–234 (Chapel Hill: University of North Carolina Press, 1992).

25. Bagley and Tokatlian, "Dope and Dogma." Robert O. Keohane and Joseph S. Nye argue that realists underestimate various other factors, such as linkages between states. Two forms of interdependence exist: complex and asymmetric. The relationship between Canada and the United States can be described as a complex interdependence. That these two countries will enter into war is extremely unlikely because they share many linkages. See Robert O. Keohane and Joseph S. Nye Jr., *Power and Interdependence: World Politics in Transition* (Boston: Little Brown, 1977). Liberalism, therefore, emphasizes the role and importance of cooperation. Colombia and the United States have many linkages, but Colombia depends on the United States for aid. In addition, the United States and Colombia started negotiating free trade agreements but the relationship between Colombia and the United States is not one of complex interdependence.

26. Keohane and Nye, *Power and Interdependence*, 315; Robert O. Keohane, ed., *Neorealism and Its Critics* (New York: Columbia University Press, 1987), 378.

27. Bagley and Tokatlian, "Dope and Dogma."

28. Robert O. Keohane, *After Hegemony: Cooperation and Discord in the World Political Economy* (1984; Princeton, NJ: Princeton University Press, 2005). For more on liberalism, see Michael Doyle, "Liberalism and World Politics," *American Political Science Review* 80, no. 4 (Dec. 1986): 1151–1169; David A. Baldwin, ed., *Neorealism and Neoliberalism: The Contemporary Debate* (New York: Columbia University Press, 1993).

29. Thanks to Bruce Bagley for pointing this out to me during a conversation in May 2013.

30. This book also invokes the use a constructivist framework the Copenhagen School developed. The Copenhagen School revolutionized security studies, challenging the fundamental principles of security for other theories. Buzan and his colleagues argue that security is a contested concept, and we must consider security for what and for whom. In order for something to become securitized, an existential threat must exist. Political actors, such as the president, must convince the citizens that the topic attempting be securitized is serious and a potential threat. What is needed is the designation of an existential threat

requiring emergency action or special measures and the acceptance of that designation by a significant audience. There will be instances in which the word "security" appears without this logic and other cases that operate according to that logic with only a metaphorical security reference. See Buzan, Weaver, and de Wilde, *Security*, 239; Wendt, "Anarchy," 391.

Chapter 2. The Colombian Puzzle in Historical Context

1. Peter H. Smith, *Drug Policy in the Americas* (Boulder, CO: Westview, 1992), 366; Juan Gabriel Tokatlian, *Drogas, dilemas y dogmas: Estados Unidos y la narcocriminalidad organizada en Colombia* (Santafé, Colombia: C.E.I, Universidad de los Andes/Tercer Mundo Editores, 1995).

2. Peter Lupsha, "Drug Trafficking: Mexico and Colombia in Comparative Perspective," *Journal of International Affairs* 35, no. 1 (1981): 95; Richard Craig, "Colombian Narcotics and U.S. Colombian Relations," *Journal of Interamerican Studies and World Affairs* 2, no. 3 (Aug. 1981): 243–70; Marco Palacios, *Between Legitimacy and Violence: A History of Colombia, 1875–2002* (Durham, NC: Duke University Press, 2006), 299.

3. Bruce Michael Bagley, *Drug Trafficking, Political Violence and U.S. Policy in Colombia in the 1990s* (Miami, FL: University of Miami, 2001), http://www.as.miami.edu/international-studies/pdf/Bagley%20Drugs%20and%20 violence%20final3.pdf, 1.

4. Ibid., 1; Government Accountability Office, *Drug Control: Narcotics Threat from Colombia Continue to Grow* (Washington, DC: GAO/NSAID, 1999), 4–5.

5. Peter Andreas, "Free Market Reform and Drug Market Prohibition: U.S. Policies at Cross Purposes in Latin America," *Third World Quarterly* 16, no. 1 (1995): 75–88; Bagley, *Drug Trafficking, Political Violence*, 1–31; Bruce Michael Bagley, "The New Hundred Years War? U.S. National Security and the War on Drugs in Latin America," *Journal of Interamerican Studies and World Affairs* 30, no. 1 (Spring 1988): 161–182.

6. Bagley, *Drug Trafficking, Political Violence*, 1–31, esp. 2; *Drug Control: Narcotics Threat*, 99–136.

7. Bagley, *Drug Trafficking, Political Violence*, 1–31.

8. Ibid.; Crandall, *Driven by Drugs*, 193; Crandall, "Clinton, Bush and Plan Colombia," 159.

9. Bagley, *Drug Trafficking*, 1–31; *Drug Control: Narcotics Threat*, 99–136. For more on Colombia and drug cultivation, see Francisco E. Thoumi, "Why the Illegal Psychoactive Drugs Industry Grew in Colombia," in *Drug Trafficking in the Americas,* ed. Bruce M. Bagley and William O. Walker III, 77–96 (Coral Gables, FL: North-South Center Press at the University of Miami, 1996), 77–87.

10. Bagley, *Drug Trafficking*, 1–31.

11. Bruce Bagley, *Drug Trafficking and Organized Crime in the Americas: Major Trends in the Twenty-First Century* (Washington, DC: Woodrow Wilson Center Press, 2012), 3; Patrick L. Clawson and Rensselaer W. Lee III, *The Andean Cocaine Industry* (New York: St Martin's Griffin, 1998).

12. Bagley, *Drug Trafficking, Political Violence*, 1–31, esp. 3; for more on Peru, see Edmundo Morales, "The Andean Cocaine Dilemma," in *Drug*

Trafficking in the Americas, ed. Bruce M. Bagley and William O. Walker III, 161–177 (Coral Gables, FL: North-South Center Press at the University of Miami, 1996); David Scott Palmer, "Peru, Drugs, and Shining Path," in *Drug Trafficking in the Americas*, ed. Bruce M. Bagley and William O. Walker III, 179–197 (Coral Gables, FL: North-South Center Press at the University of Miami, 1996); David Scott Palmer, "United States–Peru Relations in the 1990s: Asymmetry and its Consequences," in *Latin America and the Caribbean Contemporary Record: 1989–1990*, vol. 9, ed. Eduardo Gamarra and James Malloy (New York: Holmes and Meier, 1992).

13. For more on Bolivia and drug trafficking, see Eduardo A. Gamarra, "U.S.–Bolivia Counternarcotics Efforts during the Paz Zamora Administration: 1989–1992," in *Drug Trafficking in the Americas*, ed. Bruce M. Bagley and William O. Walker III, 217–256 (Coral Gables, FL: North-South Center Press at the University of Miami, 1996); see Eduardo Gamarra, "The United States, the 'War on Drugs' and Bolivian Democracy," in *Latin American and Caribbean Contemporary Record,* vol. 9 (New York: Holmes and Meier, 1992); Clare Hargreaves, *Snowfields: The War on Cocaine in the Andes* (New York: Holmes and Meier, 1992).

14. *Colombia's Strategy for Strengthening Democracy and Promoting Social Development, 2007–2013* (Washington, DC: National Planning Department, 2007); Crandall, *Driven by Drugs*, 193.

15. See Bagley, *Drug Trafficking, Political Violence*, 2; Bagley and Tokatlian, "Dope and Dogma"; Bruce Michael Bagley, "U.S. Foreign Policy and the War on Drugs: Analysis of a Policy Failure," in "Assessing the Americas' War on Drugs," special issue, *Journal of Interamerican Studies and World Affairs* 30, no. 2–3 (Summer-Autumn 1988): 189–212; Bagley, "New Hundred Years War?" 161–182.

16. Bagley, *Drug Trafficking, Political Violence*, 1–31, esp. 2.

17. Ibid., 2.

18. Steven Dudley, *Walking Ghosts: Murder and Guerrilla Politics in Colombia* (New York: Routledge, 2004); Crandall, *Driven By Drugs*.

19. Bagley, "New Hundred Years War?" 161–182; Bagley, *Drug Trafficking, Political Violence*, 1–31.

20. Crandall, *Driven by Drugs*, 193, 81–82.

21. Crandall, *Driven By Drugs*; Peter Andreas, "Dead-End Drug Wars," *Foreign Policy*, no. 85 (1991): 106–128; Bagley, "U.S. Foreign Policy," 189–212.

22. Crandall, *Driven by Drugs*, 193, 83. See Sewall H. Menzel, *Cocaine Quagmire: Implementing the U.S. Anti-Drug Policy in the North Andes Colombia* (Lanham, MD: University Press of America, 1997), 213.

23. Bagley, *Drug Trafficking and Organized Crime*, 7–11.

24. Bagley, *Drug Trafficking and Organized Crime,* 4; Andreas, "Dead-End Drug Wars," 106–128.

25. In an interview, Sanho Tree noted the massive size of Colombia as well as the geography of the country; Sanho Tree (Director, Drug Policy Project), interview by author, Aug. 15. 2012. The Institutional Review Board of the University of Miami approved this interview.

26. Beatriz Acevedo, Dave Bewley-Taylor, and Coletta Youngers, *Ten Years of Plan Colombia: An Analytical Assessment* (Oxford, UK: Beckley Foundation, 2008).

27. Crandall, *Driven by Drugs*, 193, 83; Juan Tokatlian, *The United States and Illegal Crops in Colombia* (Berkeley: Center for Latin American Studies, 29; Juan G. Tokatlian, *Globalización, Narcotráfico y Violencia: Siete Ensayos Sobre Colombia* (Buenos Aires, Argentina: Editorial Norma, 2000).

28. Chester A. Crocker, *Grasping the Nettle: Analyzing Cases of Intractable Conflict* (Washington, DC: U.S. Institute of Peace Press, 2005), 410; Cynthia J. Arnson, *In the Wake of War: Democratization and Internal Armed Conflict in Latin America* (Washington, DC: Woodrow Wilson Center Press, 2012), 430; Cynthia J. Arnson, *Comparative Peace Processes in Latin America* (Washington, DC: Woodrow Wilson Center Press, 1999), 493.

29. Colombia had a long civil war that lasted from 1899 to 1902. This conflict is referred to as the "War of a Thousand Days." DeShazo, Primiani, and McLean explain that the war "pitted the Liberal and Conservative parties against each other on a national scale, leaving deep political scars that were re-opened during 'La Violencia' from 1948 to the mid-1950s." See Peter DeShazo, Tanya Primiani, and Phillip McLean, *Back from the Brink: Evaluating Progress in Colombia, 1999 to 2007* (Washington, DC: Center for Strategic and International Studies, 2007), 3.

30. Arnson, *In the Wake of War*, 430; Crocker, *Grasping the Nettle*, 410; Marc W. Chernick, *Negotiations and Armed Conflict: The Colombian Peace Process, 1982–1986* (New York: Columbia University, Institute of Latin American and Iberian Studies, 1988), 48; Palacios, *Between Legitimacy and Violence*, 299; Richard Downes, *Land and Ambiguous Warfare: The Challenge of Colombia in the Twenty-First Century* (Carlisle, PA: Strategic Studies Institute, 1999).

31. Crandall, *Driven by Drugs*, 193, esp. 60; Craig, "Colombian Narcotics," 243–270.

32. Crandall, *Driven by Drugs*, 61.

33. Bagley, *Drug Trafficking, Political Violence,* 1–31.

34. Ibid., 10.

35. Ibid., 11; For more information on the conflict in Colombia, see also Holmes, Sheila Amin Gutiérrez de Piñeres, and Kevin M. Curtin, *Guns, Drugs and Development in Colombia* (Austin: University of Texas Press, 2008), 87.

36. DeShazo, Primiani, and McLean, *Back from the Brink*, 5.

37. Crandall, *Driven by Drugs*, 193, esp. 62.

38. Bagley, *Drug Trafficking, Political Violence,* 37; Crandal, *Driven By Drugs,* 64.

39. DeShazo, Primiani, and McLean, *Back from the Brink*, 6; Jennifer S. Holmes, Sheila Amin Gutiérrez de Piñeres, and Kevin M. Curtin, "Drugs, Violence, and Development in Colombia: A Department Level Analysis," *Latin American Politics and Society* 48, no. 3 (2006): 157–184, 48.

40. Bagley, *Drug Trafficking, Political Violence,* 1–31.

41. Crandall, *Driven by Drugs*, 193, esp. 85; Ibid; Crandall, "Clinton, Bush and Plan Colombia," 159; Gamarra, *Entre La Droga*.

42. Crandall, *Driven by Drugs*, 85; Max Manwaring, *Nonstate Actors in Colombia: Threat and Response* (Carlisle, PA: Strategic Studies Institute, 2002); See also R. L. Maullin, *Soldiers, Guerrillas, and Politics in Colombia* (Lexington, MA: Lexington Books, 1973).

43. Eduardo Pizarro and Pilar Gaitán, "Plan Colombia and the Andean Regional Initiative," in *Addicted to Failure: U.S. Security Policy in Latin*

America and the Andean Region, ed. Brian Loveman, 53–79 (Lanham, MD: Rowman and Littlefield, 2006), 70.

44. Ibid., 70.

45. Ibid., 70.

46. Crandall, *Driven by Drugs*, 193; Crandall, "Clinton, Bush and Plan Colombia," 159; Crandall, *Driven By Drugs,* 101–41.

47. Brian Loveman, ed., *Addicted to Failure: U.S. Security Policy in Latin America and the Andean Region* (Lanham, MD: Rowman and Littlefield, 2006), 367.

48. Marc W. Chernick, *Colombia's "War on Drugs" vs. the United States' "War on Drugs"* (Washington, DC: Washington Office on Latin America, 1991), 11.

49. Crandall, "Explicit Narcotization," 95–120.

50. Crandall, *Driven by Drugs*, 102. From 1990 to 1993, Mr. McLean held the position of Deputy Assistant Secretary of State for Inter-American Affairs.

51. For more on realism, see Mearsheimer, *Tragedy of Great Power Politics*; Waltz, *Theory of International Politics*.

52. For more on realism, see John Mearshiemer, *The Tragedy of Great Power Politics*. See also Bagley and Tokatlian, "Dope and Dogma"; Crandall, *Driven by Drugs*, 193; Crandall, "Clinton, Bush and Plan Colombia," 159; Crandall, "Explicit Narcotization," 95–120.

53. Crandall, *Driven by Drugs*, 193, esp. 109.

54. Crandall, *Driven by Drugs*, 109; "Standing Guard for Uncle Sam," *Economist*, 1995.

55. The certification process occurred in 1986 under the Reagan administration, a period that witnessed tremendous amount of drug use, often called the "crack epidemic." The U.S. Congress required the executive branch to certify countries in order to ensure that they are complying with U.S.-set standards; see *Passing Judgment: The U.S. Drug War Certification Process*, drugstrategies.com, http://www.drugstrategies.com/pdf/PassingJudgement98.pdf, 1; Bill Spencer, "Drug Certification," *Foreign Policy in Focus* 6, no. 5 (2001): 1.

56. *Passing Judgment*, 7.

57. Juan Gabriel Tokatlian, "Drogas: Cambio De Estrategia." *El Tiempo*, Jan. 29, 1995, http://www.eltiempo.com/archivo/documento/MAM 300319 (accessed June 21, 2012).

58. Crandall, *Driven by Drugs*, 114.

59. Juan G. Tokatlian, "Desertificación Silenciosa," *El Tiempo*, Jan. 11, 1998, 1; Adrián Bonilla, "U.S. Andean Policy, the Colombian Conflict, and Security in Ecuador," in *Addicted to Failure: U.S. Security Policy in Latin America and the Andean Region*, ed. Brian Loveman, 103–129 (Lanham, MD: Rowman and Littlefield, 2006), 129; Spencer, "Drug Certification," 1.

60. Unlike other countries in the region, Colombia not only has drug traffickers but also has a long history of an internal armed conflict.

Chapter 3. The Origins of Plan Colombia

1. Marc W. Chernick (Director, Center for Latin American Studies [CLAS], Georgetown University), interview by author, Aug. 9, 2012. The Institutional Review Board of the University of Miami approved this interview.

2. Thanks to an anonymous reviewer for pointing out that the United States did not embrace Pastrana because of the Republican majority in Congress, but instead supported Pastrana because he was not connected to drug traffickers.

3. Crandall, *Driven by Drugs*, 193, esp. 143.

4. Thanks to an anonymous review for highlighting this point.

5. DeShazo, Primiani, and McLean, *Back from the Brink*; Doug Stokes, *America's Other War: Terrorizing Colombia* (London: Zed Books, 2005), 147; Nini M. Serafino, *Colombia: Conditions and U.S. Policy Options* (Washington, DC: Congressional Research Service, 2001), 1–44.

6. DeShazo, Primiani, and McLean, *Back from the Brink*, 8.

7. "William J. Clinton: The President's News Conference with President Andres Pastrana of Colombia," 2000, http://www.presidency.ucsb.edu/ws/index.php?pid=55165 (accessed Sept. 20, 2012), 1.

8. Serafino, *Colombia: Conditions and U.S. Policy Options*, 1–44.

9. Acevedo, Bewley-Taylor, and Youngers, *Ten Years of Plan Colombia*, 1–13; Serafino, *Colombia: Conditions and U.S. Policy Options*, 1–44.

10. "William J. Clinton," 4.

11. Ibid., 5.

12. Ibid., 2.

13. Bagley, *Drug Trafficking, Political Violence*, 1–31, esp. 12.

14. Ingrid Vaicius and Adam Isacson, *The "War on Drugs" Meets the "War on Terror": The United States' Military Involvement in Colombia Climbs to the Next Level* (Washington, DC: Center for International Policy, 2003), 2; Jerry Seper, "Drug Czar Rips Clinton, Congress on Funding," *The Washington Times*, December 2.

15. DeShazo, Primiani, and McLean, *Back from the Brink*, 9.

16. Chernick interview, 2012.

17. Ibid.

18. Sandra Borda Interview. Thanks also to Arlene Ticker for her insight; Arlene B. Tickner (Professor, Los Andes University), interview by author, Aug. 6, 2012 (the Institutional Review Board of the University of Miami approved this interview); Arlene B. Tickner, "Colombia and the United States: From Counternarcotics to Counterterrorism," *Current History* 1026, no. 661 (2003): 72.

19. Tickner interview; Chernick interview.

20. Ibid.

21. Chernick interview.

22. Chernick interview.

23. Marijuana quotes: Bill Clinton, "I didn't inhale," https://www.youtube.com/watch?v=CeXGnSpjgNM (accessed 2013, published 2012).

24. Chernick interview.

25. Ibid.

26. Acevedo, Bewley-Taylor, and Youngers, *Ten Years of Plan Colombia*, 1–13; DeShazo, Primiani, and McLean, *Back from the Brink*, 3.

27. Crandall, *Driven by Drugs*, 193; Crandall, "Clinton, Bush and Plan Colombia," 159.

28. Crandall, *Driven by Drugs*, 149.

29. Ibid., 151.

30. Ibid., 152.

31. Ibid., 153; DeShazo, Primiani, and McLean, *Back from the Brink*; Vaicius and Isacson, *"War on Drugs."*

32. Chernick interview; Ingrid Vaicius, *El Plan Colombia: El Debate En Los Estados Unidos* (Washington, DC: Center for International Policy, 2000), 11; Gen. Barry M. McCaffrey, director, Office of National Drug Control Policy, "Remarks to the Atlantic Council of the United States" (Washington: November 28, 2000) <http://www.ciponline.org/colombia/112801.htm>.

33. Vaicius and Isacson, *"War on Drugs,"* 11; Gen. Barry R. McCaffrey, director, Office of National Drug Control Policy, "Remarks to the Atlantic Council of the United States" (Washington: November 28, 2000) <http://www.ciponline.org/colombia/112801.htm,

34. Crandall, *Driven By Drugs,* 150.

35. Waltz, *Theory of International Politics*; Mearsheimer, *Tragedy of Great Power Politics.* For information on classical realism, see E. H. Carr, *The Twenty Years' Crisis, 1919–1939: An Introduction to the Study of International Relations*, 2nd ed. (London: Macmillan, 1962); Hans Morgenthau, *Politics among Nations: The Struggle for Power and Pace*, 5th ed. (New York: Knopf, 1973).

36. Bonilla, "U.S. Andean Policy"; Juan Gabriel Tokatlian, "The End of the Monroe Doctrine," 2009, http://www.project syndicate.org/commentary/the-end-of-the-monroe-doctrine (accessed June 21, 2012).

37. Bonilla, "U.S. Andean Policy," 129; Loveman, *Addicted to Failure*, 367; Mearsheimer, *Tragedy of Great Power Politics*; Waltz, *Theory of International Politics*; Kenneth A. Schultz, *Democracy and Coercive Diplomacy* (West Nyack, NY: Cambridge University Press, 2001); Robert Art and Patrick M. Cronin, *The United States and Coercive Diplomacy* (Washington, DC: U.S. Institute of Peace Press, 2003), 442.

38. Joseph S. Nye, Jr., *Soft Power: The Means to Success in World Politics* (New York: Public Affairs, 2004), 191.

39. John J. Mearsheimer, "The False Promise of International Institutions," *International Security* 19, no. 3 (Winter 1994): 5–49. For more on realism, see Waltz, *Theory of International Politics*; Mearsheimer, *Tragedy of Great Power Politics.* Mearsheimer, however, argues that a state can only strive to be a regional hegemon due to the seas.

40. Waltz, *Theory of International Politics*; Waltz, *Man, the State and War*; Mearsheimer, *Tragedy of Great Power Politics.*

41. Waltz, *Theory of International Politics.* Realism, therefore, has it weaknesses. For more on U.S. trade with Colombia, see USTR, Trade Facts, "Free Trade with Colombia: Summary of the United States-Colombia Trade Promotion Agreement," June 2007.

42. M. Angeles Villarreal, *The U.S.-Colombia Free Trade Agreement: Background and Issues* (Washington, D.C.: Congressional Research Service, 2014; Bagley and Tokatlian, "Dope and Dogma"; Keohane and Nye, *Power and Interdependence*, 315; Keohane, *Neorealism and Its Critics*, 378.

43. Wendt, "Anarchy Is What States," 391.

44. Ethan Nadelmann, "Addicted to Failure," *Foreign Policy*, no. 137 (July–Aug. 2003): 94; Andreas, "Dead-End Drug Wars," 106–128; Andreas, "Free Market Reform," 75–88.

45. Ted Galen Carpenter, *Bad Neighbor Policy: Washington's Futile War on Drugs in Latin America* (New York, NY: Palgrave Macmillan, 2003).

156   Notes to Chapter 3

46. Connie Veillette, *Plan Colombia: A Progress Report* (Washington, DC: Congressional Research Service, 2005), 1.

47. This is fiscal year.

48. Connie Veillette, *Plan Colombia*, 1.

49. Connie Veillette, *Plan Colombia*; Gabriel Marcella, *Plan Colombia: The Strategic and Operational Imperatives* (Carlisle, PA: Strategic Studies Institute, U.S. Army War College, 2001), 29.

50. Adam Isacson, "Mission Creep: The U.S. Military's Counter-Drug Role in the Americas," in *Drug Trafficking, Organized Crime, and Violence in the Americas Today*, ed. Bruce M. Bagley and Jonathan D. Rosen (Gainsville: University Press of Florida, forthcoming, 2015), 1.

51. M. P. Moloeznik, "The Military Dimension of the War on Drugs in Mexico and Colombia," *Crime, Law, and Social Change* 40, no. 1 (2003): 107–112.

52. Adam Isacson, "Mission Creep: The U.S. Military's Counter-Drug Role in the Americas," 2.

53. Juan G. Tokatlian, "A New Doctrine of Security? U.S. Military Deployment in South America," *NACLA Report on the Americas* 41, no. 5 (2008): 6.

54. Juan Gabriel Tokatlian, "Militarizing the Andes," http://www.project-syndicate.org/commentary/militarizing-the-andes (accessed June 21, 2012).

55. Isacson, "The U.S. Military," 15–60; Isacson, "Mission Creep"; Holmes, de Piñeres, and Curtin, "Drugs, Violence, and Development in Colombia," 157–184.

56. In an interview approved by the Institutional Review Board of the University of Miami, Arlene Tickner of Los Andes University argued that the percentage spent on the military or hard components decreased over time. For more on the phases of Plan Colombia, see John Bailey, *Plan Colombia and the Mérida Initiative: Policy Twins or Distant Cousins?* (Washington, DC: N.p., 2009).

57. 500 military personnel and 300 personnel; DeShazo, Primiani, and McLean, *Back from the Brink*. Congress later increased in the number in 2004. Bailey, *Plan Colombia and the Mérida Initiative*, 10; Veillette, *Plan Colombia: A Progress Report*, 1–11.

58. The year 2007 saw the shift to manual eradication. Adam Isacson, *Don't Call Plan Colombia a Model: On Plan Colombia Tenth Anniversary, Claims of "Success" Don't Stand Up to Scrutiny* (Washington, DC: Washington Office on Latin Affairs, 2010); Adam Isacson, *Plan Colombia—Six Years Later: Report of a CIP Staff Visit to Putumayo and Medellin, Colombia* (Washington, DC: International Policy Report, 2006); Isacson, "The U.S. Military," 1–15; Adam Isacson, "Optimism, Pessimism, and Terrorism: The United States and Colombia in 2003," *Center for International Policy* X, no. 2 (2004): 245–255.

59. David Buffin and Topsy Jewell, *Health and Environmental Impacts of Glyphosate*, ed. Pete Riley, Mary Taylor, Emily Diamand, and Helen Barron (London: Pesticide Action Network, 2001), 7. See Alejandro Gaviria Uribe and Daniel Mejía Londoño, eds., *Politicas Antidroga En Colombia Éxitos, Fracasos y Extravíos* (Bogotá, Colombia: Universidad de los Andes, 2011), 445; Janelle Conaway, "Study of Aerial Spraying," *Organization of American States, Sales and Promotion Division* 56, no. 3 (2004): 57.

60. Buffin and Jewell, *Health and Environmental Impacts of Glyphosate*, 9–10.

61. María Clemencia Ramírez Lemus, Kimberly Stanton, and John Walsh, "Colombia: A Vicious Circle of Drugs and War," in *Drugs and Democracy in Latin America: The Impact of U.S. Policy*, ed. Coletta A. Youngers and Eileen Rosin, 61–98 (Boulder, CO: Rienner, 2005); Buffin and Jewell, *Health and Environmental Impacts*, 1–38; Conaway, "Study of Aerial Spraying," 57; "Transnational Institute: Plan Colombia's Aerial Spraying. A Failure Foretold," 2003, http://www.tni.org/archives/drugscolombia docs_plan-e (accessed Aug. 22, 2012); americas.org/en/project/plancolombia (accessed Aug. 22, 2012); Lynne Peeples, "Dangers Posed by Pesticides during Pregnancy," *Huffington Post*, Apr. 5, 2012, http://www.huffingtonpost.com/2012/04/05/pesticides-pregnancy-babies health_n_1406468.html (accessed Aug. 27, 2012).

62. "Drugs and Democracy, Ecuador: 'Collateral Damage' from Aerial Spraying on the Northern Border," Dec. 1, 2003, http://www.tni.org/article/Ecuador-collateral-damage-aerial-spraying-northern-border (accessed Aug. 28, 2012); "Letter to Colombian President Uribe Requesting No Aerial Spraying in National Parks," americas.org/en/lettertoUribe (accessed Aug. 28, 2012); "People's Daily Online—Colombian President Defends Aerial Spraying of Coca Crops," Dec. 25, 2006, http://english.peopledaily.com.cn/200612/25/eng20061225_335656. html (accessed Aug. 28, 2012).

63. Ramírez Lemus, Stanton, and Walsh, "Colombia: A Vicious Circle," 118.

64. Acevedo, Bewley-Taylor, and Youngers, *Ten Years of Plan Colombia*, 1–13.

65. Ramírez Lemus, Stanton, and Walsh, "Colombia: A Vicious Circle," 119–121.

66. Isacson, "Mission Creep," 27; Isacson, "The U.S. Military," 1–15; Holmes, de Piñeres, and Curtin, "Drugs, Violence, and Development in Colombia," 157–184.

67. Ramírez Lemus, Stanton, and Walsh, "Colombia: A Vicious Circle," 61–98, 121; "Plan Colombia: The Harmful Impacts"; "Transnational Institute."

68. Daniel Mejía (Associate Professor, Los Andes University), interviewed by author in Colombia, Aug. 6, 2012. This interview was approved by the Institutional Review Board of the University of Miami.

69. Ramírez Lemus, Stanton, and Walsh, "Colombia: A Vicious Circle," 61–98, 117; Gaviria, *Politicas Antidroga En Colombia*, 445.

70. Francisco E. Thoumi, *The Size of the Illegal Drugs Industry in Colombia* (Coral Gables, FL: North-South Center Press, University of Miami, 1996), 20.

71. Francisco E. Thoumi, *Illegal Drugs, Economy, and Society in the Andes* (Washington, DC: Woodrow Wilson Center Press, 2003), 416, esp. 31. See also Daniel Vidart, *Coca, Cocales y Coqueros En América Latina* (Bogotá, Colombia: Editorial Nueva América, 1991); Gaviria, *Politicas Antidroga En Colombia*, 445; Gamarra, *Entre La Droga*.

72. Thoumi, *Illegal Drugs, Economy*, 416, 31. Thoumi, *Size of the Illegal Drugs Industry*, 20; Tokatlian, *Globalización, Narcotráfico y Violencia*; Tokatlian, *The United States and Illegal Crops*, 29.

73. Tree interview.

74. Marten Brienen (former Director, Academic Programs in Latin American Studies, University of Miami), interview by author, Aug. 1, 2012. Brienen is currently at Oklahoma State University. This interview was approved by the Institutional Review Board of the University of Miami.

75. Carpenter, *Bad Neighbor Policy*.

76. Thoumi, *Size of the Illegal Drugs Industry*, 20; Tokatlian, *Globalización, Narcotráfico y Violencia*; Tokatlian, *The United States and Illegal Crops*, 29.

77. Mejía, interview; Daniel Mejía and Pascual Restrepo, "The War on Illegal Drugs in Producer and Consumer Countries: A Simple Analytical Framework," Social Science Research Network, Feb. 1, 2001, http://papers.ssrn.com/sol3/papers.cfm?abstract_id=1764005.

78. Brienen interview.

79. Daniel Mejía argued that these statistics are wrong. He stated that coca growers earn much more money when they develop the past or base. Mejía interview; Carpenter, *Bad Neighbor Policy*, 107.

80. Carpenter, *Bad Neighbor Policy*, 109.

81. Brienen, interview. For more on this topic, see Francisco E. Thoumi, *Political Economy and Illegal Drugs in Colombia* (Boulder, CO: Rienner, 1995); Thoumi, *Illegal Drugs, Economy*.

82. Brienen, interview.

83. Carpenter, *Bad Neighbor Policy*, 108. Thoumi, *Size of the Illegal Drugs Industry*, 20; Vidart, *Coca, Cocales y Coqueros*.

84. Veillette, *Plan Colombia: A Progress Report*.

85. Bagley, "U.S. Foreign Policy," 189–212; Bagley, *Drug Trafficking, Political Violence*, 1–31; Smith, *Drug Policy in the Americas*, 366.

86. Carpenter, *Bad Neighbor*; Isacson, "The U.S. Military," 1–15.

87. Bagley, "U.S. Foreign Policy," 189–212; Bagley, "New Hundred Years War?" 161–182; Nadelmann, "Addicted to Failure," 94.

88. For more on constructivism, see Wendt, "Anarchy Is What States," 391.

89. Crandall, "Deep into the Anti-Drug Mire"; Crandall, "Clinton, Bush and Plan Colombia," 159; Crandall, *Driven by Drugs*, 193.

90. Neack, *New Foreign Policy*.

91. For more on realism, see Waltz, *Theory of International Politics*.

92. Bagley and Tokatlian, "Dope and Dogma"; Keohane, *Neorealism and Its Critics*, 378.

93. Waltz, *Theory of International Politics*; Mearsheimer, *Tragedy of Great Power Politics*; Mearsheimer, "False Promise of International Institutions," 5–49; Layne, *The Peace of Illusions*, 290; Robert Jervis, "Cooperation under the Security Dilemma," *World Politics* 30, no. 2 (1978): 167–214.

94. Crandall, *Driven By Drugs,* 101–32.

Chapter 4. Uribe and the Fusion of the War on Drugs with the War on Terrorism

1. Veillette, *Plan Colombia: A Progress Report*, 1–11, esp. 2; "Under Uribe, the Dark Side of Colombia-New York," *NY Latino Journal*, Apr. 18, 2007, http://nylatinojournal.com/home/eagles-in-fall,-lions-in-spring/analysis/under-uribe,-

the-dark-side-of-colombia.html (accessed Aug. 28, 2012); Robert Long and Jose O'Brien, "Colombia's War on Terror," May 24, 2009, http://hpronline.org/world/colombia's-war-on-terror/ (accessed Aug. 28, 2012).

2. An anonymous reviewer argued that Uribe did not reverse the formula. This individual declared that legalization to combat the "terrorists" in Colombia started as early as February 2002, and Uribe came to office in May 2002. The reviewer stated that this demonstrates that the shift toward the war on drugs had already begun prior to Uribe. I disagree and believe that Uribe was crucial in reorienting Plan Colombia. I also disagree that the events are chronologically wrong. In a September 2013 email correspondence with Bruce Bagley, Bagley argues that the original version of Plan Colombia passed in July 2002 prohibited U.S. assistance for combatting the guerrillas. Bagley argues that the Colombians were extremely unhappy with this policy. Bagley states that both Bush and Uribe sought to modify the original conditions the U.S. Congress imposed. Bagley highlights that the logic was that the FARC members were not only drug traffickers but also terrorists.

3. Crandall, "Explicit Narcotization," 95–120; Barry Buzan, "Will the 'Global War on Terrorism' Be the New Cold War?" *International Affairs* 82, no. 6 (Nov. 2006): 1101–1118; Crandall, *Driven by Drugs*, 193; Tokatlian, *Globalización, Narcotráfico y Violencia.*

4. "Transcript of President Bush's Address," CNN News, Sept. 20, 2001, http://articles.cnn.com/2001–09–20/us/gen.bush.transcript_1_joint-session-national-anthem-citizens?_s=PM:US (accessed Aug. 28, 2012).

5. This defies realist logic. Bush was a neoconservative realist, which combines realism with Wilsonianism. Mohammed Nuruzzaman, "Beyond Realist Theories: 'Neo-conservative Realism' and The American Invasion of Iraq" *International Studies Perspective* no. 7. (2006:) 239–53.
Daalder, *America Unbound,* 246.

6. Ibid.

7. Buzan, "Will the 'Global War on Terrorism,'" 1101–1118; Buzan, Weaver, and de Wilde, *Security,* 239; for more on the threat of terrorism, see Jennifer S. Holmes, *Terrorism and Democratic Stability* (Manchester, UK: Manchester University Press, 2001).

8. For more on constructivism, see: Wendt, "Anarchy Is What States," 391; Wendt, *Social Theory of International Politics,* 429.

9. Washington has failed to learn from lessons of the past and is surprised that a poor, underdeveloped region begins to harbor terrorists. Chalmers Johnson developed the term "blowback" to describe such a situation. A larger point also can be learned about the contradictions in IR when examining history. During the cold war, the United States supported the Mujahedeen and Osama Bin Laden and helped arm them in order to defeat the Soviets in Afghanistan. The United States willingly supported this group because it viewed the former Soviet Union as the major threat and enemy of the United States. This teaches us that today's friend is tomorrow's enemy. See Chalmers A. Johnson, *Blowback: The Cost and Consequences of American Empire* (New York: Holt, 2004), 268.

10. David A. Baldwin, "The Concept of Security," *Review of International Studies* 23, no. 1 (1997): 5–26.

11. Buzan, Weaver, and de Wilde, *Security,* 239

12. "President Bush's Speech to Congress Declaring War on Terror," Sept. 20, 2001, http://middleeast.about.com/od/usmideastpolicy/a/bush-war-on-terror-speech_2.htm (accessed July 21, 2012), 1; George W. Bush and John W. Dietrich, *The George W. Bush Foreign Policy Reader: Presidential Speeches and Commentary* (Armonk, NY: M. E. Sharpe, 2005), 320.

13. "President Bush's Speech to Congress," esp. 3.

14. Pizarro and Gaitán, "Plan Colombia and the Andean Regional Initiative," 80.

15. Vaicius and Isacson, *"War on Drugs,"* 11. Isacson, "Extending the War on Terrorism to Colombia"; Rui Ferreira, "Las FARC se asemejan a Bin Laden," *El Nuevo Herald*, September 29, 2001

16. Vaicius and Isacson, 11; Pizarro and Gaitán, "Plan Colombia and the Andean Regional Initiative"; Isacson, "Extending the War on Terrorism to Colombia"; Anthony Boadle, "Pastrana Seeks U.S. Aid to Fight 'Narco-Terrorism,'" Reuters (Washington: November 9, 2001).

17. Vaicius and Isacson, 11; Ambassador Francis X. Taylor, State Department coordinator for counterterrorism, Press conference at the OAS (Washington: October 15, 2001) <http://www.oas.org/OASpage/eng/videos/pressconference10_15_01.asf>.69.

18. Ramírez Lemus, Stanton, and Walsh, "Colombia: A Vicious Circle," 61–98, esp. 111.

19. Álvaro Uribe, Inaugural Speech by Alvaro Uribe, Council on Foreign Relations, Aug. 7, 2002. http://www.cfr.org/americas/inaugural-speech-alvaro-uribe/p4738.

20. Ibid.; Ramírez Lemus, Stanton, and Walsh, 112.

21. Ramírez Lemus, Stanton, and Walsh, 112.

22. Waltz, *Theory of International Politics*; Mearsheimer, *Tragedy of Great Power Politics*; Layne, *The Peace of Illusions*, 290.

23. CNN, "Professor Bruce Bagley on the Crisis in Colombia."

24. Buzan, Weaver, and de Wilde, *Security*, 239.

25. Crandall, *Driven by Drugs*, 193, 91; Crandall, "Clinton, Bush and Plan Colombia," 159.

26. Daalder, *America Unbound*, 246.

27. Ibid.

28. Isacson, "Optimism, Pessimism, and Terrorism," 245–255, 252; Isacson, "Mission Creep"; Isacson, "The U.S. Military," 1–15.

29. Pizarro and Gaitán, "Plan Colombia and the Andean Regional Initiative," 69, 80; Vaicius and Isacson, *"War on Drugs."*

30. Pizarro and Gaitán, "Plan Colombia and the Andean Regional Initiative," 69, 80.

31. Ibid., 69.

32. Crandall, "Explicit Narcotization," 95–120; Crandall, "Clinton, Bush and Plan Colombia," 159; Daalder, *America Unbound*, 246; Juan G. Tokatlian, "Estados Unios y Latinoamérica, Más Distanciados," *El Tiempo*, Sept. 10, 2002.

33. Chernick interview.

34. Ibid.

35. Alexander Moens, *The Foreign Policy of George W. Bush: Values, Strategy, and Loyalty* (Burlington, VT: Ashgate, 2004), 227; Daalder, *America Unbound*, 246.

36. Juan A. Alsace, *All Bush's Horses and All Bush's Men: How Far Should the U.S. Go to Help Put Colombia Back Together Again?* (Washington, DC: National Defense University, National War College, 2003), 1.

37. Joyce P. Kaufman, *A Concise History of U.S. Foreign Policy* (Lanham, MD: Rowman and Littlefield, 2010), 223.

38. Ibid; the notion of maintaining its position as the hegemon is a realist concept. See Waltz, *Theory of International Politics,* for more on defense realism. For more on offensive realism, see Mearsheimer's *Tragedy of Great Power Politics.*

39. Pizarro and Gaitán, "Plan Colombia and the Andean Regional Initiative," 80, esp. 55.

40. Alsace, *All Bush's Horses*, 9; Vaicius, *El Plan Colombia*; James Traub, "Think Again: Failed States," *Foreign Policy*, June 20, 2011, http://www.foreignpolicy.com/articles/2011/06/20/think_again_failed_states?page=full (accessed Aug. 29, 2012).

41. Alsace, *All Bush's Horses*, 9.

42. For the link to such statements, see http://www.colombia.ru/eng/index2.php?option=com_content&do_pdf=1&id=110, 1.

43. Ibid.

44. "All Bush's Horses," 9; Angela Rabusa and Peter Chalk, *Colombian Labyrinth: The Synergy of Drugs and Insurgency and Its Implications for Regional Security* (Santa Monica, CA: RAND, 2001); see *CIA* [Central Intelligence Agency] *Guide to the Analysis of Insurgency* (Washington, DC: Government Printing Office, 1997).

45. Alsace, *All Bush's Horses,* 8.

46. Ibid.

47. Alsace, *All Bush's Horses.*

48. Ibid., 7.

49. Joseph Ganitsky (Director, UM Center for International Business Education and Research), interview by author, Aug. 1, 2012. This interview was approved by the Institutional Review Board of the University of Miami.

50. Ibid.

51. Michael LaRosa, *Colombia: A Concise Contemporary History* (Lanham, MD: Rowman and Littlefield, 2012), 265; Steven L. Taylor, *Voting Amid Violence: Electoral Democracy in Colombia* (Boston, MA: Northeastern University Press, 2009), 240.

52. Sibylla Brodzinksy, "Uribe, a Bush Ally, Treads on Shaky Ground," *Time*, Feb. 20, 2007, http://content.time.com/time/world/article/0,8599,1592017,00.html (accessed June 21, 2012).

53. Uribe, Inaugural Speech, 6.

54. Bagley, *Drug Trafficking, Political Violence*, 1–31; Bagley, *Drug Trafficking and Organized Crime.*

55. Carpenter, *Bad Neighbor Policy*, 65; Karen DeYoung, "U.S. May End Curbs on U.S. Aid to Colombia," *Washington Post*, Mar. 15, 2002, A01.

56. Carpenter, *Bad Neighbor Policy*, 66. Karen DeYoung, "House Rejects Bush Request on Colombia," *Washington Post,* July 25, 2001, A17.

57. Ibid., 65.

58. Ibid., 86; Max G. Manwaring, *Implementing Plan Colombia: Strategic and Operational Imperatives for the U.S. Military* (Washington, DC: Strategic Studies Institute, U.S. Army War College, 2000).

59. Carpenter, *Bad Neighbor Policy*, 87; Manwaring, *Implementing Plan Colombia*, 1–4.

60. *Drug Reduction Goals Were Not Fully Met*, 12.

61. Holmes, de Piñeres, and Curtin, "Drugs, Violence, and Development in Colombia," 157–184; DeShazo, Primiani, and McLean, *Back from the Brink*; Loveman, *Addicted to Failure*, 367, ch. 2.

62. *Drug Reduction Goals Were Not Fully Met*, 115, esp. 12.

63. *Report of the High Commissioner for Human Rights on the Situation of Human Rights in Colombia* (New York: U.N. Economic and Social Council, 2005), 10.

64. *Drug Reduction Goals Were Not Fully Met*, 14.

65. Ibid.; Holmes, de Piñeres, and Curtin, "Drugs, Violence, and Development in Colombia," 157–184; DeShazo, Primiani, and McLean, *Back from the Brink*.

66. Giugale M. Marcelo, Olivier Lafourcade, and Connie Luff, eds., *Colombia: The Economic Foundation of Peace* (Washington, DC: World Bank, 2003), 994; Adam Isacson, "Plan Colombia and Beyond," blog entry, Center for International Policy, 2009, http://www.cipcol.org/?m=200908 (accessed Sept. 20, 2012); DeShazo, Primiani, and McLean, *Back from the Brink*.

67. This is the fiscal year. U.N. High Commissioner for Refugees, "Colombia," http://www.unhcr.org/pages/49e492ad6.html (accessed Aug. 28, 2012); DeShazo, Primiani, and McLean, *Back from the Brink*.

68. *Drug Reduction Goals Were Not Fully Met*, 115, 33; Holmes, de Piñeres, and Curtin, "Drugs, Violence, and Development in Colombia," 157–184; DeShazo, Primiani, and McLean, *Back from the Brink*; Crandall, *Driven by Drugs*, 193; Tokatlian, "A New Doctrine of Security?" 6.

69. *Drug Reduction Goals Were Not Fully Met*, 115, 34; DeShazo, Primiani, and McLean, *Back from the Brink*; Holmes, de Piñeres, and Curtin, "Drugs, Violence, and Development in Colombia," 157–184; Isacson, "Mission Creep."

70. *Drug Reduction Goals Were Not Fully Met*, 115, esp. 27.

71. Ibid., esp. 29.

72. Ibid., 32.

73. *Drug Reduction Goals Were Not Fully Met*, 115, esp. 32; DeShazo, Primiani, and McLean, *Back from the Brink*.

74. *Drug Reduction Goals Were Not Fully Met*, 35.

75. Ibid., 37.

76. Ibid., 38.

77. "IV. A Comprehensive Approach, 7. Reducing the Supply of Illegal Drugs," Office of National Drug Control, 1999, https://www.ncjrs.gov/ondcppubs/publications/policy/99ndcs/iv g.html (accessed Aug. 22, 2012);Gaviria, *Politicas Antidroga En Colombia*, 445; Carpenter, *Bad Neighbor Policy;* "Interdiction,"

Embassy of the United States, http://bogota.usembassy.gov/nas interdiction. html (accessed Aug. 28, 2012); Matt Phillips, "*USS Nicholas* Supports Drug Interdiction," U.S. Navy, May 9, 2012, http://www.navy.mil/submit/display. asp?story_id=67063 (accessed Aug. 28, 2012).

78. Carpenter, *Bad Neighbor Policy*, 93; "Drug Interdiction," June 25, 2012, U.S. Coast Guard, http://www.uscg.mil/hq/cg5/cg531/drug_interdiction. asp (accessed Aug. 22, 2012);

79. See Bruce Bagley, "Seminario De Seguridad" (El Colegio de La Frontera Norte), July 8, 2012, YouTube, http://www.youtube.com/watch?v=sMeqNJzWXCo.

80. Thanks to an anonymous review for pointing this out. For more information, see the National Drug Intelligence Center, "National Drug Threat Assessment" (Washington, DC: U.S. Department of Justice, 2011), http://www. justice.gov/archive/ndic/pubs38/38661/cocaine.htm.

81. Carpenter, *Bad Neighbor Policy*, 95; Gamarra, *Entre La Droga*; Brienen interview; Thoumi, *Illegal Drugs, Economy*, 416; Thoumi, *Size of the Illegal Drugs Industry*, 20.

82. *Drug Reduction Goals Were Not Fully Met*, 48.

83. Ibid., 49.

84. Ibid., 50.

85. Connie Veillette, *Andean Counterdrug Initiative (ACID) and Related Funding Programs: FY2005 Assistance* (Washington, DC: Congressional Research Service, 2004), 10; Daniel W. Christman, John G. Heimann, and Julia E. Sweig, *Andes 2020: A New Strategy for the Challenges of Colombia and the Region* (New York: Council on Foreign Relations Center for Preventive Action, 2004).

86. Isacson, "Optimism, Pessimism, and Terrorism," 245–255, 247.

87. *Drug Reduction Goals Were Not Fully Met*, 115, 25; Veillette, *Plan Colombia: A Progress Report*, 1–11; Christman, Heimann, and Sweig, *Andes 2020*.

88. *Drug Reduction Goals Were Not Fully Met*, 25.

89. Laura Zelenko and Matthew Bristow, "Colombia Uribe Says Venezuela is Paradise for Terrorist," *Bloomberg News*, Apr. 26, 2012, http://www.bloomberg. com/news/2012–04–26/colombia-uribe-says-venezuela-is-paradise-for-terrorist. html (accessed Aug. 22, 2012); Toby Muse, "Colombia: Chavez Funding FARC Rebels," *The Washington Post*, March 24, 2008, http://www.washingtonpost. com/wp-dyn/content/article/2008/03/03/AR2008030300355_pf.html.

90. "Venezuela Expels Colombian Ambassador," *El Universal*, Mar. 3, 2008, http://www.eluniversal.com/2008/03/03/en_colcd_art_venezuela-expels-col_03A1405123.shtml (accessed Aug. 22, 2012).

91. Bagley, *Drug Trafficking, Political Violence*, 1–31; Bagley, *Drug Trafficking and Organized Crime;* Christman, Heimann, and Sweig, *Andes 2020*.

92. David Mares (Professor of Political Science, University California, San Diego), Interview by author, Aug. 24, 2012; David R. Mares, *Drug Wars and Coffeehouses: The Political Economy of the International Drug Trade* (Washington, DC: Congressional Quarterly Press), 188.

93. Dr. Calvani notes that such opinions are his own and he is not speaking on behalf of the U.N. Office on Drugs and Crime. This interview was approved by the Institutional Review Board of the University of Miami.

94. *Drug Reduction Goals Were Not Fully Met*, 25.

95. Isacson, "Optimism, Pessimism, and Terrorism," 245–255, esp. 251–252.

96. *Drug Reduction Goals Were Not Fully Met*, 26.

97. Bagley, *Drug Trafficking and Organized Crime*, 17; "Conozca Cómo Las Bandas Criminales Se 'Reparten' Zonas De Colombia," *El País*, Feb. 16, 2012, http://www.elpais.com.co/elpais/judicial/noticias/exclusivo-conozca-como-bandas-criminales-reparten-zonas-del-pais (accessed Aug. 22, 2012); "En Colombia Hay 10 Bandas Criminales Dedicadas Al Narcotráfico," Caracol.com. co, May 20, 2009, http://www.caracol.com.co/noticias/judicial/en-colombia-hay-10–bandas-criminales-dedicadas-al-narcotrafico-segun-las-autoridades/20090520/ nota/815259.aspx (accessed Aug. 22, 2012); Elvira Maria Restrepo and Bruce Bagley, eds., *La Desmovilizacion De Los Paramilitaries En Colombia: Entre La Esperanza y El Escepticismo* (Bogotá, Colombia: Uniandes, 2011).

98. Bagley, *Drug Trafficking and Organized Crime*, 17; "Nuevas Bandas Criminales Amenazan Seguridad En Colombia: Naranjo," *Semana*, Jan. 25, 2011, http://www.semana.com/nacion/nuevas-bandas-criminales-amenazan-seguridad-colombia-naranjo/150722–3.aspx (accessed Aug. 22, 2012); "Conozca Cómo Las Bandas Criminales"; Isacson, *Plan Colombia—Six Years Later*, 1–19; Restrepo and Bagley, *La Desmovilizacion De Los Paramilitaries*.

99. "Nuevas Bandas Criminales Amenazan."

100. The summer of 2010.

101. "World Report 2011: Colombia, Human Rights Watch," Human Rights Watch, 2011, http://www.hrw.org/world-report-2011/world-report-2011–colombia (accessed Aug. 29, 2012).

102. Veillette, *Plan Colombia: A Progress Report*, 1–11, 8.

103. Chernick interview.

104. Ibid.

105. *Drug Reduction Goals Were Not Fully Met*, 115, 27.

106. Noam Chomsky, *Failed States: The Abuse of Power and the Assault on Democracy* (New York: Metropolitan Books, 2006), 311; Alsace, *All Bush's Horses*; Isacson, *Plan Colombia—Six Years Later*, 1–19.

107. DeShazo, Primiani, and McLean, *Back from the Brink*; Holmes, de Piñeres, and Curtin, "Drugs, Violence, and Development in Colombia," 157–184; Holmes, de Piñeres, and Curtin, "Drugs, Violence, and Development in Colombia," 157–184.

108. Veillette, *Plan Colombia: A Progress Report*, 1–11, 12.

109. Ibid.

110. "Uribe: Yo no Me Reuní Con Paramilitares," *Semana*, 2008, http://www.semana.com/on line/uribe-no-reuni-paramilitares/111223–3.aspx (accessed June 21, 2012); "Cousin of Colombian President Arrested in Death Squad Probe," *Washington Post*, Apr. 22, 2008, http://www.washingtonpost.com/wp dyn/content/article/2008/04/22/AR2008042201144.html?hpid=sec world (accessed June 21, 2012); U.N. High Commissioner for Refugees, *Human Rights Watch World Report 1998—Colombia*, Jan. 1, 1998, http://www.unhcr.org/refworld/ country,,HRW,,COL,,3ae6a8c417,0.html (accessed June 21, 2012); BBC News, "Uribe Defends Security Policies," Nov. 18, 2004, http://news.bbc.co.uk/2/hi/ americas/4021213.stm (accessed June 21, 2012); Brodzinksy, "Uribe, a Bush Ally"; Ashley Hamer, "Fight against Drug Trafficking in Colombia Is Failing:

Experts," *Colombia Reports*, n.d., http://colombiareports.com/colombia news/ news/6939–fight-against-drug-trafficking-in-colombia-is-failing-experts.html (accessed June 21, 2012).

111. "Uribe: Yo no Me Reuní"; "Cousin of Colombian President Arrested"; BBC News, "Uribe Defends Security Policies"; Garry Leech, "The Paramilitary Spearhead of Plan Colombia," *Colombia Journal*," Nov. 20. 2000, http:// colombiajournal.org/colombia40.htm (accessed June 21, 2012); Brodzinksy, "Uribe, a Bush Ally."

112. Isacson, *Don't Call Plan Colombia a Model*, 1–13, 4.

113. Sibylla Brodzinksy, "Uribe, A Bush Ally, Treads on Shaky Ground," *Time*, Feb. 20, 2007. Sibylla Brodzinsky, "Colombian Establishment Rocked by Death Squad Scandal," *Guardian*, Nov. 29, 2006, http://www.guardian.co.uk/ world/2006/nov/29/colombia.sibyllabrodzinsky (accessed June 21, 2012).

114. Isacson, *Don't Call Plan Colombia a Model*, 1–13, 4.

115. Brodzinsky, "Colombian Establishment Rocked," 2.

116. DeShazo, Primiani, and McLean, *Back from the Brink*, 35; Isacson, *Plan Colombia—Six Years Later*, 1–19.

117. Christan Leonard, "Impunity Remains High for Crimes against Colombian Unionists," *Colombia Reports*, 2012, http://colombiareports.com/ colombia-news/news/22800-impunity-remains-high-for-crimes-against-colom- bian-unionists.html (accessed Aug. 22, 2012); Isacson, *Don't Call Plan Colombia a Model*, 7–8.

118. Dan Kovalik, "U.S.-Sponsored Crimes in Colombia Referred to International Criminal Court," *Huffington Post*, June 4, 2012, http://www.huffington- post.com/dan-kovalik/colombia-international-criminal-court_b_1562748.html, 1.

119. Adriaan Alsema, "False Positives," *Colombia Reports*, Aug. 2012, http://colombiareports.co/false-positives/.

120. Brodzinsky, "Colombian Establishment Rocked"; BBC News, "Colombian Soldiers Jailed for 'False Positive' Killings," July 6, 2011, http:// www.bbc.co.uk/news/world-latin-america-14055765 (accessed Aug. 8, 2012); Isacson, *Don't Call Plan Colombia a Model*, 1–13; Center for International Policy, "New Report on Mistakes of Plan Colombia and Lessons for Latin America," news release, Nov. 10, 2011, http://www.ciponline.org/press-room/ article/new-report-on-mistakes-of-plan-colombia-and-lessons-for-latin-america (accessed June 21, 2012).

121. Kovalik, "U.S.-Sponsored Crimes."

122. DeShazo, Primiani, and McLean, *Back from the Brink*, 25.

123. "Annual Survey of Violations of Trade Union Rights 2012—Colom- bia," International Trade Union Confederation, June 6, 2012, http://survey.ituc csi.org/Colombia.html?lang=en (accessed Aug. 26, 2012).

124. DeShazo, Primiani, and McLean, *Back from the Brink*, 26; Soli- darity Center, *Justice for All: The Struggle for Worker Rights in Colombia* (Washington, DC: Solidarity Center, 2006), http://www.solidaritycenter.org/ files/ColombiaFinal.pdf (accessed Aug. 26, 2012).

125. DeShazo, Primiani, and McLean, *Back from the Brink*, 27.

126. Sandra Borda (Associate Professor, Los Andes University), interview by author, Aug. 8, 2012. This interview was approved by the Institutional Review Board of the University of Miami.

127. Bagley and Tokatlian, "Dope and Dogma"; Keohane and Nye, *Power and Interdependence*, 315.

128. M. Angeles Villarreal, U.S.-Colombian Trade Promotional Agreement (Washington DC: Congressional Research Service, 2006), 1–6.

129. Ibid., 6; Jim Wyss, "Colombian Unions Hope Trade Deal Doesn't Mask Continued Violence," *Miami Herald*, Oct. 13, 2011, http://www.miami-herald.com/2011/10/13/2452957/colombian-unions-hope-trade-deal.html (accessed Aug. 26, 2012). For more on the trade agreement, see USTR, *Trade Facts: Free Trade with Colombia, Summary of the United States-Colombia Trade Promotion Agreement*, June 2007.

130. "Latinobarómetro Poll: Latin Americans, Despite Stereotype, Are Political Moderates," *World Public Opinion*, Jan. 10, 2007, http://worldpubli-copinion.org/pipa/articles/brlatinamericara/299.php?lb=brla&pnt=299&nid=&id= (accessed June 21, 2012); "Bush Pushes Trade Pact to Aid Colombia and His Legacy," *Los Angeles Times*, Nov. 13, 2008, http://articles.latimes.com/2008/nov/13/world/fg-colombia13 (accessed June 21, 2012); Jorge, Domínguez, "A Legacy of Mixed Messages," *Boston Globe Magazine*, 2006.

131. U.S. White House, "President Bush Honors Presidential Medal of Freedom Recipients," news release, Jan. 13, 2009, http://georgewbush-whitehouse.archives.gov/news/releases/2009/01/20090113-7.html (accessed June 21, 2012).

132. Borda interview.

133. Laura Gómez-Mera, *Power and Regionalism in Latin America: The Politics of Mercosur* (Notre Dame, IN: University of Notre Dame Press, 2013).

134. Bruce M. Bagley y Magdalena Defort, (comp.) *¿La hegemonía norteamericana en declive? El desafío del ALBA y la nueva integración lati-noamericana en el siglo XXI* (Cali, Colombia, ICESI, 2014)

135. Bagley, *Drug Trafficking and Organized Crime*; Wendt, *Social Theory of International Politics*, 429; "War-Torn Colombia Less Violent in 2003, Government Says," Reuters, Jan. 6, 2004; Christman, Heimann, and Sweig, *Andes 2020*.

136. Crandall, "Clinton, Bush and Plan Colombia," 159; Crandall, "Explicit Narcotization," 95–120; Crandall, *Driven by Drugs*, 193.

137. Waltz, *Theory of International Politics*; Keohane, *Neorealism and Its Critics*, 378.

138. Barry Buzan further discusses framing the issue and defining the problem; see Barry Buzan, Ole Waever, and Jaap de Wilde, *People, States, and Fear: An Agenda for International Security Studies in the Post-Cold War Era* (Chapel Hill: University of North Carolina Press, 1997), 262; Buzan, "Will the 'Global War on Terrorism,'" 1101–1118; Buzan, Weaver, and de Wilde, *Security*, 239; Isacson, *Don't Call Plan Colombia a Model*, 1–13; Isacson, *Plan Colombia—Six Years Later*, 1–19.

139. Chernick interview; Crandall, *Driven by Drugs*, 193.

140. John Otis, "U.S. Military Base Plan Puts Colombia in Hot Water," *Time*, Aug. 12, 2009, http://www.time.com/time/world/article/0,8599,1915825,00.html#ixzz0rehy8KtO (accessed June 21, 2012); BBC News, "Uribe Defends Security Policies"; Brodzinksy, "Uribe, a Bush Ally"; Nye, *Soft Power*, 191.

141. Transcript: Colombian President Alvaro Uribe, *Fox News*, Sept. 19, 2005, http://search.proquest.com/docview/463932713.

142. Thanks to Bruce Bagley for pointing this out. This argument is founded in the Neo-Liberal Institutional Framework. For more on this, see Robert Keohane, *After Hegemony*.

143. "A Legacy of Mixed Messages," Weatherhead Center for International Affairs; "Bush Pushes Trade Pact," *Los Angeles Times*; "Latinobarómetro Poll," *World Public Opinion*; Brodzinksy, "Uribe, a Bush Ally"; Nye, *Soft Power*, 191.

144. U.S. White House, "President Bush Honors," 2.

145. "U.S.: Award to Uribe Sends Wrong Message," *Human Rights Watch*, Jan. 12, 2009, http://www.hrw.org/news/2009/01/12/us-award-uribe-sends-wrong-message (accessed Aug. 26, 2012).

146. Sandra Borda interview. She is referring to strategic intelligence as opposed to mental capacity.

147. Bagley, *Drug Trafficking and Organized Crime*, 7; Isacson, *Don't Call Plan Colombia a Model*, 1–13; Isacson, *Plan Colombia—Six Years Later*, 1–19.

148. Pizarro and Gaitán, "Plan Colombia and the Andean Regional Initiative," esp. 80, 72.

149. Pizarro and Gaitán, "Plan Colombia and the Andean Regional Initiative," esp. 80, 72; "Partners Colombia—Partners for Democratic Change."

150. "Coca Cultivation Rises in Colombia, U.N. Says," *Washington Post*, June 18, 2008, http:// http://www.washingtonpost.com/wp-dyn/content/article/2008/06/18/AR2008061802950.html (accessed June 21, 2012); *Drug Reduction Goals Were Not Fully Met*, 115; Veillette, *Plan Colombia: A Progress Report*, 1–11; Veillette, *Andean Counterdrug Initiative*, 1–36.

Chapter 5. Beyond Plan Colombia and Desecuritization

1. "Interview: President Juan Manuel Santos of Colombia" (London: Chatham House, 2012)," http:// chathamhouse.org/publications/twt/archive/view/185137 (accessed Sept. 20, 2012), 1.

2. Buzan, Weaver, and de Wilde, *Security*; Wendt, "Anarchy Is What States," 391.

3. Tickner, "Colombia and the United States," 72; Tickner interview; Vaicius, *El Plan Colombia*; Tickner, "Colombia and the United States," 72; Crandall, *Driven by Drugs*, 193.

4. Mares interview.

5. DeShazo, Primiani, and McLean, *Back from the Brink*.

6. For more, see DeShazo, Primiani, and McLean, *Back from the Brink*.

7. Thanks to Marc Chernick who told me this in an interview at Los Andes University, which was approved by the Institutional Review Board of the University of Miami.

8. Isacson, *Plan Colombia—Six Years Later*, 1–19; Isacson, "Mission Creep"; Isacson, "The U.S. Military," 1–15; *Drug Reduction Goals Were Not Fully Met*, 115.

9. Francisco E. Thoumi, "Debates recientes de la Organización de las Naciones Unidas acera del régimen internacional de drogas: Fundamentos, limitaciones e (im) posibles cambios," in *Drogas y prohibición: Una vieja Guerra, un nuevo debate*, ed. Juan Gabriel Tokatlian (Buenos Aires, Argentina: Libros del zorzal, 2010), 27–56.

10. Mejía interview.

11. Bruce Bagley argued this in a lecture in his course "Drug Trafficking in the Americas," University of Miami, fall 2008. For more on constructivism, see Buzan, Weaver, and de Wilde, *Security*.

12. U.N. Office on Drugs and Crime, *Coca Cultivation Survey,* (Bogotá, Colombia: UNODC, 2009), 17

13. Ibid. Also, I would like to thank an anonymous review for pointing this out to me.

14 U.N. Office on Drugs and Crime, *Colombia: Coca Cultivation Survey 2011* (Bogotá, Colombia: UNODC, 2012), 80; "Plan Colombia: The Harmful Impacts"; Gaviria, *Politicas Antidroga En Colombia*, 445; Isacson, *Don't Call Plan Colombia a Model*, 1–13; Isacson, *Plan Colombia—Six Years Later*, 1–19.

15. U.N. Office on Drugs and Crime, *Colombia: Coca Cultivation Survey 2011*, 8–107, 80; Vandra Felbab-Brown et al., *Assessment of the Implementation of the United States Governments' Support for Plan Colombia's Illicit Crop Reduction Components* (Washington, DC: USAID, 2009).

16. Simon Romero, "Coca Sustain War in Rural Colombia," *New York Times,* June 27, 2008, http://www.nytimes.com/2008/07/27/world/americas/27colombia.html?pagewanted=all; Isacson, *Plan Colombia—Six Years Later*, 1–19; Loveman, *Addicted to Failure*, ch. 2; U.N. Office on Drugs and Crime, *Colombia: Coca Cultivation Survey 2011*, 8–107; "Overall Picture of Coca Cultivation in Colombia Remains Stable—U.N. Agency," U.N. News Centre, July 25, 2012, http://www.un.org/apps/news/story.asp?NewsID=42554&Cr=drugs&Cr1= (accessed Aug. 26, 2012); Edward Fox, "U.S. Report on Colombia Cocaine Production Raises More Questions than Answers," *InSight Crime,* Aug. 1, 2012, http://www.insightcrime.org/insight-latest-news/item/2976-us-report-on-colombia-cocaine-production-raises-more-questions-than-answers (accessed Aug. 26, 2012).

17. Mejía interview; Mejía and Restrepo, "War on Illegal Drugs"; Daniel Mejía and Daniel M. Rico, *La Microeconomía De La Producción y Tráfico De Cocaína En Colombia* (Bogotá, Colombia: La Universidad de los Andes, 2010); Loveman, *Addicted to Failure*, 367; Thoumi, *Illegal Drugs, Economy*, 416; Tokatlian, *Globalización, Narcotráfico y Violencia*; Tokatlian, *The United States and Illegal Crops*, 29; Tokatlian, *Seguridad y Drogas*, 44.

18. Ramírez Lemus, Stanton, and Walsh, "Colombia: A Vicious Circle," 117.

19. Drug Reduction Goals Were Not Fully, 43; Mares, *Drug Wars and Coffeehouses*, 188; Mejía interview; Mejía and Restrepo, "War on Illegal Drugs"; Mejía and Rico, *La Microeconomía De La Producción*; Menzel, *Cocaine Quagmire*, 213.

20. *Drug Reduction Goals Were Not Fully Met*, 115; *Human Rights during the Juan Manuel Santos*, 1–25; Holmes, de Piñeres and Curtin, "Drugs, Violence, and Development in Colombia," 157–184; Isacson, "Mission Creep"; Isacson, *Plan Colombia—Six Years Later*, 1–19; Isacson, *Don't Call*

Plan Colombia a Model, 1–13; Isacson, "The U.S. Military," 1–15; Isacson, "Optimism, Pessimism, and Terrorism," 245–255; Adam Isacson and Abigail Poe, "After Plan Colombia: Evaluating 'Integrated Action,' the Next Phase of U.S. Assistance" *Just the Facts*, Dec. 2009, http://justf.org/content/after-plan-colombia (accessed Sept. 20, 2012); Adriaan Alsema, "Colombia's Civilian Coca Eradicators Violate Landmine Treaty," *Colombia Reports*, 2011, http://colombiareports.com/opinion/157-guests/17810-civilian-deaths-authorized-by-government-as-part-of-anti-drug-measures.html (accessed Sept. 20, 2012).

21. Isacson, *Plan Colombia—Six Years Later*, 1–19; *Human Rights during the Juan Manuel Santos*, 1–25; Aug. 22, 2012; Michael Solis, "Colombia's Internally Displaced People," *Huffington Post*, Sept. 13, 2010, http://www.huffingtonpost.com/michael-solis/colombias-internally-disp_b_715186.html (accessed Aug. 22, 2012).

22. Coletta A. Youngers and Eileen Rosin, "The U.S. 'War on Drugs': Its Impact in Latin America and the Caribbean," in *Drugs and Democracy in Latin America: The Impact of U.S. Policy*, ed. Coletta A. Youngers and Eileen Rosin, 1–14 (Boulder, CO: Rienner, 2005), 5.

23. BBC News, "Uribe Defends Security Policies"; U.S. White House, "President Bush Honors"; Otis, "U.S. Military Base Plan"; "Santos v. Uribe," *Economist*, Apr. 7, 2012, http://www.economist.com/node/21552204; Brodzinksy, "Uribe, a Bush Ally."

24. Laura Zelenko and Matthew Bristow, "Colombia Uribe Says Venezuela Is Paradise for Terrorist," April 26, 2012, *Bloomberg News*, http://www.economist.com/node/21552204.

25. Brodzinksy, "Uribe, a Bush Ally"; Hamer, "Fight against Drug Trafficking"; "Venezuela Expels Colombian Ambassador," 1. "Latinobarómetro Poll," *World Public Opinion*

26. BBC News, "Uribe Defends Security Policies"; Otis, "U.S. Military Base Plan."

27. Ibid. International Crisis Group, "Colombia: Peace at Last?" International Crisis Group, Sept. 25, 2012, http://www.crisisgroup.org/en/publication-type/media-releases/2012/latam/colombia-peace-at-last.aspx (accessed Oct. 23, 2012), esp. 1.

28. International Crisis Group, "Colombia: Peace at Last?" International Crisis Group, esp. 1.

29. Eduardo Posada Carbo, "Colombia after Uribe," *Journal of Democracy* 22, no. 1 (2011): 137–151, 137; Robert Kagan and Aroop Mukharji, "In Colombia, Democracy Is Stirred but Not Shaken," *Washington Post*, Mar. 9, 2010, http://www.washingtonpost.com/wp-dyn/content/article/2010/03/08/AR2010030803294.html.

30. "Santos v. Uribe."

31. Hannah Stone, "The War of Words over Colombia's Conflict," *InSight Crime*, May 9, 2011, http://www.insightcrime.org/insight-latest-news/item/884-the-war-of-words-over-colombias-conflict (accessed Aug. 26, 2012).

32. Amnesty International, "Afro-Descendent Communities," *Amnesty International,* 1, http://www.amnestyusa.org/our-work/countries/americas/colombia/afro-descendent-communities; International Crisis Group, "Bringing

Displaced Persons into Peace Processes: Good for Them, Good for Peace," International Crisis Group, Apr. 26, 2010, http://www.crisisgroup.org/en/ publication-type/speeches/2010/bringing-displaced-persons-into-peace-processes. aspx (accessed Oct. 23, 2012).

33. *Human Rights during the Juan Manuel Santos*, 1–25; "Santos v. Uribe," 10.

34. *Human Rights during the Juan Manuel Santos*, 1–25, 12.

35. Ibid., 12.

36. Ibid., 3. This is according to a human rights nongovernmental organization.

37. *Human Rights during the Juan Manuel Santos*, 15; "Santos v. Uribe"; "Santos Firma Decreto De Ley De Víctimas," *El Espectador*, Dec. 20, 2011, http://www.elespectador.com/noticias/politica/imagen-317740-santos-firma-decreto-de-ley-de-victimas (accessed Aug. 22, 2012).

38. "Santos Firmó Reglamentación De Ley De Víctimas y Restitución De Tierras El Pais," Dec 21, 2011, http://www.elpais.com.co/elpais/colombia/ noticias/juan-manuel-santos-firmo-decretos-dan-vida-ley-victimas-y-tierras (accessed Aug. 22, 2012).

39. *Human Rights during the Juan Manuel Santos*, 1–25, 15; Arturo Wallace, "Colombia: Las Víctimas de la Ley de Víctimas," *BBC Mundo*, Apr. 18, 2012, http://www.bbc.co.uk/mundo/noticias/2012/04/120417_ colombia_victimas_restitucion_tierras_aw.shtml (accessed Aug. 22, 2012); "Santos Aprueba La Ley De Víctimas y Restitución De Las Tierras," *El País*, Jun 11, 2011, http://internacional.elpais.com/internacional/2011/06/11/ actualidad/1307743202_850215.html (accessed Aug. 22, 2012).

40. *Human Rights during the Juan Manuel Santos*, 1–25, 16.

41. Ibid., 16.

42. Ibid., 16–18.

43. Ibid., 18; U.N. High Commissioner for Refugees, "Profile of Internal Displacement: Colombia"; Solis, "Colombia's Internally Displaced People."

44. U.N. High Commissioner for Refugees, "Profile of Internal Displacement: Colombia"; Solis, "Colombia's Internally Displaced People."

45. *Human Rights during the Juan Manuel Santos*, 14.

46. Ibid, 1–25, 13.

47. Ibid., 14.

48. Ibid., 14. In the report, the authors put this in bold for emphasis. U.N. High Commissioner for Refugees, "Profile of Internal Displacement: Colombia"; IDMC, "Internally Displaced People."

49. Kathryn Thompson, "Colombia Making Progress against Impunity: UN" *Colombia Reports*, http://colombiareports.com/colombia-news/news/16012- colombia-making-progress-against-impunity-un.html (accessed Aug. 22, 2012); "Colombia Must Fight Impunity for Sexual Violence Crimes—UN Official," U.N. News Centre, May 21, 2012, http://www.un.org/apps/news/story.asp?Ne wsID=42051&Cr=sexual+violence&Cr1 (accessed Aug. 22, 2012).

50. *Human Rights during the Juan Manuel Santos*, 3.

51. Ibid.

52. Numerous experts have debated the internal conflict in Colombia and the future of the country. Scholars have varying opinions with regard

to the peace process in Colombia and what the future holds for the country. One of the most comprehensive books is the edited volume by Elvira María Restrepo and Bruce Bagley, eds., *La desmovilización de los paramilitares en Colombia: Entre el escepticismo y la esperanza (Bogotá, Colombia: Universidad de los Andes, 2011)*.

53. Restrepo and Bagley, eds., *La desmovilización de los paramilitares en Colombia*.

54."Colombian President Calls for Global Rethink on Drugs," The Guardian, Nov. 12, 2011, http://www.guardian.co.uk/world/2011/nov/13/colombia-juan-santos-call-to-legalise-drugs (accessed Aug. 22, 2012), 3.

55. For more on constructivism, see Wendt, Social Theory of International Politics.

56. Mejía interview; Isacson, Don't Call Plan Colombia a Model, 1–13; Isacson, Plan Colombia—Six Years Later, 1–19; Mejía and Rico, La Microeconomía De La Producción; Mejía and Restrepo, "War on Illegal Drugs."

57. Mejía interview. This, however, has proved not to be true as Uruguay has legalized marijuana and other countries, such as Guatemala, have advocate for changes in drug policies.

58. Arron Daugherty, "China's Rep Visits Colombia and Meets Santos," Colombia Reports, Apr. 23, 2012, http://colombiareports.com/colombia-news/news/23611-chinas-rep-visits-colombia-and-meets-santos.html (accessed Aug. 23, 2012).

59. Thanks to Bruce Bagley for point this out.

60. Bagley, Drug Trafficking and Organized Crime, 3–5.

61. Mejía interview.

62. Mejía interview. See also Ramírez Lemus, Stanton, and Walsh, "Colombia: A Vicious Circle," 61–98, 118.

63. Veillette, *Andean Counterdrug Initiative*, 1–36; Veillette, *Plan Colombia: A Progress Report*, 1–11; *Drug Reduction Goals Were Not Fully Met*, 115.

64. Drug Reduction Goals Were Not Fully Met. Veillette, Andean Counterdrug Initiative, 1–36; Veillette, Plan Colombia: A Progress Report, 1–11; Brodzinksy, 65. Leonard, "Impunity Remains High"; "Norwegian Human Rights Fund."

65. "Uribe, a Bush Ally"; "Venezuela Expels Colombian Ambassador"; Leo Palmer, "Ecuador to Continue Investigation into DAS Wiretaps," Colombia Reports, June 5, 2010, http://www.colombiareports.com/colombia-news/news/10626-ecuador-to-continue-wire-tapping-investigations-despite-uribes-denial.html (accessed Aug. 23, 2012).

66. "Ecuador to Continue Investigation into DAS Wiretaps," Colombia Reports.

67. "Santos v. Uribe;" See Wendt, *Social Theory of International Politics*.

68. Wendt, *Social Theory of International Politics*.

69. "Sin Conflicto Armado, Uribe y Yo Iríamos Para La Cárcel: Santos," *El Colombiano*, May 14, 2011, http://www.eluniversal.com.co/cartagena/nacional/sin-conflicto-armado-uribe-y-yo-iriamos-para-la-carcel-santos-24249 (accessed Aug. 22, 2012); "Álvaro Uribe Dice Que Afirmar Que Hay Conflicto Armado Es Abrir El Camino Al Estado De Beligerancia," *El Colombiano*, May 5, 2011, http://

www.elcolombiano.com/BancoConocimiento/A/alvaro_uribe_dice_que_afirmar_
que_hay_conflicto_armado_es_abrir_el_camino_al_estado_de_beligerancia/
alvaro_uribe_dice_que_afirmar_que_hay_conflicto_armado_es_abrir_el_camino_
al_estado_de_beligerancia.asp (accessed Aug. 22, 2012); "Santos Reconoce
Conflicto Armado y Uribe Lo Controvierte," *El Espectador*, May 4, 2011,
http://www.elespectador.com/noticias/politica/articulo-267421–santos-reconoce-
conflicto-armado-y-uribe-controvierte (accessed Aug. 22, 2012).

70. A shift later occurred from aerial spraying to manual eradication
initiatives. Isacson, *Don't Call Plan Colombia a Model*, 1–13; Isacson, *Plan
Colombia—Six Years Later*, 1–19; Ramírez Lemus, Stanton, and Walsh,
"Colombia: A Vicious Circle."

Chapter 6. Desecuritizing Plan Colombia

1. Buzan, Weaver, and de Wilde, *Security*, 239

2. Thanks to an anonymous review for pointing this out to me. For more
on U.S. appropriations during this period, see *H.R. 2764 (110th): Consolidated
Appropriations Act, 2008*, Dec. 26, 2007, GovTrack, http://www.govtrack.us/
congress/bills/110/hr2764.

3. For more on drug trafficking in Mexico, see Peter Watt and Roberto
Zepeda, *Drug War Mexico: Politics; Neoliberalism and Violence in the New
Narcoeconomy* (London: Zed Books, 2012); Ted Galen Carpenter, *The Fire Next
Door: Mexico's Drug Violence and the Danger to America* (Washington, D.C.:
Cato Institute, 2012); Cynthia J. Arnson, Eric L. Olson with Chrstine Zaino,
eds, *One Goal, Two Struggles: Confronting Crime and Violence in Mexico
and Colombia* (Washington, D.C.: Woodrow Wilson International Center for
Scholars, 2014).

4. Ibid; *Colombia's Strategy for Strengthening Democracy*, 1–80.

5. Bruce Bagley, for instance, has been writing about this topic
for decades. In addition, Ethan Nadelmann has been one of the leading
advocates for harm reduction policies and the legalization of drugs. Bagley,
"New Hundred Years War?" 161–182; Bagley, "U.S. Foreign Policy," 189–212;
Bagley and Tokatlian, "Dope and Dogma"; Bagley, *Drug Trafficking, Political
Violence*, 1–31; Smith, *Drug Policy in the Americas*, 366; Nadelmann, Drugs,
24–26, 28, 30; In 2009, Gil Kerlikowske, the head of the White House Office
of National Drug Control Policy, declared an end to the war on drugs. He
states that people view the war on drugs as a war on the people. The Obama
administration is not using the terminology the war on drugs, instead focusing
on transnational organized crime groups. The argument is that drug cartels
do not only traffic drugs but also participate in a variety of illegal activities
such as extortion, kidnapping, and human trafficking. For more, see Gary
Fields, "White House Czar Calls for End to 'War on Drugs': Kerlikowske Says
Analogy Is Counterproductive; Shift Aligns With Administration Preference
for Treatment Over Incarceration" *The Wall Street Journal*, May 14, 2009.

6. Bagley, "New Hundred Years War?" 161–182; Bagley, "U.S. Foreign
Policy," 189–212; Bagley and Tokatlian, "Dope and Dogma"; Bagley, *Drug
Trafficking, Political Violence*, 1–31.

7. This is a famous line from the movie *Jerry Maguire* (Cameron Crowe, dir., Culver City, CA: Gracie Films, 1996, film).

8. See Steven Dudley.

9. *Colombia's Strategy for Strengthening Democracy*, 1–80.

10. Ibid.

11. "Daily Number: Views of the Iraq War," Pew Research Center, Nov. 23, 2011, http://pewresearch.org/databank/dailynumber/?NumberID=1370 (accessed Aug. 22, 2012); "Public Attitudes toward the War in Iraq: 2003–2008," Pew Research Center, Mar. 19, 2008, http://pewresearch.org/pubs/770/iraq-war-five-year-anniversary (accessed Aug. 22, 2012); "Iraq and Public Opinion: The Troops Come Home," Pew Research Center," Dec. 14, 2011, http://pewresearch.org/pubs/2145/iraq-backgrounder-the-troops-come-home (accessed Aug. 22, 2012).

12. Buzan, Weaver, and de Wilde, *Security*, 239.

13. "Daily Number: Views of the Iraq War"; "Public Attitudes toward the War in Iraq"; "Iraq and Public Opinion."

14. Helene Cooper and Sheryl Gay Stolberg, "Obama Declares an End to Combat Mission in Iraq," *New York Times*, Aug. 31, 2010, 1.

15. Ibid.

16. "The Taliban in Afghanistan," Council on Foreign Relations, Aug. 6, 2013, http://www.cfr.org/afghanistan/taliban-afghanistan/p10551 (accessed Aug. 22, 2012); Peter Bergen, "The Taliban, Regrouped and Rearmed," *Washington Post*, Sept. 10, 2006, http://www.washingtonpost.com/wp-dyn/content/article/2006/09/08/AR2006090801614.html (accessed Aug. 22, 2012).

17. "Gaddafi: 'Don't leave Tripoli ever to those rats . . . destroy them,'" *Guardian*, Aug. 25, 2011, http://www.guardian.co.uk/world/video/2011/aug/25/muammar-gaddafi-libya-audio-speech-august-25-2011 (accessed Aug. 27, 2012).

18. Jennifer Rubin, "Iran and Obama their own worst enemies," *The Washington Post*. Jan. 14, 2014, blog.

19. Office of Gov. Rick Perry, "Statement by Gov. Rick Perry on Obama Administration's Decision to Slash Number of National Guard Troops at U.S.–Mexico Border," news release, Dec 12, 2011, http://governor.state.tx.us/news/press-release/16786/ (accessed Aug. 27, 2012).

20. Grace Wyler, "Mexican Cartels Are Moving to the U.S." *Business Insider*, Apr. 13, 2011, http://articles.businessinsider.com/2011–04–13/politics/29970800_1_juarez-cartel-border-states-gulf-cartel (accessed Aug. 27, 2012).

21. "Mexico's Drug War: 50, 000 Dead in 6 Years," *Atlantic*, May 17, 2012, http://www.theatlantic.com/infocus/2012/05/mexicos-drug-war-50-000-dead-in-6-years/100299/ (accessed Aug. 27, 2012).

22. Linda J. Bilmes and Joseph E. Stiglitz, "The Iraq War Will Cost Us $3 Trillion, and Much More," *Washington Post*, Mar. 9, 2008, http://www.washingtonpost.com/wp-dyn/content/article/2008/03/07/AR2008030702846.html (accessed Aug. 23, 2012).

23. U.S. White House Press Office, "Remarks by President Obama at CEO Summit of the Americas," Apr. 14, 2012, http://www.whitehouse.gov/the-press-office/2012/04/14/remarks-president-obama-ceo-summit-americas (accessed

Aug. 23, 2012); U.S. White House Press Office, "Remarks by President Obama and President Santos of Colombia in Joint Press Conference," Apr. 15, 2012, http://www.whitehouse.gov/the-press-office/2012/04/15/remarks-president-obama-and-president-santos-colombia-joint-press-confer (accessed Aug. 23, 2012).

24. See Mitt Romney's Economic Vision for America (published Aug. 31, 2012) at http://www.youtube.com/watch?v=FHVJWg5ikcg.

25. "Transcript of President Bush's Address."

26. For the full text of George W. Bush's Speech to U.S. Congress declaring war on terror, see "President Bush's Speech to Congress Declaring War on Terror," *About.com,* Sept. 20, 2011, http://middleeast.about.com/od/usmideastpolicy/a/bush-war-on-terror-speech_2.htm (accessed July 21, 2012), esp. 1; Bush and Dietrich, *George W. Bush Foreign Policy Reader,* 320.

27. "President Bush's Speech to Congress," 1; Bush and Dietrich, *George W. Bush Foreign Policy Reader,* 320; "Transcript of President Bush's Address,"

28. U.S. White House Press Office, "Remarks by President Obama at CEO Summit of the Americas," 2; U.S. White House Press Office, "Remarks by President Obama and President Santos of Colombia in Joint Press Conference."

29. U.S. White House Press Office, "Remarks by President Obama at CEO Summit of the Americas," 2; U.S. White House Press Office, "Remarks by President Obama and President Santos of Colombia in Joint Press Conference."

30. U.S. White House Press Office, "Remarks by President Obama and President Santos of Colombia in Joint Press Conference." U.S. White House Press Office, "Remarks by President Obama at CEO Summit of the Americas," 2; U.S. White House Press Office, "Remarks by President Obama and President Santos of Colombia in Joint Press Conference," 2; "Colombia's Santos Urges American Engagement," *Atlantic Sentinel,* Apr. 16, 2012, http://atlanticsentinel.com/2012/04/colombias-santos-urges-american-engagement/ (accessed Aug. 23, 2012); Isacson, "Plan Colombia and Beyond," blog entry.

31. U.S. White House Press Office, "Remarks by President Obama and President Santos of Colombia in Joint Press Conference." U.S. White House Press Office, "Remarks by President Obama at CEO Summit of the Americas," 2; U.S. White House Press Office, "Remarks by President Obama and President Santos of Colombia in Joint Press Conference," 2.

32. U.S. White House Press Office, "Remarks by President Obama at CEO Summit of the Americas," 2.

33. Ibid.

34. Bonilla, "U.S. Andean Policy," 129.

35. "Remarks by President Obama at CEO Summit of the Americas | the White House," 2; White House Press Office, "President Obama and President Santos Meet in Oval Office," Apr. 7, 2011, http://www.whitehouse.gov/blog/2011/04/07/president-obama-and-president-santos-meet-oval-office (accessed Aug. 23, 2012); RealClearPolitics, Press conference with Presidents Obama and Santos, Apr. 15, 2012, http://www.realclearpolitics.com/articles/2012/04/15/press_conference_with_presidents_obama__santos_113853.html (accessed Aug. 23, 2012); U.S. White House Press Office, "Colombian-American Leaders Visit White House on Colombian Independence Day," blog entry, July 30, 2017, http://www.whitehouse.gov/blog/2012/07/30/colombian-american-leaders-visit-white-house-colombian-independence-day (accessed Aug. 23, 2012).

36. U.S. White House Press Office, "Remarks by President Obama at CEO Summit of the Americas," 2; U.S. White House Press Office, "Remarks by President Obama and President Santos of Colombia in Joint Press Conference," 2.

37. U.S. White House Press Office, "Remarks by President Obama at CEO Summit of the Americas," 2; U.S. White House Press Office, "Remarks by President Obama and President Santos of Colombia in Joint Press Conference," 2.

38. Ibid., 3.

39. U.S. White House Press Office, "President Obama and President Santos Meet in Oval Office"; RealClearPolitics, Press conference with Presidents Obama and Santos; U.S. White House Press Office, "Colombian-American Leaders Visit White House."

40. "Remarks by President Obama at CEO Summit of the Americas | the White House," 2.

41. "Remarks by President Obama at CEO Summit of the Americas | the White House," 2

42. Kirsten Begg, "Uribe Worried by Obama's Plan Colombia Cuts," Colombia Reports, Feb. 11, 2010, http://colombiareports.com/colombia-news/news/8173–colombia-concerned-about-us-funding-cuts.html (accessed Aug. 23, 2012).

43. Kirsten Begg, "Uribe Worried by Obama's Plan Colombia Cuts," Colombia Reports; Mary Cecelia Bittner, "U.S. Cuts Military Aid to Colombia by 15%," Colombia Reports, Feb. 13, 2012, http://colombiareports.com/colombia-news/news/22181–us-cuts-colombias-military-and-anti-drug-funding.html (accessed Aug. 23, 2012); Adriaan Alsema, "Plan Colombia Not Mentioned in U.S. 2011 Budget Proposal," Colombia News, Colombia Reports, Feb. 1, 2010, http://colombiareports.com/colombia-news/news/7975–plan-colombia-unmentioned-in-us-2011–budget-proposal.html (accessed Aug. 23, 2012);

44. Kirsten Begg, "Uribe Worried by Obama's Plan Colombia Cuts," Colombia Reports.

45. Alsema, "Plan Colombia Not Mentioned."

46. US Cuts Military Aid to Colombia by 15%—Colombia News | Colombia Reports: Plan Colombia and Beyond » Defense Budget see "U.S. Aid to Colombia, All Programs, 2002–2002," Just the Facts, http://justf.org/Country?country=Colombia&year1=2002&year2=2002&funding=All+Programs.

47. Plan Colombia Not Mentioned in US 2011 Budget Proposal—Colombia News | Colombia Reports "Plan Colombia and Beyond" Defense Budget.

48. Plan Colombia Not Mentioned in US 2011 Budget Proposal—Colombia News | Colombia Reports Plan Colombia and Beyond » Defense Budget; Adam Isacson and Abigail Poe, "After Plan Colombia: Evaluating 'Integrated Action,' the Next Phase of U.S. Assistance" Just the Facts,

49. Jennifer Holmes, interview.

50. Jeff Mason, "Obama Says He Inherited Economic Problems," Reuters, Aug. 8, 2011, http://www.reuters.com/article/2011/08/09/us-crisis-obama-debt-idUSTRE7776D620110809 (accessed Aug. 23, 2012); "Iraq and Public Opinion"; "Public Attitudes toward the War"; "Daily Number: Views of the

Iraq War"; John Bell, "Netanyahu's Dangerous Decision-Making on Iran,"
Opinion, *Al Jazeera English,* Aug 21, 2012, http://www.aljazeera.com/indepth/
opinion/2012/08/2012820111156829235.html (accessed Aug. 23, 2012); Barak
Ravid, Amos Harel, Zvi Zrahiya, and Jonathan Lis, "Netanyahu Trying to
Persuade Cabinet to Support Attack on Iran," *Haaretz,* Nov. 2, 2011, http://
www.haaretz.com/print-edition/news/netanyahu-trying-to-persuade-cabinet-to-
support-attack-on-iran-1.393214 (accessed Aug. 23, 2012).

51. "Iraq and Public Opinion"; "Public Attitudes toward the War"; "Daily
Number: Views of the Iraq War"; John Bell, "Netanyahu's Dangerous Decision-
Making on Iran," Opinion; Barak Ravid, Amos Harel, Zvi Zrahiya, and Jona-
than Lis, "Netanyahu Trying to Persuade Cabinet to Support Attack on Iran."

52. Carpenter, The Fire Next Door.

53. DeShazo, Primiani, and McLean, *Back from the Brink.*

54. For more on the increases in security, see DeShazo, Primiani, and
McLean, Back from the Brink. Jennifer S. Holmes (Associate Professor, Political
Economy and Political Science, University of Texas at Dallas), interview by
author, Aug. 21, 2012; Holmes, de Piñeres, and Curtin, "Drugs, Violence, and
Development in Colombia," 157–184.

55. Chernick interview.

56. Jennifer S. Holmes (Associate Professor, Political Economy and
Political Science, University of Texas at Dallas), interview by author, Aug. 21,
2012; This interview was approved by the Institutional Review Board of the
University of Miami. For more, see Holmes, de Piñeres, and Curtin, "Drugs,
Violence, and Development in Colombia," 157–184.

57. Holmes interview.

Chapter 7. Social Constructions of Colombia's Anti-Drug Campaign: An Analysis of Speech Acts from 1998 to 2009

1. This is a constructivist issue. For more on constructivism, see Wendt,
"Anarchy is what states," 391; Buzan, Weaver, and de Wilde, *Security.*

2. Thanks to Bruce Bagley for pointing this out to me in a conversation
in May 2013.

3. Douglas Farah, "Andean Coca Farming Declined in '97; U.S. Data
Show Cultivation of Cocaine's Raw Material Rose in Colombia," *Washington
Post,* Jan. 19, 1998; http://search.proquest.com/docview/408354714?account
id=14585.

4. Serge F. Kovaleski, "Colombia Hails Lifting of Sanctions; Samper
Government Continues to Assail U.S. Certification Process," *Washington Post,*
Feb. 27, 1998, http://search.proquest.com/docview/408342337?accountid=14585.

5. Ibid.

6. Serge F. Kovaleski, "Widespread Violence Threatens Colombia's
Stability; Leftist, Rightist Groups Have Killed Hundreds," *Washington Post,*
Mar. 1, 1998, http://search.proquest.com/docview/408350203?accountid=14585.

7. Laura Brooks, "Colombian Military Is Called to Account; Rebels
Outwitted Forces, Critics Say," *Washington Post,* Mar. 8, 1998, http://search.
proquest.com/docview/408375619?accountid=14585.

8. Dana Priest, "U.S. May Boost Military Aid to Colombia's Anti-Drug Effort," *Washington Post,* Mar. 28, 1998, http://search.proquest.com/docview/4 08370023?accountid=14585.

9. Douglas Farah, "Colombian Rebels Seen Winning War; U.S. Study Finds Army." *Washington Post,* Apr. 10, 1998.

10. Dana Priest, "U.S. Force Training Troops in Colombia; Exercises Involve Anti-Drug Efforts," *Washington Post,* May 25, 1998.

11. Serge F. Kovaleski, "New Colombian Chief Seeks Better U.S. Ties; Says Agenda Must Go beyond Drugs," *Washington Post,* June 23, 1998.

12. Douglas Farah, "U.S. to Aid Colombian Military; Drug-Dealing Rebels Take Toll on Army," *Washington Post,* Dec. 27, 1998.

13. Douglas Farah, "To Turn the Heroin Tide; U.S. Targets Poppy Fields to Stanch Flow from Colombia," *Washington Post,* Feb. 22, 1999, http://search. proquest.com/docview/408431748?accountid=14585.

14. Douglas Farah, "U.S. Widens Colombia Counter-Drug Efforts; Restrictions Loosened on Data Sharing." *Washington Post,* July 10, 1999, http:// search.proquest.com/docview/408507834?accountid=14585.

15. Ibid.

16. "Protecting Colombia's Integrity," *Washington Post,* July 29, 1999.

17. Bernard Aronson, "War in Colombia: The U.S. Role," *Washington Post,* August 5, 1991, A3.

18. "La Estrategia," *Semana,* Aug. 11, 1999.

19. "El Tio Conejo," *Semana,* Dec. 13, 1999.

20. "An Elder Statesman's Walk through Washington," *Washington Post,* Mar. 24, 2000.

21. "For Rebels, It's Not a Drug War; Colombian Government," *Washington Post,* Apr. 10, 2000.

22. "President, Speaker to Visit Colombia; Trip's Aim Is to Back Anti-Drug Efforts," *Washington Post,* Aug. 5, 2000.

23. Steven Dudley, "Colombian Groups Say U.S. Aid Endangers Them," *Washington Post,* Aug. 23, 2000.

24. Karen DeYoung, "Colombia Readies for Clinton; In Addition to Anti-Drug Policy," *Washington Post,* Aug. 30, 2000, A18.

25. Ibid.

26. Scott Wilson, "Europeans Scale Back Colombian Drug Aid; Package Falls Far Short of Expected $1 Billion," *Washington Post,* Oct. 19, 2000, A21.

27. Scott Wilson, "U.S. Drug Chief Tries to Boost Colombian Resolve; McCaffrey Vows Long-Term Support," *Washington Post,* Nov. 21, 2000, A22.

28. Scott Wilson, "Colombia to Ask Bush for Additional Funds; Pastrana Says Peace Process Depends on New Assistance," *Washington Post,* Feb. 16, 2001, A18.

29. George Bush, " 'I Have a Reasonable and Balanced Budget' " *Washington* Post, Feb 23, 2001, A04; George W. Bush, "Transcript of President Bush's White House News Conference," *New York Times,* Feb. 23, 2001.

30. William M. LeoGrande, "A Plan, But No Clear Objective; General Powell to Secretary Powell: We Need to Talk Colombia," *Washington Post,* Apr. 1, 2001, A4.

31. Scott Wilson, "Pastrana Takes to the Road to Sell the Softer Side of Plan Colombia," *Washington Post,* May 22, 2001, A13.

32. Judy Mann, "Money Spent on Drug War Could Be Put to Better Use," *Washington Post,* Oct. 17, 2001, C12, http://search.proquest.com/docvie w/409219773?accountid=14585.

33."The Drug-Terror Connection," *Washington Post,* Dec. 24, 2001, A16, http://search.proquest.com/docview/409255407?accountid=14585.

34. Dennis Jett, "Remember the Drug War? A Casualty of Terrorism You Haven't Heard Much About." *Washington Post,* Jan. 13, 2002, B04.

35. "Drug Users as Traitors," *Washington Post,* Feb 12, 2002.

36. Hernando Gómez Buendía, "La Nueva Alianza," *Semana,* June 10, 2012, http://www.semana.com/opinion/articulo/la-nueva-alianza/54370-3.

37. Washington in Brief, *Washington Post,* July 27, 2002, A05. Mike Allen, "Bush Asserts that Al Qaeda Has Links to Iraq's Hussein." *Washington Post,* Sept. 26, 2002.

38. Mike Allen, "Bush Asserts that Al Qaeda Has Links to Iraq's Hussein." *Washington Post,* Sept. 26, 2002.

39. Ibid.

40. Marcela Sanchez, "Getting in Deeper," *Washington Post,* Jan. 11, 2005, A27.

41. Paula Kling, "Las reformas de segunda generación," Semana, May 5, 2003, http://www.semana.com/on-line/articulo/las-reformas-segunda-generacion/ 58010-3.

42. "Las FARC: una fiera herida que sigue viva," Semana, Jan. 26, 2004, http://m.semana.com/nacion/articulo/las-farc-fiera-herida-sigue-viva/63140-3.

43. Mike Allen, "Bush Stops in Colombia, Pledges Aid for Drug War," *Washington Post,* Nov. 23, 2004, A23, http://search.proquest.com/docview/409 850740?accountid=14585.

44. Roger F. Noriega "The Good News from Colombia," Washington Post, Feb. 25, 2005, A20 http://search.proquest.com/docview/409757753?acco untid=14585.

45. Juan Forero, "In Colombia, a Dubious Disarmament; Demobilized Paramilitaries Are Sidestepping Justice, Critics and Victims Say," *Washington Post,* Oct. 17, 2006, A14, http://search.proquest.com/docview/410097314? accountid=14585.

46. "Entrevista al presidente Álvaro Uribe," Semana, Mar. 9, 2007, http:// www.semana.com/on-line/articulo/entrevista-presidente-alvaro-uribe/83858-3.

47. Duncan Smith-Rohrberg Maru, "Wasting Drug Resources," *Washington Post,* Nov. 24, 2008, A17.

48. Joshua Partlow, "Brazil's President to Seek a Change in U.S. Approach," *Washington Post,* Mar. 14, 2009, A10.

49. Juan Forero, "U.S. Plan Raises Ire in Latin America; Troops, Planes Would Use Colombian Bases in Anti-Drug Effort," *Washington Post,* Aug. 8, 2009, A06.

50. "Colombia will continue to be a valued partner of the US": Steny Hoyer," *Seamana,* Jan. 16, 2009, http://www.semana.com/international/print-edition/articulo/colombia-will-continue-to-be-valued-partner-of-the-us-steny-hoyer/99199-3.

51. Ibid.

Chapter 8. Analytic Conclusions and Policy Lessons From Plan Colombia

1. Alexander L. George, "The Two Cultures of Academia and Policy-Making: Bridging the Gap," in "Special Issue: Political Psychology and the Work of Alexander L. George," special issue, *Political Psychology* 15, no. 1 (Mar. 1994): 143–172.

2. Stephen M. Walt, "Rigor or Rigor Mortis? Rational Choice and Security Studies," *International Security* 23, no. 4 (Spring 1999): 5–48; Benjamin J. Cohen, "Are IPE Journals becoming Boring?" *International Studies Quarterly* 54, no. 3 (Sept.-Oct. 2010): 887–891.

3. See Bagley, *Drug Trafficking and Organized Crime*, 5.

4. Ibid.; also, thanks to Marc W. Chernick for his interview, which was approved by the Institutional Review Board of the University of Miami.

5. Mearsheimer, *Tragedy of Great Power Politics*; Waltz, *Theory of International Politics*.

6. Crandall, *Driven by Drugs*.

7. For more on realism, see Mearsheimer, *Tragedy of Great Power Politics*; Waltz, *Theory of International Politics*.

8. Brodzinksy, "Uribe, a Bush Ally."

9. Mearsheimer, *Tragedy of Great Power Politics*; Waltz, *Theory of International Politics*.

10. Mearsheimer, Tragedy of Great Power Politics.

11. Daugherty, "China's Rep Visits."

12. Keohane and Nye, *Power and Interdependence*, 315; Keohane, *Neorealism and Its Critics*, 378.

13. Keohane and Nye, Power and Interdependence, 315; Keohane, Neorealism and Its Critics, 378.

14. Keohane and Nye, Power and Interdependence, 315; Keohane, Neorealism and Its Critics, 378.

15. Buzan, Weaver, and de Wilde, *Security*, 239; Wendt, "Anarchy Is What States," 391; Nye, *Soft Power*.

16. Buzan, Weaver, and de Wilde, Security, 239; Wendt, "Anarchy Is What States," 391; Nye, *Soft Power*.

17. Buzan, Weaver, and de Wilde, *Security*.

18. "Colombian President Calls for Global Rethink," 3; "Drug War, Including Legalization, Hot Topic at Summit of the Americas," CNN, Apr. 14, 2012, http://articles.cnn.com/2012–04–15/americas/world_americas_summit-of-the-americas_1_legalization-drug-war-drug-issue?_s=PM:AMERICAS (accessed Aug. 22, 2012).

19. Mearsheimer, *Tragedy of Great Power Politics*; Waltz, *Theory of International Politics*.

20. Bruce Bagley, *Tráfico de drogas y crimen organizado en América Latina y el Caribe en el siglo XXI: retos de la democracia*, Ecuentro International Drogas, Usos, y Prevenciones, May 16–18, 2012, Quito, Ecuador, http://www.youtube.com/watch?v=sLbYHUs7F5c.

21. Ibid.

22. *Drug Reduction Goals Were Not Fully Met.*

23. Isacson, "Extending the War on Terrorism to Colombia"; Isacson, "The U.S. Military," 1–15; Isacson, *Plan Colombia—Six Years Later*, 1–19.

24. Ramírez Lemus, Stanton, and Walsh, "Colombia: A Vicious Circle."

25. U.N. Office on Drugs and Crime, *Colombia: Coca Cultivation Survey 2011*, 8–107, 89–102.

26. Mejía interview; Mejía and Restrepo, "War on Illegal Drugs"; Mejía and Rico, *La Microeconomía De La Producción*.

27. Mejía interview; Mejía and Restrepo, "War on Illegal Drugs"; Mejía and Rico, *La Microeconomía De La Producción*.

28. U.N. Office on Drugs and Crime, *World Drug Report* (New York: UNODC, 2011), 25; Lisa Evans, "The U.N. Drugs Report 2011: What's Happening to Cocaine and Heroin Use?" *Guardian*, June 24, 2011, http://www.guardian.co.uk/news/datablog/2011/jun/24/un-drugs-report-afghanistan (accessed Aug. 28, 2012).

29. Mejía and Rico, *La Microeconomía De La Producción*; Mejía and Restrepo, "War on Illegal Drugs"; Mejía interview.

30. U.N. Office on Drugs and Crime, *World Drug Report,* 34; *Global Report*, 476; U.N. Office on Drugs and Crime, *The Globalization of Crime: A Transnational Organized Crime Threat Assessment* (New York: UNODC, 2010).

31. U.N. Office on Drugs and Crime, *World Drug Report*, 33: "U.N. Drugs Report 2011."

32. U.N. Office on Drugs and Crime, *Colombia: Coca Cultivation Survey 2011*, 8–107, 10; U.N. Office on Drugs and Crime, *Globalization of Crime: A Transnational Organized Crime Threat Assessment* (Vienna: Austria, UNODC, 2010).

33. U.N. Office on Drugs and Crime, *World Drug Report;* Global Commission on Drug Policy, "Narcotics Body's Annual Report Highlights Alarming Trends in Drug Abuse," Feb. 24, 2010, http://www.unodc.org/unodc/en/frontpage/2010/February/narcotics-bodys-annual-report-highlights-alarming-trends-in-drug-abuse.html (accessed Aug. 28, 2012).

34. U.N. Office on Drugs and Crime, *World Drug Report*, 21; Global Commission on Drug Policy, "Narcotics Body's Annual Report"; Simon Romero, "Coca Production Makes a Comeback in Peru," *New York Times,* June 13, 2010, http://www.nytimes.com/2010/06/14/world/americas/14peru.html.

35. U.N. Office on Drugs and Crime, *World Drug Report*, 3; U.N. Office on Drugs and Crime, *Colombia: Coca Cultivation Survey 2011*, 8–107.

36. U.N. Office on Drugs and Crime, *World Drug Report,* 99.

37. "The Andean Drug Industry: The Balloon Goes Up," *Economist*, Mar. 6, 2003, http://www.economist.com/node/1622585 (accessed Aug. 28, 2012). For more on the shifting routes and recent trends, see: Bagley, *Drug Trafficking and Organized Crime*; Mares interview; Mares, *Drug Wars and Coffeehouses*, 188; U.N. Office on Drugs and Crime, *World Drug Report;* "U.N. Drugs Report 2011."

38. Carpenter, *Bad Neighbor Policy*, 114.

39. Brienen interview.

40. Ibid.

41. Romero, "Coca Sustain War in Rural Colombia."

42. Buzan, Weaver, and de Wilde, *Security*.

43. The author of these quotes noted that such statements reflect his own opinions and does not represent the opinion of the U.N. Office on Drugs and Crime.

44. Nadelmann, "Addicted to Failure," 94; Nadelmann, "Uso y Prohibicion De Drogas," 13–13; Andreas, "Dead-End Drug Wars," 106–128; Andreas, "Free Market Reform," 75–88.

45. Nadelmann, "Addicted to Failure"; Nadelmann, "Uso y Prohibicion De Drogas," 13–13; Andreas, "Dead-End Drug Wars."

46. Chernick interview.

47. DeShazo, Primiani, and McLean, *Back from the Brink*.

48. Isacson, *Don't Call Plan Colombia a Model*, 2.

49. Johnson, *Blowback*.

50. Chernick interview.

51. Tree interview.

52. Chernick interview.

53. Isacson highlighted certain words for emphasis; Isacson, *Don't Call Plan Colombia a Model*, 1–13, 1.

54. Lisa Haugaard (Executive Director of the Latin America Working Group), interview by author, 2012. The Institutional Review Board of the University of Miami approved this interview.

55. Ibid.

56. Ibid. Adriaan Alsema, "Uribe Denies having Ordered DAS Wiretaps," *Colombia Reports*," Feb. 23, 2009,, http://colombiareports.com/colombia-news/news/2999–uribe-denies-having-ordered-das-wiretaps.html (accessed Aug. 22, 2012).

57. Isacson, Plan *Colombia—Six Years Later*, 1–19; Isacson, *Don't Call Plan Colombia a Model*, 1–13.

58. Arlene Tickner pointed out to me that the funding of Plan Colombia and percentage allocated toward the hard components changed over time; Tickner interview. John Bailey also talks about the phases of Plan Colombia; see Bailey, *Plan Colombia and the Mérida Initiative*, 6.

59. "Santos v. Uribe."

60. Youngers and Rosin, "The U.S. 'War on Drugs,'" 1–15.

61. Bagley, *Drug Trafficking and Organized Crime*.

62. For more on realism, see Mearsheimer, *Tragedy of Great Power Politics*; and Waltz *Theory of International Politics*.

63. Bagley, *Drug Trafficking and Organized Crime*.

64. U.N. Office on Drugs and Crime, *World Drug Report*, 25; "U.N. Drugs Report 2011."

65. Youngers and Rosin, "The U.S. 'War on Drugs,'" 1–15; Ramírez Lemus, Stanton, and Walsh, "Colombia: A Vicious Circle"; Mejía interview.

66. Ramírez Lemus, Stanton, and Walsh, "Colombia: A Vicious Circle," 116.

Chapter 9. Back to the Future:
The Unintended Consequences of the
Partial Successes of the War on Drugs

1. Bruce Bagley, *Drug Trafficking, Political Violence*; Peter DeShazo, Johanna Mendelson Forman, and Phillip McLean, *Countering Threats to*

Security and Stability in a Failing State: Lessons from Colombia (Washington, DC: CSIS, 2009).

2. Veillette, *Plan Colombia: A Progress Report*, 1–11.

3. Ramírez Lemus, Stanton, and Walsh, "Colombia: A Vicious Circle," 61–98; Crandall, *Driven by Drugs*, 193, 91; Crandall, "Clinton, Bush and Plan Colombia," 159; Vaicius and Isacson, "The 'War on Drugs.'"

4. DeShazo, Primiani, and McLean, *Back from the Brink*.

5. *Drug Reduction Goals Were Not Fully Met.*

6. June S. Beittel, *Peace Talks in Colombia* (Washington, DC: Congressional Research Service, 2013), 5.

7. Ibid., 6; Ariel Ávila, "Las FARC: La Guerra que el País No Quiere Ver," *Arcanos*, 17 (Jan. 2012).

8. "Santos v. Uribe"; Hannah Stone, "The War of Words over Colombia's Conflict"; for an interesting interview by CNN's Christiane Amanpour with President Santos, see "Entrevista de Christiane Amanpour al Presidente Juan Manuel Santos," https://www.youtube.com/watch?v=kjP2eiVEeCQ, 2013.

9. Beittel, *Peace Talks in Colombia*, 16.

10. Ibid., 16; DeShazo, Forman, and McLean, *Countering Threats to Security.*

11. Beittel, *Peace Talks in Colombia*, 18.

12. Thanks to Bruce Bagley of the University of Miami for pointing this out to me.

13. Francisco Leal Buitrago, "Militares y paramilitares en Colombia," in *La desmovilización paramilitar en Colombia: Entre la esperanza y el escepticismo*, ed. Elvira Maria Restrepo and Bruce Bagley, 43–68 (Bogota, Colombia: Editorial Universidad de los Andes, 2011); David Adams, "Vínculos entre paramilitares y drogas: antes y después de la desmovilización," in *La desmovilización paramilitar en Colombia: Entre la esperanza y el escepticismo*, ed. Elvira María Restrepo and Bruce Bagley, 69–97 (Bogotá, Colombia: Editorial Universidad de los Andes, 2011).

14. Beittel, *Peace Talks in Colombia*, 10; Marc Chernick argues that the demobilization was a farce in an interview (approved by the Institutional Review Board of the University of Miami) at Los Andes University in 2012. For a discussion about the demobilization, see Elvira Maria Restrepo and Bruce Bagley, *La desmovilización paramilitar en Colombia: Entre la esperanza y el escepticismo* (Bogotá, Colombia: Editorial Universidad de los Andes, 2011).

15. Mariel Perez-Santiago, "Colombia's BACRIM: Common Criminals or Actors in Armed Conflict?" *Insight Crime,* July 23, 2012, http://www.insightcrime.org/news-analysis/colombias-bacrim-common-criminals-or-actors-in-armed-conflict (accessed June 4, 2013); "Rastrojos," *InSight Crime*, n.d., http://www.insightcrime.org/groups-colombia/rastrojos (accessed June 4, 2013), 1.

16. Mariel Perez-Santiago, "Colombia's BACRIM: Common Criminals or Actors in Armed Conflict?" *Insight Crime,* Jul 23, 2012, http://www.insightcrime.org/news-analysis/colombias-bacrim-common-criminals-or-actors-in-armed-conflict (accessed June 4, 2013); "Rastrojos," *InSight Crime*, n.d., http://www.insightcrime.org/groups-colombia/rastrojos (accessed June 4, 2013), 1.

17. "Rastrojos," 3.

18. Beittel, *Peace Talks in Colombia*, 11; Christopher Looft, "Study: BACRIMs Continue Steady Expansion across Colombia," *Insight Crime*, Feb. 22, 2012, http://www.insightcrime.org/news-briefs/study-bacrims-continue-steady-expansion-across-colombia (accessed June 4, 2013).

19. "Rastrojos," 2–3.

20. Ibid., 1.

21. Thanks to Marc Chernick.

22. Bagley, *Drug Trafficking and Organized Crime*, 3–5.

23. Ibid; U.N. Office on Drugs and Crime, *World Drug Report,* 1–272.

24. Bagley, Drug Trafficking and Organized Crime, 3–6.

25. For a debate on the FARC peace talks, see "Colombian Commentator Views U.S. Perspective on FARC Talks," BBC News, Dec. 7, 2012; Beittel, *Peace Talks in Colombia.*

26. For more on the reintegration of combatants, see María Victoria Llorente and Juan Carlos Palou, "La reintegración de excombatientes en Medellín: ¿de dónde venimos y dónde estamos?" in *La desmovilización paramilitar en Colombia: Entre la esperanza y el escepticismo*, ed. Elvira Maria Restrepo and Bruce Bagley, 423–464 (Bogotá, Colombia: Editorial Universidad de los Andes, 2011).

27. Bruce Bagley made the argument about Santos becoming a war president if the peace process failed. He participated in a Coral Gables, Florida, conference proceeding regarding this topic titled, "Re-thinking the Colombian Conundrum: Talking Peace in a Changing Landscape" (panel events by Miami Consortium for Latin American and Caribbean Studies, University of Miami, Feb. 15, 2013); "Forum: Colombia's Security Challenges—The Peace Process and Its Chances for Success" (panel events, University of Miami Center for Hemispheric Policy, Nov. 2012).

28. Bittner, "U.S. Cuts Military Aid"; "Plan Colombia and Beyond: Defense Budget"; Alsema, "Plan Colombia Not Mentioned"; Beittel, *Peace Talks in Colombia*; Crandall, *Driven By Drugs*, 1

29. Darcy Crowe, "Colombian President's Approval Ratings Plunge amid Nationwide Strikes," *Wall Street Journal,* Sept. 4, 2013, http://online.wsj.com/news/articles/SB10001424127887324123004579055630272308744.

30. Bruce Bagley, "Re-thinking the Colombian Conundrum."

Index

185